Grief and Romantic Relationship Dissolution

Grief and Romantic Relationship Dissolution

Shawn Blue

LEXINGTON BOOKS
Lanham • Boulder • New York • London

Published by Lexington Books
An imprint of The Rowman & Littlefield Publishing Group, Inc.
4501 Forbes Boulevard, Suite 200, Lanham, Maryland 20706
www.rowman.com

Unit A, Whitacre Mews, 26-34 Stannary Street, London SE11 4AB

British Library Cataloguing in Publication Information Available

Library of Congress Cataloging-in-Publication Data Available

ISBN 978-1-4985-6855-5 (cloth : alk. paper)
ISBN 978-1-4985-6856-2 (electronic)

∞™ The paper used in this publication meets the minimum requirements of American National Standard for Information Sciences—Permanence of Paper for Printed Library Materials, ANSI/NISO Z39.48-1992.

Printed in the United States of America

Contents

Acknowledgments vii

Preface ix

Introduction xiii

1 Connection: The Foundation of Romantic Relationships 1

2 Digital Relationships: The Role of Technology and Social Media in the Formation and Maintenance of Romantic Relationships 35

3 The Relationship between Grief and Connection 57

4 Digital Relationships: The Role of Technology, Social Media, and Media on the Dissolution of Romantic Relationships 99

5 Diagnosis and Treatment 115

6 Romantic Relationship Grief in Psychotherapy 137

7 The Case of Shana and Jared 147

8 Media Depictions of Love and Grief 161

Conclusion 169

References 177

Index 203

About the Author 205

Acknowledgments

I would like to sincerely thank everyone who supported my process in completing this book. I would like to thank Dr. Salman Akhtar for supporting and encouraging my writing from the beginning of our professional relationship. I would like to thank my *dear* friend and colleague, Dr. Deanna Nobleza, for her professional support and friendly encouragement throughout the writing process. I would like to thank Jan Wright for her advice and assistance related to the logistical aspects of writing this book. I appreciate my editors, Kasey Beduhn, Becca Rohde, and Laura Chappell, for their patience and guidance. I am grateful to my family and friends who supported me through this book but also through multiple times of personal grief. Special thanks go to June Blue, Sheena Blue, Catherine McGlown, Natalie Alexander, Dr. Erica Walker and Dr. Daria Valentine, Corinne Zupko, Saleda Bryant, and Latrice Coleman. Further acknowledgment goes to June Blue; thank you for always being my biggest cheerleader. I am grateful to Dr. Beatrice Salter for her reassurance and helpful anecdotes related to the book writing process. I am grateful to all of my clients and patients who have shared their personal experiences of grief with me in psychotherapy. Finally, I thank my father, Willie Blue, who passed away during the writing of this book and was unable to view the final product.

Preface

I was compelled to write this book after witnessing numerous experiences of loss, especially in the form of romantic relationships. I began to see similarities of how loss is experienced in both romantic relationship dissolution and with death. As I observed my patients go through responses of grief I began using my knowledge of grief models in working with these patients. I found that these models fit well in helping patients understand their emotional experience. However, what I also began to become aware of was others' experience of understanding romantic relationship dissolution as a type of grief.

Surprisingly, most individuals are hesitant to categorize a romantic relationship breakup as a grief experience. Unfortunately, society still has difficulty dealing with grief surrounding death and therefore has difficulty understanding and managing grief surrounding breakups. This observation of those experiencing grief following romantic relationship breakups and society's delayed and complicated understanding of grief as a concept in romantic relationship breakups led to the creation of this book. It is imperative to have a resource that sheds light on this process in the hopes that all types of grief would be better understood and respected.

The attachment and connection within romantic relationships not only play a pivotal role in the experience of that relationship but also in the grief felt following the ending of that relationship. Multiple factors are involved in the attachments formed in romantic relationships. Attachment theory, a psychological theory that describes the origin and process of attachments, explains how individuals' attachment styles can influence how they view themselves and the world but also how they interact in all relationships.

The multiple attachments formed in romantic relationships influence one's experience of grief following a breakup.

Grief is often described in terms of the emotions experienced after a death. However, clinical practice suggests that a similar grief process is experienced following a romantic relationship breakup. By considering breakups in this way allows us to highlight the significance of these events in an individual's life. It also provides the opportunity to help one experience the grief of breakups and find resolution in a healthy way. Hopefully it will decrease society's practice of minimizing one's experience of a romantic relationship breakup and provide a new opportunity of community support and healing. It is hoped that after reading this book, one's understanding of grief will be expanded and eventually society will be better at reacting to and responding to grief, especially in the dissolution of romantic relationships.

In my clinical work, I've noticed that individuals feel pressured to move on too quickly from a romantic relationship breakup and are encouraged to begin dating/remarry again. Not only does this inhibit the process of grief, it also minimizes the loss that is present in any romantic relationship ending. It is important to honor this love and allow the opportunity for healing in order to enhance future romantic relationships. In addition, individuals enter treatment and it appears that they have internalized societal assumptions that they should not be affected so deeply by relationship breakups. This belief also inhibits grief because it doesn't allow the individual to feel the right to be able to grieve the loss of someone who has served as an attachment figure. It is important for the individual experiencing the loss, as well as others in the individual's life, to understand the significance of romantic endings and how they can have an effect on the emotional experience of the individual.

Life involves a multitude of losses. We are inundated with so many losses that we become immune to what is considered loss. We accept different events in our lives as a normal consequence of life but sometimes fail to go the next step in acknowledging, accepting, and treating it as a loss. Given the abundant amount of loss we endure (death, pet loss, miscarriage, infertility, unemployment, friendship breakups, and so on), romantic relationship breakups are only one of many losses that one will endure in a lifetime. By beginning to better understand and experience loss of romantic relationship breakups it is hoped that we will become better equipped to experience and support others through loss. The bigger and indirect goal of this book is to eventually nurture a better understanding and support of all types of loss.

Coincidently, as I was writing this book my father suddenly and unexpectedly passed away. In some ways, the author of my first "love" story died and with him died the origin of my love schema. I find it significant that I witnessed my father's death while nearing the finishing of this book, a book related to grief of romantic relationship breakups. A firm believer in the connection between parental attachment models and later relationships (i.e., romantic relationships) I understand the importance of my father's death and my resulting grief. My grief provided an additional reverence of the process of grief of all losses. It is with this view that I offer the following.

Introduction

Romantic love has been extensively studied for decades. Taking into account its complexity, multiple antecedents of love have been observed and investigated. Regardless of the process of love, it can be easily argued that romantic partners play a pivotal role in one's life. Romantic partners are a varied source of strong emotional processes. The existence, absence, or loss of a romantic relationship can elicit many different, yet strong, affective states. There are many theories that attempt to explain the role and function of romantic love. One theory that potentially encompasses the strong emotional impact that romantic relationships serve in one's life is attachment theory. Attachment theory, as formulated by John Bowlby, delineates the process of forming strong and close bonds, similar to those which occur in romantic relationships. This theory also provides evidence for the resulting loss and grief that is experienced when the attachment of a romantic relationship is dissolved.

Recently the loss of romantic relationships has been acknowledged as an influential event in one's life that causes an experience of loss and grief. This has been clearly illustrated in the case of divorce of romantic partners. Although positive outcomes can occur in the loss of romantic relationships, the importance of the loss process should be acknowledged and in some cases resolved. Many individuals are able to navigate the loss of a romantic union and even achieve a more positive outcome after the dissolution. Others experience symptoms and affective states that seriously impact their functioning and can have negative consequences on their mental and physical lives. Yet a few others have an even more significant influence on their functioning and are unable to resolve their loss without professional treatment or intervention. Society, as a whole, has difficulty understanding, accepting, and expressing grief and loss. Grief and loss related to death continue to be a difficult process for individuals to obtain and provide support in a healthy way. Grief and loss as it relates to the loss of romantic relationships is another area that proves difficult in the area of the provision or acceptance of support to those who are affected.

In this book, a brief description of romantic relationships, including a discussion of various theories of romantic love and the physiological foundation of love will be provided. In addition, an exploration of connective behaviors between animals and humans will be offered culminating in a description of the attachment process that is inherent within relationships. Next, grief will be analyzed by evaluating various models of grief accompanied by illustrations of clinical case material. In addition, traditional and ritualistic behavior related to grief and emotional and cognitive consequences of grief will be offered. An exploration of how cognitions play a role in grief will also be highlighted along with examples from clinical cases. A full depiction of a clinical case exploring all five stages of Kubler-Ross's stage theory as well as attachment theory is utilized to reflect the value of this theory in the understanding of romantic relationship breakups. Technology, social media, and multimedia will be explored as it relates to love and romantic relationship breakups. Due to the significance that technology holds in most areas of daily life, including romantic relationships, a chapter will be devoted to an exploration of how social media and multimedia play in grief and relationship dissolution. Finally, a chapter on treatment implications will be offered with recommendations for couple and marital counseling.

Chapter One

Connection

The Foundation of Romantic Relationships

THEORETICAL FRAMEWORKS OF LOVE

Before delving into an investigation into how grief is experienced as a result of romantic relationship breakups and divorce, it is only appropriate that first a relevant discussion of the origin and development of romantic relationships is provided. A framework of various theories of love will be offered to set the foundation for a clearer understanding of love. Evolutionary and social theories, as well as psychoanalytic and psychodynamic conceptualizations of love, will be discussed and evaluated.

The Role of Attraction

An evolutionary theory of romantic attachment highlights gender differences as being based on differing needs for genetic survival and procreation. In an evolutionary sense, for men, a woman's value is her ability to procreate. On the other hand, women tend to value commitment and the ability to provide and they base value on a man's ability to provide resources. Men's search for sexual partners has both short and long-term goals. In the short term, males seek females who are sexually available but in the long term, men seek women who are faithful and committed. Women seek men who are able to provide resources that will provide care for them and any potential offspring. Seeking men who will be committed helps ensure that men will be available and will continue to provide care. Charles Darwin's theory of natural selection, also based on survival, proposes that change occurs to ensure that traits that are more adaptable will survive. Related to humans, individuals who are better able to adapt are better able to survive. Modern evolutionary theory has elaborated upon Darwin's ideas and describes a concept called parental investment. This concept involves romantic attraction and mate selection resulting from the largest difference between genders in their parental investment. Historically, because women spent so much more time and effort in raising children when compared to men, women made careful attempts to ensure that offspring would survive and therefore women's parental investment was higher.

Social theory proposes another explanation for differences in romantic attachment. One argument suggests that social forces (i.e., norms, gender stereotypes, social roles, differences in social power) create different preferences (Aron & Aron, 1986; Davis, 1990; Pines, 2005). Related to romantic attraction, individuals might be attracted to others due to being attracted to stereotypes. In fact, it has been theorized that individuals experience a dilemma over past and current cultural values (Ickees, 1993). Apparently, gender differences are smaller than expected and perceived (Pines, 2005) and are based on societal gender stereotypes. Social theory argues that social forces influence romantic attraction (Aron & Aron, 1986; Davis, 1990; Pines, 2005). In addition, social forces serve as stimuli for what is preferred in terms of romantic attraction. Furthermore, sexual roles and scripts differ for men and women and have an effect on their particular perceptions of attraction in potential partners (Chafetz, 1975; Pines, 2005).

Psychoanalytic theory provides yet another approach to explain gender differences in romantic attraction (Chodorow, 1978; Pines, 2005; L. Rubin, 1983). Due to the role that women play in motherhood (i.e., birthing and nursing), they tend to be the source of the first *love object* for both women and men. It is argued that it is this first bond that individuals attempt to model when forming romantic relationships later in life. This early bond with mother is both emotional and erotic. Gender identity forms when male and female children are able to develop a separate self and are able to build relationships with others. After this occurs, the process begins to differentiate for male and female children. Boys must begin to transition their emotional attachment from mother by beginning to identify with father. The boy's sexual organ is recognized as a mutual identifying factor for the relationship between the boy and father. Boys develop defenses in order to maintain any emotional needs that were met in the past by mother. Because this transition begins at such an early age for boys, they are best equipped to become independent; however, the more difficult skill for boys to develop is intimacy. When men experience falling in love, they are able to regain the opportunity to build an emotional union with a woman (as they did early on with mother). Conflict in men arises due to the desire for union with the mother, which also represents intimacy, but experience anxiety due to the past early loss with both mother and intimacy. Therefore, in romantic relationships, men might desire the ability to be intimate but also experience fear and anxiety in the existence of intimacy. The early erotic bond with mother that was suppressed is later played out in relationships with other women. On the other hand, girls do not experience separation from the mother like boys do. Therefore, girls, unlike boys, are better able to be intimate and also continue to identify with the mother. However, girls find it difficult to build independence as boys are able to do. Girls suppress their erotic bond with mother but it is later transferred to the father. This erotic attachment is later transferred again in relationships with other men. However, girls are able to retain their emotional attachment with the mother (Chodorow, 1978; Pines, 2005; L. Rubin, 1983).

This theory explains why emotional intimacy and sexual intimacy is significant for different genders. For men, sexual intimacy plays a significant role in romantic relationships due to their earlier denial of an emotional connection but also with their sexual attachment being maintained. For women, emotional intimacy plays a significant role in romantic relationships due to their earlier denial of a sexual attachment to mother but having their emotional attachment maintained. Furthermore, men's emphasis on sexual intimacy also means they identify the process of intimacy with physical connection, whereas women who place a higher value on emotional intimacy, identify with words or emotional expression. When searching for potential romantic partners, men tend to value physical attributes, such as appearance or sexual desire. Women on the other hand value components that increase emotional intimacy, such as security and commitment. Due to these different processes of how each gender approaches intimacy within romantic relationships, what often plays out is an interaction between the desire for expression of intimacy and attempts to stop or withhold it or experience conflict when confronted with it (Chodorow, 1978; Pines, 2005; L. Rubin, 1983).

Ayala Malach Pines is a clinical, social, and organizational psychologist. When discussing romantic love, she contends that the role of proximity plays a significant role in the behavior of attraction (Pines, 2005). The closer one is to a potential dating partner increases the likelihood that the couple will get married. In addition, a process of repeated exposure is involved in attraction, with positive feelings toward a person increasing with the number of times that he or she is seen and this also increases the likelihood of being perceived as attractive. This is also influenced by one's tendency to be attracted to familiar faces and to individuals that look similar to one's self. However, the caveat to this tendency includes the finding that the process of repeated exposure reinforces the dominant emotion experienced, and can be either positive or negative. Also related to the role of attractiveness, involves a bias toward beauty. Pines (2005) suggests that the role of arousal as related to attraction, no matter what the origin of the arousal, will lead to increased attraction to another. However, arousal does not always lead to falling in love. The other components needed to contribute to arousal and lead to the chances of falling in love include preferred characteristics of appearance, age, education, and social class.

When considering the effect of separation on the experience of romance, the emotional status of the couple dictates the outcome. For example, for couples who share an emotional closeness, a brief separation can be beneficial and increase the experience of romance. On the other hand, for couples lacking emotional closeness, a separation can be detrimental and could potentially lead to a breakup or divorce. Several characteristics are found to be most significant on the influence of romantic partners and include age, education, race, religion, and ethnic background (Pines, 2005).

Reactance theory is offered as an explanation for why obstacles tend to increase love and attraction. One tends to be attracted to and love those that they had to overcome an obstacle to obtain. Mood also plays an important role in attraction. The more positive one feels about oneself and the more positive mood one is experiencing will lead to increased attraction of another. The opposite is true as well and the less positive one feels about oneself and if the mood one is experiencing is negative, the result will be the decreased likelihood that one would be attracted to another. Self-fulfilling prophecies are also involved in the experience of romantic attraction. It appears that when romantic partners idealize each other more at the start of a relationship, they experience increased satisfaction and less conflict. As the relationship matures, each partner begins to integrate the partner's perceptions and tends to see him or herself more positively. Apparently, self-love and self-actualization also play a role in attraction. Pines (2005) suggests that the more one has a sense of self, one is more able to be intimate and love others. She has found that individuals who have a stronger sense of self and are self-actualized typically have romantic relationships that are unselfish and intimate.

The Experience of Love

Sigmund Freud (1856–1939) was an Austrian neurologist and psychoanalyst and has been identified as the father of psychoanalysis. Psychoanalytic treatment focuses on one's unconscious thoughts, including an exploration of one's defenses, conflicts, wishes, desires, and fears. Related to the study of love, Freud believed that love is expressed through the sexual instinct. His theory of the sexual instinct involved painful bodily tension with the goal of seeking relief. Furthermore, inherent within this theory, the removal of this sexual tension is the goal of one's sexual desire. Successful removal of one's sexual tension results in sexual satisfaction (Freud, 1963).

Freud's original view on romantic love involved the integration of friendship and erotic desire between two non-familial adults. Based on this view, Freud described two *currents*, affectionate (friendship) and sensual (erotic desire) currents, needed in order to have a normal experience of love. The affectionate current developed earlier than the sensual current and occurs during the early relationship with the mother. The other current, the sensual current, develops during puberty and sexual development, and eventually is combined with the affectionate current in order to allow appropriate romantic and sexual relationships (Akhtar, 1996; Freud, 1912, 1963). Freud's later view of love involved two categories of love, *narcissistic and anaclitic* love (Akhtar, 1996; Freud, 1914). Narcissistic love, Freud conceptualized as fulfilling needs of the ego. On the other hand, anaclitic love involves the need to obtain aid from the object of desire. In addition, Freud (1914, 1915, 1930) acknowledged the pain within romantic love. He discussed the process by which one identifies with a love interest and attempts to achieve his or her ideal ego attainment. In a later view of Freud's (1930), he acknowledged the avoidance of the loss of love by integrating one's love toward the love object, mankind, and cultural institutions.

Freud conceptualized three conditions of love (Freud, 1963). The first condition includes his idea of the *need for an injured third party*, where a man chooses an attached woman, one who is married, engaged, or a friend to another man. The second condition, Freud called *love for a harlot*, and involved a man desiring a woman who is sexually disloyal or a woman who participates in infidelity. Freud acknowledged that a third condition occurs in normal love and there is a combination of tender feelings and sensual feelings. For men, a woman's value is based on her sexual integrity. He also believed that men have a need to rescue the women they love, especially to help them maintain their sexual respectability.

Freud (1963) theorized that one's experience of love is based on fixated feelings for the mother. He believed that romantic love objects are so similar to mothers that they act as mother surrogates. This connection to the mother is evident in Freud's first condition of love, where the woman belongs to the man. Related to the mother, this condition is satisfied due to the mother belonging to the father. The second condition is also relevant to the relationship with mother. The adult male wishes to think of his mother as having sexual purity. Based on the Oedipus complex, the male begins to desire the mother and hate the father. Because the mother has chosen to engage in sexual intercourse with the father and not the male son, the mother is seen as being sexually unfaithful to the son. In order to manage the conflict that is caused by desiring the mother and hating the father, the son engages in fantasies of the mother being unfaithful to the father with the son. The son wishes to *rescue* the mother by repaying her with an equal gift to the gift she gave him (i.e., birth) and the son wishes to satisfy this by giving her a child (i.e., similar to himself). By *rescuing* the mother, the son is able once again to identify with the father. By incorporating all instincts, the male is able to fulfill his wish of becoming the *father of himself*. For the woman, her husband also serves as a surrogate for the father. Whether the woman accepts or rejects the husband is dependent on the level of fixation to her father. Freud (1963) described a transition from an immature stage of love to a mature stage, where individuals move from an immature idealization of the other to a more mature and accurate view of the loved one. He believed that this process of idealizing a loved one was a process of projection of an ideal self. Freud viewed love as involving the projection of one's unattained ideals onto a partner. He hypothesized that a sex drive provided energy for this process. The primary goal of love, Freud believed, was sexual union.

Erich Fromm (1900–1980) was a psychologist, psychoanalyst and social philosopher. Fromm (1956) conceptualized love as including romantic love, brotherly love, erotic love, self-love, the love of God and the love of offspring. Fromm (1956) believed love was more than the relationship with another person but involved love in a broader sense. In this way he encompassed love toward all humanity. He described love as an active task that does not involve solely the attainment of one object or representation of love, but in fact explained love as including self, humanity, the world, and life. Fromm (1956) described two types of unions when discussing love. The first form of union he called symbiotic union. Symbiotic union involves the *mother* and her *fetus* and reflects their shared experience and existence. Both mother and child impact one another, with mother providing food and protection to the child and the child positively influencing the mother. Fromm (1956) further classified symbiotic union as having both masochistic and sadist aspects. The passive or masochistic aspect of symbiotic union involves submission and is characterized by an individual who uses escape to avoid the experience of isolation by attaching to another individual who has power over one (i.e., authority, protection). On the other hand, the active or sadist aspect of symbiotic union involves domination. This individual also uses escape to avoid the experience of isolation by attaching to another individual and taking power over that individual (i.e., authority, protection). Both individuals (sadist and masochist) are dependent on each other, and the only distinguishing difference between the two individuals is one exploits and the other individual is exploited. However, most individuals behave in both sadistic and masochistic ways to different individuals.

Fromm (1956) defined mature love as the ability to preserve integrity. Mature love also connects individuals with others and provides them with the resources to conquer the experience of isolation. Mature love allows individuals to merge and become one union but also remain as two individuals. Fromm (1956) offered four basic components to all forms of love: care, responsibility, respect, and knowledge. In addition, he described a biological need for love that involves feminine and masculine polarities. Fromm (1956) also outlined his theory of the developmental stages of love. He described the earliest stages of life involving a child's experience of the mother providing nourishment and protection. Eventually, the child becomes older and begins to differentiate among objects and begins to learn how behaviors influence mother. For example, the child begins to understand that crying behaviors elicit comfort and eating will elicit satisfaction. The child then begins to interpret that he or she is *loved*. Fromm (1956) explained that the child experiences love from the mother in a passive way. The child does not have to do anything to obtain the love but likewise is unable to produce the love from mother, as in situations of absent motherly love. The form of love described here is identified as an ideal love and Fromm (1956) recognized that all mother/child relationships do not exist in this way. Fromm (1956) distinguished this early childhood experience of passively being loved from a new developmental milestone (ages eight and a half to ten) where the child's behavior becomes active and he or she begins to give love. The child begins to incorporate the needs of others and desires to satisfy those needs. By moving into this stage of giving love, the child now creates a union with another. Later, as the child continues to mature into adulthood, one begins to integrate his or her mother and father. The mature adult integrates both motherly love and fatherly reason and judgment. In order to achieve successful achievement and optimal emotional health, the mature adult must experience a balance of both mother and father attachments.

Fromm (1956) defined love as more than a relationship to a specific individual but as a behavior between an individual and his or her connection to the world. He further clarified that there are different types of love and provided theories regarding brotherly love, motherly love, erotic love, self-love, and love of God. He offered that the most fundamental form of love is *brotherly love* and defined it as love for humankind. *Motherly love* is defined as the unconditional care and attention between mother and child. Fromm (1956) established motherly love as the highest love of all types of love. Inherent within motherly love, the mother cares and attends to the child's needs but the mother must also desire and encourage separation. This unselfish quality differentiates an affectionate mother from a loving mother. A loving mother is able to tolerate and encourage separation without withholding love during the process. *Erotic love* involves the exclusive union with another individual. Fromm (1956) characterized erotic love as the most deceptive love of all loves. *Self-love* involves the idea that in order to love others fully and authentically one must also love one's self. Fromm (1956) debated the argument that to love one's self is selfish. He argued that self-love and selfishness are opposite behaviors and proposed that selfishness is a reflection of an individual lacking love for him or herself, even to the experience of hating oneself. Finally, *love of God*, like most forms of love originates from a desire to obtain union in order to avoid separation. Similar to the mature adult described above whom eventually integrates both father and mother, the mature adult also integrates God. Furthermore, an individual must accomplish true integration of a balance of both mother and father before one can successfully develop a mature love of God. Mature love, as conceptualized by Fromm (1956), involves an integration of attachments with mother and father. In addition to mature love, including care, responsibility, respect, and knowledge, it also allows for the existence of both dependence and independence.

According to object relations theory, an object is an internal representation. It can involve an individual, object, or experience. Because object relations theory includes an exploration of both objects and the relationship between objects, one's internal representation will include both objects and relationship between objects. Related to romantic relationships, one holds internal representations of romantic partners as well as other emotional and intimate relationships. A romantic image is an unconscious model that represents who one is attracted to and falls in love with and involves emotional experiences that are created early in life. Parental caretakers play a major role in the development of romantic images and an integration of both positive and negative experiences make up the romantic image.

Apparently, one seeks out repressed elements of themselves in romantic partners. Due to an individual's difficulty in acknowledging and addressing these repressed parts, one seeks others that express or embody them. This allows individuals to address their repressed parts without having to directly deal with their personal experience with their repressed selves. Others are able to integrate repressed parts and see them as positive complements to their romantic relationship. Whether one will seek out repressed parts in a romantic partner as a method of denial of one's internal repressed parts or will integrate repressed parts and view them as a complement to their romantic relationship is based on a process described by an object relations theorist, named Margaret Mahler. Mahler (1974) theorized a developmental process called *psychological birth* that occurs between the ages of six months and three years. In her theory, the early relationship with mother is very important (especially the union with mother) and is the foundation for building romantic relationships. She described a specific experience of separation-individuation that occurs throughout one's lifetime and there are distinct periods for the process of separation-individuation during adolescence, marriage, and becoming a parent. Successful achievement of this process is called *differentiation*. One who is differentiated is individuated and is able to have secure relationships. To be undifferentiated, one most likely experienced unmet needs, abandonment or rejection. This undifferentiated individual experiences splits in identity due to a history of unmet needs, which are then repressed because they are too painful to address and become internalized. Those who deny their repressed parts and seek them out in romantic partners can be thought of as being undifferentiated. Furthermore, those who integrate repressed parts and view repressed parts of themselves in romantic partners as complementary can be thought of as being differentiated.

Harville Hendrix is a pastoral counselor, educator, and therapist. He, along with his wife, Helen LaKelly Hunt, a psychologist and women's activist, founded a couples' treatment approach called Imago Relationship Therapy (Hendrix, 1988). Hendrix believed that individuals choose partners that have similar traits of one's caretakers. He theorized that individuals attempt to re-create relationships from childhood. Romantic partners are selected to attempt to fix the emotional issues obtained from childhood. Interestingly, individuals are attracted to or are drawn to both the positive and negative traits of their parents in potential romantic partners. In most cases, the negative characteristics tend to be more powerful in mate selection. When an individual chooses a partner that only shares a few similar traits with parental caretakers, he or she will initially experience a mild attraction, less passion, and less problems. The reason this occurs is because the individual is drawn to seek a partner that gratifies the parental conflict and the conflict is not triggered as strongly as it would be if the partner had more similar traits with caretakers. In certain situations, romantic partners can project the traits of caretakers onto their romantic partners. This provides an opportunity to elicit a similar and familiar response and triggers conflicts experienced in childhood. In many ways, individuals unconsciously choose romantic partners with the wish that they will serve as surrogate parents that will fix the deficits experienced in childhood. Hendrix (1988) posited that romantic attraction occurs between two individuals stuck at similar developmental stages and who experienced similar psychological injuries.

Robert Sternberg (1986) proposed a triangular theory of love. He conceptualized love as involving intimacy, passion, and decision/commitment which form the vertices of a triangle. Intimacy (closeness, connectedness and bondedness) involves the intimate feelings and behaviors experienced in a relationship. Passion (romance, physical attraction, and sexual consummation) is tied to motivation and arousal. Decision/commitment (decision to love, maintenance of love) is based on cognitive decision making. Sternberg argued that love should be viewed as a whole system involving both genetic behaviors but also social role modeling. These components of love have differing properties. For example, intimacy and decision/commitment components tend to maintain stability in close and loving relationships. However, the passion component tends to be unstable and unpredictable. Related to control and presuming that an individual is aware of one's feelings in a relationship, this individual would have high control over the decision/commitment component, some control over the intimacy component, and little control over the passion component experienced in loving relationships. Each of these components' significance differs and is dependent on the duration of the relationship. The passion component will typically play a large part, the intimacy component plays a moderate part and decision/commitment component plays little to no part at all in short-term relationships. Alternatively, both the intimacy and decision/commitment component tend to play a large part with the passion component playing a moderate part (with some decline over time) in long-term relationships. In addition, these three components of loving relationships also differ in the types of relationships experienced. The intimacy component tends to form the foundation of most types of loving relationships, whereas the passion component usually only exists in specific relationships such as romantic relationships. The decision/commitment component can exist at different levels across a range of loving relationships. Finally, these three components differ in psychophysiological involvement, with the passion component having a high involvement, the intimacy component having a moderate involvement, and the decision/commitment component having a low involvement. Sternberg (1986) further divided love into eight subsets. *Nonlove* involves relationships where none of the three components of love exist (casual relationships). *Liking* involves relationships that only involve intimacy (friendships). *Infatuated love* involves relationships that only involve passion. *Empty love* involves relationships that only involve decision/commitment. *Romantic love* involves relationships with both intimacy and passion. *Companionate love* involves both intimacy and decision/commitment. *Fatuous love* involves both passion and decision/commitment. *Consummate love* involves all three components of intimacy, passion, and decision/commitment.

When comparing the three components (intimacy, passion, and decision/commitment), there are also differences found in the course of loving relationships. For the loving component, there occurs a decreasing experience of intimacy. In a romantic relationship, the positive consequence of this decrease in intimacy is the increase in interpersonal connection which results in a closer relationship. The negative consequence is reflected in the fact that the relationship begins to resemble no relationship at all due to the lack of perceivable or displayed intimacy. Within the passion component, there are two processes that occur that influence the course of the relationship. The first process often develops quickly and diminishes quickly. The second process often slowly develops and slowly fades. The decision/commitment component is greatly influenced by the success of the relationship. Usually commitment begins to increase after one meets a romantic partner. In relationships that last long-term, commitment increases at a gradual level at first and then gains momentum. Later, the amount of commitment levels off (graphically representing an S-curve). During a conflictual period, a decrease in commitment is experienced. Finally, in preparation for a relationship ending, the commitment can move back down to baseline, the level experienced before meeting or getting to know the individual (Sternberg, 1986).

An important related aspect to consider in this discussion includes real and ideal triangles. The real triangle involves the love one has for another in a close and loving relationship. The ideal triangle involves an ideal relationship which is based both on previous relationships and expectations of close and loving relationships. Satisfaction plays a role in the presence or lack of overlap in the corresponding triangles. For example, the area between the real and ideal triangles that is overlapping is thought to represent satisfaction, with dissatisfaction representing the non-overlapping areas between these two triangles. Intuitively, if the amount of discrepancy between the real and ideal triangles is too large, the relationship is vulnerable to dissolution (Sternberg, 1986). Another aspect that is also important to consider is the expression of love within close and loving relationships. Each individual's expression of love can influence the course, maintenance, and quality of love. Both feelings and behaviors interact to influence one's, or the relationship's, experience. Moreover, feelings influence behaviors in loving relationships and behaviors influence feelings in a relationship. Relationship behaviors lead to additional behaviors which eventually culminate into a network of relationship behaviors. On the other hand, the lack of behaviors expressed in a relationship can result in continued lack of behaviors in the relationship. One's individual behaviors are assumed to influence how the other individual in the relationship feels about him or herself (and will influence the other individual's self-triangle of love). Lastly, each individual's behavior in the relationship will have an influence on the other's behaviors leading to reinforcing patterns of behavior (Sternberg, 1986).

John Alan Lee (1988) used the analogy of color in his theory of love. His love styles include eros (passionate love), storge (affectionate love), and ludus (game playing love). He considered these three categories to be the primary love styles and he believed that other love styles originate from these primary colors. His secondary love styles included mania, pragma (combination of ludus and storge), and agape (selfless, giving, altruistic), which is a combination of eros and storge. Lee (1988) provided examples of each of his love styles and provided insight into each love styles' childhood experiences and adult romantic urges and preferences. He used a color wheel and geometric forms (circles and triangles) to represent the various love styles. His love styles are represented in the form of circles and triangles and create a chart of the structure of the love styles. This chart can be used to identify the match between love styles. Lee's typology included a study of love within gay and lesbian populations and found that it fits well within his theory of love.

Barbara Fredrickson (2013) described the activity of love and connection (which she calls positivity resonance) as involving:

- Shared positive emotions between two people
- Synchrony of biochemistry between two people
- Motivation to nurture and enhance another's well-being

Because she argued that positivity resonance occurs within interpersonal relationships, she contended that love is imbedded in connection. She provided two necessary conditions for love: safety and connection. She explained that this integration of components expands connection and produces a positive energy that maintains this connection. The power of this energy can only be created by love and connection, and other positive emotions do not have enough strength to produce the charge that positivity resonance does. This energy increases biochemical adaptations that increase attraction and bonding. The more opportunities that positivity resonance has to take place the larger the probability that a relationship will form. She further purported that love produces changes in one's body and brain, which in turn elicit change in another individual's body and brain. She identified particular contextual factors that must exist for positivity resonance to occur: perceived safety and connection. Connective behaviors that are important in the process of positivity resonance include physical presence, eye contact, touch, voice, and mirrored bodily gestures. When loneliness is experienced, the opposite of connection, cortisol increases in the blood. This results in a lowered immune system and susceptibility to inflammatory conditions. An even more interesting link between connection and physical health is that one who perceives or thinks of being disconnected has more devastating health results than actual disconnection (Fredrickson, 2013).

The perceptions of one's romantic partners' and the meaning one interprets from their behaviors has a lot to do with the emotional connection experienced in the relationship. Sue Johnson (2013) describes how there are *micromoments and micromoves of connection and disconnection* in a romantic relationship. Romantic relationships involve transitioning from connection and disconnection and this transitioning process is a normal experience of all romantic relationships. It is important to honestly acknowledge the presence of both connection and disconnection in the process of a healthy romantic relationship. By acknowledging it, one is better able to manage it instead of assuming that it is a sign of dysfunction within the relationship. Affect regulation during periods of disconnection can help one move from a space of disconnection to connection.

The theories and conceptualizations of love offered above represent the multifaceted experience of loving relationships. The process of love is complex and is not simply explained. Inherent within many of the theories discussed above is the fundamental aspect of connection. Whether it is explicitly described or implicitly inferred, connection forms the basis for love to occur, exist, and be maintained. Connection also forms the attachment experienced in all relationships and provides the framework for why grief is experienced when that connection is lost. Below, a discussion of connection witnessed in animals and humans will be offered as well as the biochemistry involved within connective behaviors.

Dunbar (2012) conducted numerous studies on pairbonded species and found that these species are highly sensitive to the needs of its mate in order to know how to organize its day. In her study of miniature klipspringer antelope in East Africa, she observed how the male of the species constantly follows the female mate around. The male never strays more than ten yards away from the female in order to maintain protection of her. Therefore, the male and female never feed at the same time. While one feeds, the other watches and protects. When one is full and is desiring rest the other mate will come closer and begin to stand guard. These mates never leave each other's side. Dunbar describes this process as necessary for survival and acknowledged that it can be psychologically taxing. Studies of this species highlight the importance of making a good decision when selecting a mate. Presumably, the antelope must find a mate who will ultimately be responsive, attentive, and protective. Choosing the wrong mate can have dire outcomes. What seems potentially implied by this research is that this species appears to be highly connected. The mates need to be connected and attuned to each other's needs, whereabouts, and safety. This is done constantly throughout their lives and without it they would not be able to survive. Although it is recognized as a psychological burden, its significance is present in its existence (Dunbar, 2012).

Within both humans and animals, there are a number of neurotransmitters involved in the process of attraction and connection. Oxytocin is a neurotransmitter and a hormone (Cassidy & Shaver, 2008, 2016; Mikulincer & Shaver, 2007, 2016). Its role is to encourage bonding by stimulating feelings of connection, trust, and calm, as well as release stress. It also blocks fear, anxiety, and panic reactions. Oxytocin is made in the hypothalamus, where it then travels to the pituitary gland and is released into the bloodstream. It has been proposed to be helpful in the treatment of autism, addictions, sexual dysfunction, cancer, and men's health issues. There are even claims that oxytocin allows one to experience grief in a manageable way and inhibits debilitating negative obsessive behavior (Stoller, 2012). Oxytocin is present at times of deep emotional connection. In parent-child relationships, oxytocin is present during breast feeding. In romantic partners, it occurs during orgasm. It has been found that just the mere thought of a romantic partner can induce the flow of oxytocin. This confirms how powerful this type of connection is that one's romantic partner does not even need to be present in order to elicit this response. Just thinking of the partner can induce this deep connection with another. Individuals are able to accomplish this by creating and maintaining symbolic representations of others that they are able to elicit in later situations. When a deep emotional connection is experienced, this symbolic representation is conjured up and maintains feelings of connection with that individual (Cassidy & Shaver, 2008, 2016; Johnson, 2013; Mikulincer & Shaver, 2007, 2016; Stoller, 2012). Even human brain size is biologically adapted to provide for opportunities of connection. Human brain size allows for complex tasks of predicting others' behaviors and analyzing one's own behaviors and its consequences on others. Given how much of the human body and brain are primed for connection, it seems apparent that connection is not only important but essential for survival (Johnson, 2013).

One chemical in the brain that appears to be involved in attraction and romantic love is dopamine. Dopamine is associated with attention and motivation. In addition, dopamine is associated with many of the feelings connected with an experience of ecstasy (i.e., exhilaration, hyperactivity, sleeplessness, loss of appetite, and a pounding heart). Another chemical identified in the process of attraction and romantic love is norepinephrine, which is a derivative of dopamine. Norephinephrine is also connected to the feelings of exhilaration discussed before (Cassidy & Shaver, 2008, 2016; Johnson, 2013; Mikulincer & Shaver, 2007, 2016; Stoller, 2012). The exact details of the activity of a third chemical, serotonin, are unknown. However, lowered levels of serotonin are hypothesized to be involved in the process of attraction. Serotonin levels are dependent on dopamine and norepinephrine and it is believed that as dopamine and noreponephrine increase, levels of serotonin decrease.

This combination of reactionary chemicals is thought to result in obsessional thinking and fantasizing about a romantic partner (Cassidy & Shaver, 2008, 2016; Johnson, 2013; Mikulincer & Shaver, 2007, 2016; Stoller, 2012).

Another important brain area associated with attraction and romantic behavior is the caudate nucleus, located in the reward system of the brain. In addition to bodily movement, this area is also involved in arousal, pleasure, and reward acquisition. Involved within reward acquisition, the caudate nucleus includes the perception, discrimination, preference, anticipation, and expectation of a reward. When an individual experiences increased levels of passion, increased activity is witnessed in the caudate nucleus. The length of a relationship has also been associated with two regions of the caudate nucleus. The anterior cingulate cortex and the insular cortex have been shown to show more activity when individuals were in longer romantic relationships. To provide more insight into why this occurs, it is important to understand the purpose of these two regions. The anterior cingulate cortex plays a role in emotions, attention, and working memory. Furthermore, the insular cortex is involved with obtaining information from external touch and temperature, internal pain, and stomach reactions (i.e., "butterflies in the stomach"). The longer one is in a romantic relationship correlates with changes that are experienced in the brain related to emotions, memory, and attention. It is hypothesized that these changes play a role in the process of attachment (Cassidy & Shaver, 2008, 2016; Johnson, 2013; Mikulincer & Shaver, 2007, 2016; Stoller, 2012).

The role of oxytocin in connection has been extensively studied in both animals and humans. When observing female rats, it is clear that they have little maternal instincts of nurturing before becoming mothers (Young & Alexander, 2012). Before motherhood, female rats can often be fearful of, attack, and even kill newborn rats. When baby rats are placed in the non-mother rats' proximity, they initially exhibit fear or anxiety. These emotions begin to dissipate after a few days and the female rats begin to come closer to the baby rats. After a week, these female rats begin resembling actual mothers. Even though they were not biological mothers, their brain chemistry became triggered and activated to allow them to display mothering behaviors. This is also reflected in the fact that when the blood of pregnant rats was injected into non-mother female rats they also began to exhibit mothering qualities when introduced to baby rats. When oxytocin is injected into the brains of non-mother female rats, they also begin to exhibit mothering qualities (Young & Alexander, 2012). Because estrogen triggers an increase in oxytocin receptors, when both estradiol and oxytocin are injected into non-mother female rats more of them begin to display mothering qualities. Estrogen, oxytocin, and prolactin hormones trigger mothering behaviors and qualities. Pregnant female rats begin preparing nests in advance of giving birth. And after birth, they begin to display caring and nurturing behaviors.

Oxytocin increases in the uterus during late pregnancy (Young & Alexander, 2012). This allows the uterus to contract during childbirth. During labor, oxytocin is three hundred times the amount present before pregnancy. The amount of oxytoxic receptors (as well as prolactin, which stimulates milk production) also increases in a woman's breasts too. These receptors allow for the opportunities of birth and connection with offspring. Oxytocin and connective behaviors are also evident in the activity of breast feeding (Young & Alexander, 2012). During breastfeeding, newborn babies massage their mother's nipples and this begins the messaging and signaling for the experience of both feeding and connection. The massage created by the newborn's hands triggers oxytocin to be released in the mother's brain. In typical situations, the newborn sticks his or her tongue out and feeding begins, although there are some situations of feeding difficulties. Once the newborn's tongue connects with the mother's nipple, the newborn will continue to massage the mother's breast. This activity involves two crucial activities between mother and child, feeding and connection. The more oxytocin found in a woman's blood will increase the amount of mothering behaviors exhibited during breast feeding (Young & Alexander, 2012). Touching, grooming, gazing, cuddling, and talking behaviors increase as the levels of oxytocin increases. This bond is powerful and is reflected in the evidence that a mother's amygdala becomes activated when she recognizes her child. Dopamine is triggered when a mother cares for her child and through sensory communication with her child (i.e., sights, sounds, and smells). This connective communication occurs between both mother and child (Young & Alexander, 2012). Through the acts of the mother touching, grooming, gazing, cuddling, and talking with her child, she feels needed and depended upon (for everything). The child also begins to make decisions about his or her mother, especially whether she is available or responsive. The child also feels important, cared for, and loved.

Oxytocin also has a special role in empathy and the ability to read faces and emotional expressions (Young & Alexander, 2012). Eyes, along with other language cues, are used to identify the emotions of others. It is argued that one first acquires this skill during childhood with one's interactions with one's mother. Mothers look at their children and listen to the sounds they make. Children look back at the mother and communicate with sounds. These behaviors are maintained and reinforced by oxytocin. If these behaviors occur appropriately, it begins the process of obtaining skill in identifying and expressing emotions. Studies show that when oxytocin is injected into the bloodstream, individuals are able to better identify the emotions of others (Young & Alexander, 2012). It has been proposed that individuals might have difficulty regulating their emotions, being empathic, and accurately reading the emotions of others due to a lack of appropriate nurturing and connection during childhood. When oxytocin is administered to individuals who have trouble identifying the emotions of others, empathy increases. Other studies have been conducted that involve the romantic bond of adults and the connection with oxytocin receptors (Young & Alexander, 2012). When shown pictures of celebrity actors, strangers, relatives, and their lovers, female brain activity looked very similar to the brain receptors activated when mothers look at pictures of their babies. This furthers the idea, that sex fulfills not only needs for procreation but also for romantic bonds and connection.

Vasopressin might be associated with bonding and mating, particularly in men (Young & Alexander, 2012). Studying male prairie voles, vasopressin was involved in both mating and showing a preference for a particular partner. When vasopressin was inhibited, even if they mated, male prairie voles would not show preference for a partner. Other studies observed male prairie vole behavior after mating and living with a female. The outcome of mating and cohabitating with a female vole, changed the male vole's brain and resulted in an abundance of vasopressin. This also resulted in an enhanced romantic bond with the female vole and motivated care of offspring. Also, similar to how oxytocin increases the ability to read the emotions of others in females, vasopressin increases a male's ability to better identify happy or angry emotions. However, they were not as accurate when it came to neutral faces and emotions.

It appears that levels of oxytocin might have a generational pattern (Young & Alexander, 2012). Studies reveal that oxytocin and vasopressin levels are shared genetically from parent to child. Lower levels of oxytocin are associated with lowered nurturing behaviors between mothers and their children. This makes sense when considering the hypothesis that children who grow up with unresponsive parents are not modeled the skills needed for providing nurturing behaviors to their own children. Furthermore, there is potentially a correlation between childhood abuse and levels of oxytocin (Young & Alexander, 2012). Individuals who have experienced a history of emotional or physical abuse tended to have lower levels of oxytocin compared to individuals who did not. In fact, this seems to be especially true in the case of emotional abuse (Young & Alexander, 2012).

Shelley Taylor (2002) constructed a theory describing two social behaviors called *tending* and *befriending*. Tending refers to maternal care and protection of offspring. Oxytocin plays a major role in the tending component of this theory. In addition to being a stress hormone, Taylor (2002) argued that oxytocin is also a social hormone and is associated with maternal tending. Vasopressin, also a stress hormone might be responsible for tending in men.

Befriending refers to obtaining social support in order to avoid or reduce situations of risk and increase protection. The critical implications of this theory provide an alternative argument to the fight or flight response that has historically been used to describe stress reactions.

Marriage can be viewed as a tending system with emotional and physical benefits to both men and women (Taylor, 2002). However, these benefits are differentially dependent on gender. In heterosexual relationships, women's care of men tends to have better benefits for men's emotional and physical health. In some heterosexual relationships women tend to have multiple obligations and responsibilities in addition to work, such as the care of the home and children. In these relationships, after a workday, men tend to relax. In these same relationships, women tend to experience continued increased levels of catecholamines due to the continued stress of household, work, and childhood tasks before they are able to relax and prepare for sleep. It is hypothesized that due to the prolonged stress arousal state of women in some heterosexual relationships, men tend to reap more of the benefits of marriage than women.

Another theory explaining the experience of building interpersonal relationships involves the *belongingness* hypothesis, which is based on a human drive or motivation (Baumeister & Leary, 1995). Two criteria are necessary for the fulfillment of the belongingness theory: positive interactions with others on a frequent basis and the existence of a mutual concern for each other's well-being. The need to belong theory includes the belief that the motivation to build and maintain relationships is innate and universal to all humans. In addition, the theory has an evolutionary foundation manifested through both survival and reproductive needs. Meeting both criteria increases survival and reproductive chances.

Unlike Freud's and Bowlby's conceptions of interpersonal relating, the need to belong theory does not emphasize a specific relationship or individual (Baumeister & Leary, 1995). In fact, the need to belong theory can involve any human being and when a relationship is lost it can be replaced with another individual. In situations of a loss of belongingness, humans would experience stress, as well as negative health and emotional conditions. As a result, behaviors directed at the formation of relationships would ensue. The satisfaction of the drive to form and maintain relationships is based on the criteria of quality and quantity. Therefore, extra relationships will result in less satisfaction and less distress when experiencing the ending of these relationships. Empirical study of the belongingness theory has resulted in several conclusions (Baumeister & Leary, 1995). First, relationships appear to be established in a natural and spontaneous manner. Time and effort are both placed into these relationships in order to maintain them and obtain support. When external factors threaten the relationship, these relationships are strengthened. Individuals strongly avoid the ending of relationships. Individuals put a great deal of thought into the other individuals in their relationships, as well as make interpretations about events related to their relationships and extend ways of processing information about the self into how relationships are processed. In addition to thought, individuals experience strong positive and negative emotions related to their relationships. Acceptance results in the experience of positive emotions and rejection results in the experience of negative emotions. The belongingness theory also explains the distress that is experienced in such events as divorce or death. Emotion forms the foundation of behavior regulation in the creation and maintenance of interpersonal relating. When individuals maintain relationships with infrequent interactions, they still find these relationships to be valuable; however, they suffer related to the interactional infrequency of these relationships. In addition, relationships considered to be negative or problematic do not provide the benefits that the belongingness theory offers. An individual's first relationships appear to hold the most value and additional relationships hold less value. Individuals can derive satisfaction and value from new relationships created to replace lost relationships. Although some relationships cannot be replaced with new relationships, obtaining new relationships with similar qualities can provide value.

ATTACHMENT THEORY

Connections among humans originated with studies done by John Bowlby, a psychologist, psychiatrist and psychoanalyst who studied the connections and relationships between people (Bowlby, 1988). Bowlby was a major proponent of attachment theory, which grew out of psychodynamic theory (Bowlby, 1988). Attachment is a process that includes a set of organized behaviors a child and caregiver engage in that serve the function of obtaining and maintaining proximity to a caregiver who is perceived to provide the child with protection. The critical period for the formation of attachment occurs within the first year of life (Blue, 2006; Bowlby, 1988). However, attachment is considered to continue to develop throughout the lifespan. Parent-child interactions that are mutually rewarding and caregiving responses that are consistent and attuned with the infant's needs are considered essential to the development of a secure attachment. The quality of attachments formed in early childhood influences the development of relationships later in life (Blue, 2006; Bowlby, 1988). Primary caregivers have the greatest influence on later development (Blue, 2006; Main, Kaplan, & Cassidy, 1985).

From a biological sense, the attachment system evolved as a method of protection. Bowlby theorized that children who sought out responsive caregivers had a better prognosis for survival and procreation. The attachment system is regulated by oxytocin, vasopressin, adrenaline, cortisol, amygdala and the hypothalamic-pituitary-adrenal (HPA) axis. Cortisol plays a particularly important role in the context of separation and loss. It has been identified in high levels when separation or loss is experienced. It is clear that the attachment system comprises two components that are essential for attachment to occur. Oxytocin is present and serves the role of promoting bonding and closeness. However, when an individual is stressed as a result of loss or separation, cortisol enters the situation. This attachment system is present both in childhood and adulthood and is activated during times of stress when an individual reaches out for support from an attachment figure (Cassidy & Shaver, 2008, 2016; Mikulincer & Shaver, 2007, 2016).

Everyone cannot serve as an attachment figure. An individual identified as an attachment figure has a special and deep emotional bond. It is the individual who is sought out during times of stress, threat and need. This individual is distinguished from other close relationships and involves an individual that is viewed as a *secure base* (Cassidy & Shaver, 2008, 2016; Mikulincer & Shaver, 2007, 2016). When a threatening event occurs, individuals unconsciously and quickly bring up mental representations of attachment figures. Individuals also attempt to gain close proximity to attachment figures in a process called *proximity seeking*. This process provides a protective buffer against perceived threats (Cassidy & Shaver, 2008, 2016; Mikulincer & Shaver, 2007, 2016).

Rothbaum et al. (2000) voiced concerns that attachment theory was not a universal construct. They argued that attachment theory is based on cultural assumptions that do not hold true for all cultures. However, van IJzendoorn and Sagi-Schwartz (2008) concluded that secure, avoidant, and ambivalent attachment styles can be found in every culture. They observed that most cultures prefer secure children and secure attachment behavior seems to be the result of sensitive parenting. They suggested that attachment theory can be referred to as having cross-cultural validity (Mesman, van IJzendoorn, & Sagi-Schwartz, 2016; van IJzendoorn & Sagi-Schwartz, 2008).

Attachment in Childhood

Attachment behaviors were first studied amongst six-year-old children and it was found that mothers who were assumed to be the child's primary caregiver played a greater role in the child's internal representations of self and others when compared to secondary caregivers, such as the father

(Blue, 2006; Main, Kaplan, & Cassidy, 1985). Included in attachment is a mental representation of self and others, which includes the perceptions, beliefs, and expectations involved with it (Blue, 2006; Hazan & Shaver, 1994). In addition, this representation is influenced by all of the important relationships an individual has experienced but is most impacted by the relationship with the primary caregiver. Four attachment styles were observed in parent-child interactions and are offered as descriptive categories to characterize attachment behaviors (Ainsworth, 1979; Blue, 2006; Main, Kaplan, & Cassidy, 1985). A standardized laboratory procedure called the Strange Situation provided the characteristics of three parent-child interactions (Ainsworth, 1979; Blue, 2006). Ainsworth observed infants with their caregivers in separation and reunion episodes and recorded their interactions during these periods. Observations gained from the Strange Situation revealed the presence of three types of attachments. Infants who used their caregivers as a *secure base* from which they were likely to explore their environment were characterized as having a secure attachment. During separation, these infants ceased exploration and exhibited distress at the absence of the caregiver. Once the caregiver returned, these infants were likely to reestablish contact with the caregiver. Anxious-Ambivalent attachment was characterized by infants who displayed anxiety with their caregivers. During separation these infants were extremely distressed and once the caregiver returned these infants were likely to show ambivalence. Anxious-Avoidant attachment was characterized by avoidant behavior between infants and caregivers. During separation, these infants were likely to show no emotion and upon the caregiver's return either showed avoidance or ignoring behaviors. A subsequent attachment category has been studied and is called Disorganized attachment (Main, Kaplan, & Cassidy, 1985). Upon separation, these infants exhibited unpredictable behavior and at their caregiver's return they were inconsolable (Blue, 2006).

These observations of parent-child interactions led to categories of attachment styles (Ainsworth, 1979; Blue, 2006; Main, Kaplan, & Cassidy, 1985). Attachment styles involve patterns of relating to others and parent-child observations consisted of ways of relating between infants and caregivers. Their classifications are extremely important because they provide the foundation for not only understanding parent-child relationships but also relationships later in life. Attachment styles have also been theorized to have evolved as a process to increase survival. The secure attachment style has been maintained throughout history as a result of humans living in closely united groups. Secure attachment behavior allowed humans to experience greater security related to offspring and survival. However, other attachment styles also were needed to ensure chances of surviving in environments that were less than ideal (i.e., hostile or rejecting environments). Therefore, the avoidant and anxious attachment styles emerged as well (Levine & Heller, 2010). Most theorists contend that childhood attachment is highly associated with romantic attachment (Bartholomew & Horowitz, 1991; Collins & Read, 1990; Feeney & Noller, 1990; Hazan & Shaver, 1987). The work of social psychologists and their study of romantic attachment in adults has led to the development of several methods of assessing romantic attachment processes. Their research proposes that individuals choose partners that are similar to the attachments made with their parents. Romantic partners are selected that confirm and validate their attachment styles and individuals continue to exhibit the same secure, anxious or avoidant behavior that was witnessed in their childhood with their parents in their current adult relationships (Bartholomew & Horowitz, 1991; Collins & Read, 1990; Feeney & Noller, 1990; Hazan & Shaver, 1987).

Working Models

Bowlby posited that children eventually begin to internalize their experiences with their caregivers (Blue, 2006; Bowlby, 1973). These early attachment relationships form a prototype for later relationships in life, including peers and sexual partners. He used the term *working models* to describe these internal representations of attachment relationships and hypothesized two components that are involved within these working models. The first component of a working model involves the child's model of others, and these are individuals that are generally judged to be capable to be called upon in situations when support and protection are needed. The second component includes the child's image of the self, and involves whether the child feels that he or she is the type of individual that someone else is willing to support and protect. It is suspected that these internal representations of early attachment relationships are related to the formation of subsequent relationships later in life (Blue, 2006; Bowlby, 1973). In infancy, working models have a sensorimotor, procedural, and nonlinguistic nature (Cassidy & Shaver, 2008, 2016; Mikulincer & Shaver, 2007, 2016). These working models are a representation of interactions with early caregivers that occurred before linguistic skill and introspection were learned and are often at the pre-verbal level. These models (especially because they are unconscious and automatic) often are reactivated during close relationships in later life and modify an individual's behavior, emotions and expectations. This is often reflected in witnessing an individual's tendency to be drawn to similar patterns of relationships. In addition to this seeking out process, individuals also tend to behave in later relationships in similar ways that match their early working models.

Securely and insecurely attached individuals have specific working models relevant to their particular attachment style. When describing romantic partners, insecurely attached individuals often have negative appraisals of their partners (i.e., predictability, dependability, faithfulness, support). Appraisals of romantic partners by insecurely attached individuals also include rejection and disappointment. On the other hand, when describing romantic partners, securely attached individuals tend to have positive appraisals of their partners. Attachment related working models influence one's expectations of their partner's behaviors. Securely attached individuals tend to have positive mental representations of others and therefore tend to have positive expectations of their partner's availability, support, and responsiveness. Alternatively, insecurely attached individuals tend to have negative working models of others and as a result tend to have negative expectations of their partner's availability, support, and responsiveness. Unlike securely attached individuals, insecurely attached individuals are unable to incorporate contextual influences to partner behavior.

Bowlby (1973) theorized that individuals are often romantically attracted to partners who fit their working model of others. Furthermore, attachments are formed that are congruent to the individual's attachment experiences at the current time and his/her preexisting working models of attachment. Moreover, adult attachment relationships are formed by interactions with early attachment figures and attachment related experiences later in one's life that (challenge) working models formed earlier in life. Several researchers have observed the influence of early internal representations on later relationships in life (Collins & Read, 1990; Hazan & Shaver, 1987). An individual's attachment style and working model play a role in the types of beliefs and perceptions that an individual holds about relationships (Blue, 2006; Collins & Read, 1990; Hazan & Shaver, 1987). Extending this line of thinking, it also was proposed that these dimensions not only influence beliefs and perceptions about relationships, but also about self and others in general (Hazan & Shaver, 1987). Overall, research suggests that working models play a role in adult romantic attachment relationships. An individual's attachment style formed by the relationship with his or her caregiver is related to the development of subsequent working models. It seems that the models formed in childhood provide the foundation for the creation and development of later relationships and experiences. It also appears that these models produce unique sets of perceptions of not only others, but also perceptions of self (Blue, 2006).

Attachment patterns are similar to personality structures and tend to remain stable during one's life and relationships (Cassidy & Shaver, 2008, 2016; Mikulincer & Shaver, 2007, 2016). However, discontinuities in attachment interactional patterns can occur in the lifespan. These patterns along with working models can be modified as a result of personal, familial, and social factors. Both negative and positive life events can interact to change attachment patterns and working models. Related to romantic relationships, an individual experiencing a negative life event (death or loss of a romantic partner) or a positive life event (having a relationship with a supportive and loving romantic partner) can have an effect on his or her attachment patterns and schemas. Stressful life events could influence an individual's attachment style and could result in a shift from secure attachment to an insecure attachment style. Context and environmental factors, such as the formation of new supportive, responsive, and available relationships can alter attachment styles and ultimately one's working models. On the other hand, obtaining similar relationships to those experienced in childhood can result in the continuity of attachment styles.

Attachment in Adulthood

Studying attachment in adulthood, it appears that adults can have multiple attachment figures (Cassidy & Shaver, 2008, 2016; Mikulincer & Shaver, 2007, 2016). How an individual chooses among attachment figures to select one that serves as the principal one is dependent on developmental stage, needs at the current time, and the quality of the relationship. However, the individual's specific attachment style can have an effect on the resulting selection of the principal attachment figure. There have been multiple self-report measures created by researchers to measure adult romantic attachments. The first measure developed by Hazan and Shaver (1987) evaluated behaviors in romantic relationships. The researchers utilized three descriptions that correlated with Ainsworth's (1979) childhood attachment style observations.

- The first description described *securely attached* individuals. These individuals tend to be comfortable with intimacy. They also tend to be comfortable depending on others and having others depend on them. They are able to trust others and behave in trustworthy ways. When a threat of conflict occurs, securely attached individuals are able to utilize constructive solutions.
- The second description identified *avoidantly attached* individuals. These individuals tend to be uncomfortable with intimacy and trusting others. They also tend to be uncomfortable depending on others. They often avoid allowing others to become close to them. They often are distant, self-reliant, and independent. They will deal with stress and conflict by utilizing avoidance.

- The third description classified *anxiously attached* individuals. These individuals tend to desire closeness but feel that others do not want to be as close with them as they prefer. They often fear abandonment or have worries of others love for them. They worry that their partners will not value them in their relationships. They also worry that if they become too close to others their partners will not be available, responsive, or will leave them.

Affect Regulation

In attachment theory, emotions occur when an individual perceives a change in their internal or external world (Cassidy & Shaver, 2008, 2016; Mikulincer & Shaver, 2007, 2016). This change is often automatic and unconscious and is judged dependent on an individual's particular goals at the moment. An individual makes a decision of whether the change is favorable (in which case the emotion would be favorable) or whether the change is unfavorable (in which case the emotion would be unfavorable). This emotion regulation process can be affected by competing goals that in some way make the emotion unattractive (i.e., defenses or personal conflicts). When these competing goals are present, the individual must make an additional decision to modify or eliminate the emotion in order to achieve a state or emotional experience that is more desirable. In securely attached individuals, this emotion altering process is not necessary.

Affect regulation is very important in the maintenance of healthy romantic relationships. Securely attached individuals are effective at regulating their own affect and therefore are able to meet the needs of their partners. It is an important skill to build in order to interact more effectively in a healthy relationship. Before one is able to communicate and interact with a romantic partner, one must work on becoming proficient at regulating one's own affect (Cassidy & Shaver, 2008, 2016; Johnson, 2013; Mikulincer & Shaver, 2007, 2016). Having available and supportive attachment figures has been shown to reduce the experience of distress. Due to the safety that the attachment figure provides, individuals avoid experiencing stress. When observed in childhood this process can exist within the experiences of thinking of attachment figures and/or retrieving positive memories. Securely attached individuals tend to have constructive coping skills and can effectively manage distress (Cassidy & Shaver, 2008, 2016; Mikulincer & Shaver, 2007, 2016). However, insecurely attached individuals tend to have less effective coping skills, experience more intense distress, and have more difficulty managing distress. As a result, insecure individuals are more vulnerable at developing severe emotional problems.

Interpersonal Dynamics

During an interpersonal interaction, an individual must organize and plan his or her behavior (Cassidy & Shaver, 2008, 2016; Mikulincer & Shaver, 2007, 2016). In order to obtain the outcome one desires, an individual must direct his or her plan in order to influence his/her partner's views or responses. In attachment theory, the desirable outcome is influenced by an individual's behaviors in the purpose of obtaining support and the attachment figure's response to this behavioral interaction. In order for this interaction to be successful, the individual must engage in successful execution of behaviors and inhibit any competing behaviors (intrapersonal behaviors). However, it also involves communication, acknowledgment of the attachment partner's needs and desires, and an ability to adjust plans, if needed, dependent on the attachment partner's responses (i.e., interpersonal behaviors). Inherent in the effective communication needed within this interpersonal regulation process involves expressiveness, sensitivity, and conflict management.

Regarding intimacy, attachment styles can influence interpersonal goal setting (Cassidy & Shaver, 2008, 2016; Mikulincer & Shaver, 2007, 2016). Anxiously and avoidantly attached individuals differ in their interpersonal goals. Anxiously attached individuals are focused on needs of protection and intimacy. Because of this focus, anxiously attached individuals are sometimes perceived of as *clingy* and *dependent*. They are often unable to obtain reliable love from a partner. Anxiously attached individuals also experience fears of rejection and abandonment. However, avoidantly attached individuals are focused on needs for autonomy and distance. In addition, they fear closeness and interdependence. Securely attached individuals can utilize both intimacy and distance without a fear of losing their autonomy. However, insecurely attached individuals attempt to fulfill their unmet needs, lower their fears, and maintain their defenses.

Anxiously attached individuals experience a wish to be loved and accepted and seek closeness (Cassidy & Shaver, 2008, 2016; Mikulincer & Shaver, 2007, 2016). They tend to be hypervigilant to rejection, which in some instances inhibits opportunities to approach their partners in an interaction, again to avoid the threat of rejection. Because of this fear of rejection and their negative working models of others, anxiously attached individuals experience anxiety when partners express interest. They might be consumed with obsessive rumination about their behaviors. This cycle can open anxiously attached individuals up to situations of abuse, non-mutually desired sexual encounters, rejection, or being hurt. Avoidantly attached individuals seek autonomy and distance (Cassidy & Shaver, 2008, 2016; Mikulincer & Shaver, 2007, 2016). They have a tendency to inhibit their emotions. Similar to anxiously attached individuals they also have a negative working model of others and therefore avoidantly attached individuals tend to distrust others. They have a view of themselves as being *self-reliant* and *strong* and accordingly have difficulty expressing weakness or dependency. Despite their limitations to closeness they still manage proximity in an avoidance of being rejected or abandoned if the partner loses interest.

Both anxiously and avoidantly attached individuals react in defensive ways that disrupt interpersonal interactions (Cassidy & Shaver, 2008, 2016; Mikulincer & Shaver, 2007, 2016). Anxiously attached individuals overexaggerate their emotional experiences, but especially those that involve distress, vulnerability, and neediness. Because of their self-preoccupation they are distracted from being able to accurately analyze or interpret others' behaviors and needs. Honest and positive behaviors from others might be dismissed and misinterpreted because anxiously attached individuals tend to be distrustful that others would be able to love and accept them. On the other hand, they are also prone to misinterpret negative behaviors since these behaviors trigger their negative self-representations of being unlovable. Avoidantly attached individuals tend to not disclose personal information and can be perceived as being secretive or concealing. Self-disclosure goes against the avoidantly attached individual's goal of avoiding closeness and intimacy but is also related to their lack of trust. Similarly, avoidantly attached individuals have difficulty employing nurturing behaviors toward their partners and might misinterpret signs of nurturance needs as well, especially when expressed needs are related to intimacy or reassurance. In addition, avoidantly attached individuals also tend not to encourage disclosure from their partners.

Conflict management is an important task of interpersonal relationships, and specifically in romantic relationships. Securely attached individuals are able to see conflict as a challenge as opposed to a threat. Securely attached individuals have the viewpoint that they can effectively deal with conflicts. They are able to reduce conflict due to their skills in communication and compromise. Finally, they are successful in being able to see both their own sides and their partner's sides during a conflict (Cassidy & Shaver, 2008, 2016; Mikulincer & Shaver, 2007, 2016). On the other hand, insecurely attached individuals tend to view conflict as a threat. For anxiously attached individuals, when conflict occurs their fear of rejection is triggered. Their tendency to overexaggerate emotions, analyze the conflictual situation in catastrophic ways, and engage in obsessive rumination, challenges them from truly understanding their partners' behaviors and needs. Unlike securely attached individuals, anxiously attached individuals have a harder time with communication, compromise, or negotiation. Anxiously attached individuals react to conflictual situations either through submission or domination. Avoidantly attached individuals avoid conflict and have poor strategies for dealing with conflict as well. Avoidantly attached individuals will most likely dismiss or minimize the importance of the conflictual topic. This aids in the avoidantly attached individuals' escape from the conflict by providing emotional distance from the partner and the conflict itself. Similar to anxiously attached individuals, avoidantly attached individuals are less likely to use communication, compromise, or negotiation. An avoidantly attached individual would also most likely react to conflict with domination, if complete avoidance or escape is impossible (Cassidy & Shaver, 2008, 2016; Mikulincer & Shaver, 2007, 2016).

Attachment and Same Sex Romantic Relationships

Same sex relationships appear to operate similarly to heterosexual relationships (Cassidy & Shaver, 2008, 2016; Herek, 2006; Kurdek, 2005; Mohr, 2008; Mohr & Jackson, 2016; Ridge & Feeney, 1998) and both seem to have similar attachment styles and express similar attachment behavior (Cassidy & Shaver, 2008, 2016; Kurdek, 2005; Mohr, 2008; Mohr & Jackson, 2016). However, traditional gender processes might play a role in same sex romantic relationship attachment behavior (Cassidy & Shaver, 2008, 2016; Fassinger & Arseneau, 2007). Unfortunately, there has not been extensive empirical study of same sex relationships based on attachment theory. However, based on the limited studies available it does appear that both same sex and heterosexual romantic relationships operate in similar ways. Most of the available research on same sex relationships shows a connection between relationship factors and attachment security, such as relationship quality, commitment, and communication patterns (Elizur & Mintzer, 2003; Gaines & Henderson, 2002; Kurdek, 1997, 2002; Mohr, 2008; Mohr & Jackson, 2016).

A study comparing committed gay and lesbian couples with committed and non-committed heterosexual couples resulted in several findings (Roisman et al., 2008). In this study, gay males and lesbians had similar and positive views of their romantic relationships as opposite sex married men and women. However, when compared to the couples in long-term romantic relationships, dating couples, and engaged women endorsed more positive views of their relationships. All committed couples (heterosexual and same sex) exhibited higher quality interpersonal interactions when compared to heterosexual non-committed couples. Engaged heterosexual men exhibited less secure attachment behavior than gay men, lesbians, and engaged women. It does appear that differences within same sex relationships might exist based on traditional gender patterns (Mohr, 2008; Mohr & Jackson, 2016). However, the limited research available provides confusing observations related to gender concerns. There have been several studies showing differing levels of anxiety in lesbian, gay, and bisexual individuals. Despite this difference, there appears to be similarity in relationship functioning and attachment in both genders in same sex romantic relationships, except for one difference related to the interaction between partner attachment behaviors. Specifically, in lesbian relationships one partner's attachment style was dependent upon the other partner's attachment style. Another factor related to gender processes includes sexual exclusivity. Limited research shows that gay couples participate in sexual activities outside of their romantic relationship at rates higher than other relationships. It is hypothesized that sexual infidelity might not represent the same negative consequences to the attachment relationship as it has traditionally been considered in heterosexual relationships (Mohr, 2008; Mohr & Jackson, 2016).

Inherent within any exploration of same sex relationships must also involve a discussion of factors related to prejudice, discrimination, and rejection as well as internalized negative views (i.e., internalized homonegativity). The importance of exploring these dynamics is further supported by research that implies that the relationship quality of same sex relationships has an inverse relationship to factors related to discrimination and stigma (Mohr & Fassinger, 2006; Otis, Riggle, & Rostosky, 2006). Furthermore, the fear system in same sex individuals is hypothesized to become activated in identity development due to the need to perceive threats to safety and due to the experience of emotions, such as fear, shame and anger. This is reflected in studies that support that negative identity development and the process of concealing one's sexual orientation is associated with attachment insecurity (Elizur & Mintzer, 2003; Jellison & McConnell, 2003; Mohr & Fassinger, 2003; Wells & Hansen, 2003). Mohr (2008) proposes that same sex romantic relationships might experience similar double bind processes to parent-child relationships. In same sex romantic relationships, partners potentially experience conflict as a result of their participation in same sex relationships that might be opposite from their values and beliefs. This process involves a fluctuation between a *push-pull*, from engaging in a desire to participate in the relationship but also an urge to distance oneself from a partner who triggers the conflict of values and beliefs. This also is reflected in research that identifies a risk factor of internalized homonegativity for conflict experienced in same sex romantic relationships (Mohr & Fassinger, 2006), as well as links between internalized homonegativity and attachment insecurity (Balsam & Szymanski, 2005; Elizur & Mintzer, 2003; Mohr & Fassinger, 2006). It is hypothesized that internalized homonegativity may negatively impact the ability to build trust and closeness in same sex unions (Mohr, 2008). Negative societal views related to the longevity and commitment of same sex romantic relationships might be internalized by same sex partners and might lead to several relationship dynamics (Mohr, 2008). These views could lead to romantic relationship breakups or the perception that same sex relationships are not considered as significant when compared to heterosexual relationships due to absent legal and societal support (Ainsworth, 1985; Brown, 1995). These views can also influence same sex relationship partners who are insecurely attached by increasing the probability of jealousy (Brown, 1995; Collins & Read, 1990; Sharpsteen & Kirkpatrick, 1997).

Given the importance of early caregivers in Bowlby's theory of attachment, it is important to explore the experience of parent-child relationships as it relates to same sex orientation and to romantic relationship development and processes. What is not known very well is the process of parent-child processes within families of same sex orientation (Mohr, 2008; Mohr & Jackson, 2016). However, empirical support has been provided for the finding that the relationship quality of same sex romantic relationships has an inverse relationship with the experience of parental disapproval with sexual orientation identifications (Murphy, 1989; Smith & Brown, 1997). Considering attachment processes and identity development in same gender sexual orientation individuals, the experience of identifying one's same sex orientation to caretakers can involve rejection, shame, ridicule, and denial. In addition, this identification is made to attachment figures that are (in ideal situations) supposed to provide security, comfort, reassurance, and acceptance. In parent-child relationships that involve insecure attachment patterns, the identification process can potentially be even more problematic. One study of same gender sexual orientation adults found that their memories of parental attachment styles have associations with levels of parental rejection of same gender sexual orientation (Mohr & Fassinger, 2003). Working models of individuals with same gender sexual orientation might have positive or negative consequences based on parental views regarding same sex orientation. Therefore, having a positive (affirming) or negative (non-affirming) coming out process with parents, can positively or negatively influence working models. This is consistent with Bowlby's (1988) ideas that working models can change through subsequent experiences throughout the lifespan. A positive coming out process leads to positive romantic relationship attachment security (Mohr & Fassinger, 2003) and can even serve as a preventative factor of victimization and violence (Hershberger & D'Augelli, 1995).

In 2015, same sex couples were granted the right to legally marry. Up until that time same sex couples utilized other methods to signify their commitment, such as cohabitation, civil unions, domestic partnerships, designated beneficiaries, and reciprocal beneficiaries. Given that marriage has historically been granted to heterosexual couples, it is argued that the institution of marriage is a product of heteronormativity and represents the normality or privilege assumed for the traditional practice of marriage (Duggan, 2003). However, in the absence of the legalized opportunity to marry, same sex couples have lacked clear and identifiable symbolizations of romantic relationship milestones, especially regarding the beginning of relationships. Many same sex couples decided to utilize the first time that they had a sexual encounter, the date that they began cohabitation, the date they mutually purchased a home, or the date of their civil union or other ceremony to identify the commitment of their relationships (Patterson, Ciabattari, & Schwartz, 1999; Reczek, Elliott, & Umberson, 2009; Stiers, 1999). Given that Riggle, Rostosky, and Horne (2010) found that legal recognition of same sex couples results in reports of lowered psychological distress and increased meaning and well-being, it is apparent that the legalization of marriage has many benefits.

Attachment and Transgender Romantic Relationships

There is little research available regarding the romantic relationships of trans individuals (Brown, 2010; Kins et al., 2008; Pfeffer, 2008) and most importantly the attachment behavior of this population. Originally, there was a focus of research conducted with male-to-female (MtF) trans individuals (Cromwell, 1999; Devor, 1997; H. Rubin, 2003). However, recently more research is being conducted with female-to-male (FtM) trans individuals (Brown, 2010; Devor, 1997; Fleming et al., 1984; Huxley, Kenna, & Brandon, 1981b; Kins et al., 2008; Lev, 2004). In some of the research conducted with MtF trans individuals, it has been noted that their disclosure of the transitioning process had concerning consequences on the relationship. The heterosexual partners in these couples experienced disrupted perceptions and expectations of their relationships (i.e., the future of the relationship) (Brown, 2010; Buxton, 2007). As a result, most of the marriages ended in separation or divorce (Buxton, 2007; Huxley, Kenna, & Brandon, 1981a). When comparing female-to-male (FtM) trans individuals and their partners to heterosexual non-trans couples, no differences were found in the areas of relationship and sexual satisfaction, psychological well-being, and sex roles (Fleming et al., 1984; Huxley, Kenna, & Brandon, 1981b; Kins et al., 2008). In the past, there have been assumptions that FtM's were attracted to women (Huxley, Kenna, & Brandon, 1981b; Pauly, 1974). In a study observing the sexual orientation of FtM's, conclusions regarding attraction were revealed. FtM's who reported being attracted to women found both heterosexual and lesbian women desirable. However, heterosexual women were evaluated to be more desirable than lesbian women (Chivers & Bailey, 2000). In another earlier study, FtM's endorsed a sexual preference for males or both females and males (Steiner & Bernstein, 1981).

However, recent research suggests that FtM's are sexually attracted to men (Bockting, Benner & Coleman, 2009; Meier, Pardo et al., 2013). While transitioning it has been suggested that FtM's sexual attraction changes from men or women only to a bisexual or queer sexual orientation (Meier, Sharp, et al., 2013). Despite the lack of relevant research of trans individuals in romantic relationships, recent studies have suggested that many FtM's hold romantic relationships (Brown, 2010; Devor, 1997; Lev, 2004). However, what remains unknown includes rates of romantic relationships of trans individuals, the process and rates of dissolution of romantic relationships with trans individuals, protective factors for maintaining romantic relationships, as well as the attachment process of trans romantic relationships.

Attachment and Singlehood

Schachner, Shaver, and Gillath (2008) applied attachment theory to single adults and made several hypotheses regarding their attachment behavior compared to committed romantic couples. They theorized whether single adults were more avoidantly attached or anxiously attached than partnered or married adults. Furthermore, they questioned whether single adults are similar to partnered or married adults regarding reliance on attachment figures and attachment security. In addition, they wondered whether single adults' choice of attachment figures might be individuals besides romantic partners, such as friends or family members. The results of their study showed no significant differences in attachment security between single adults and partnered or married adults. However, they did find an association between single males and attachment anxiety. They attributed this finding to be a result of traditional gender roles, which potentially promote the encouragement of males to initiate relationships and thereby risk being rejected. In addition, they found long-term singlehood to be linked to the experience of depression, general anxiety, and sexual dissatisfaction. Furthermore, they found an association between attachment insecurity, singlehood, and the experience of loneliness (Schachner, Shaver, & Gillath, 2008).

Single adults within this study also endorsed childhood relationships with both parents as being troubled (i.e., neglect, indifference). Related to the selection of attachment figures in adulthood, single adults tended to utilize their attachment figures differently than partnered and married adults. Single adults reported utilizing familial relatives (i.e., sister) and friends, whereas coupled adults reported utilizing romantic partners and children as attachment figures. Despite this difference, they still utilized attachment figures to provide a secure base, similar to partnered and married adults, and had as many attachment figures as coupled adults (Schachner, Shaver,

& Gillath, 2008). The study's authors (Schachner, Shaver, & Gillath, 2008) proposed the need for additional study of singlehood as it relates to attachment theory and behavior. Due to their finding of troubled childhood parental reports of the single adults within their study, they also indicated that the parent-child relationship especially might have an influence on long-term singlehood. More research in this area would provide greater clarity to the understanding of singlehood and its origins in attachment theory.

PATTERNS OF MATE SELECTION

Wachtel's (1993) concept of *cyclical psychodynamics* has utility when explaining the patterns of mate selection. Cyclical psychodynamics is founded in psychodynamic theory and incorporates repetitive patterns of interactional dynamics between individuals as it is played out within intrapersonal processes and everyday living. This theory observes how individuals play out patterns in everyday life (Wachtel, 1993). Intrapersonal processes manifest in a repetitive and causative pattern resulting in a problematic lifestyle and impaired interpersonal interactions. According to this theory, a *vicious circle* occurs because even with insight into the origin of the pattern the individual will continue to play out the pattern *until* the experience of anxiety and fear no longer exceed the insight of the origin of the pattern (or more simply put, until the anxiety and fear are processed and revolved). Although the individual's patterns are often connected to the past, within cyclical psychodynamics, the past no longer maintains the pattern. The individuals' present behaviors maintain the pattern. To fully address the pattern, one must take into consideration the individual's entire process, how it originated in the past but also how it is being maintained in the present. Cyclical psychodynamics is different from *repetition compulsion*, a concept discussed by Sigmund Freud (Freud, 1920). Within the concept of repetition compulsion, the individual intentionally and actively replays out a pattern with the hope or wish of *mastering* the trauma (or to change it in some way). However, in cyclical psychodynamics the individual is not trying to intentionally re-create the pattern. In this case, the individual is trying to avoid the situation from happening. Although this is the individual's intention, in the end, the individual causes the outcome that he or she is ultimately trying to prevent. It is suspected that either or both of the concepts of cyclical psychodynamics and repetition compulsion play a role in the interactional dynamics of couples. It is known that individuals play out attachment patterns and inherent within these patterns might be contributing experiences resulting from aspects of both of these concepts. Whether the activity of playing out these patterns is intentional or not and whether there is priority placed on the origin of the need for the pattern or not, it seems plausible that these concepts could be a contributing factor.

CONCLUDING REMARKS

There are many theories as to how love and romantic attachments develop. Theoretical foundations and psychological models were described and offered as the framework for the understanding of love and romantic relationships. Attachment theory has also been offered and provided as an option of understanding the impact that attachment relationships have in the loss and associated grief of these relationships. However, there are many other theories that propose to explain what occurs in romantic relationships. One connection of all of these theories involves the presence of utilizing conscious or unconscious factors in selecting a mate. It is perhaps a lack of understanding or insight of these unconscious factors that play a role in the distress and grief experienced during a romantic relationship breakup. The power of working models is often observed in psychotherapy. Upon inquiry of childhood experiences, individuals in psychotherapy often describe an origin of attachment patterns existing since childhood. The ways in which these individuals behave with their romantic partners often mimic these childhood interactions, especially in times of stress and rejection. By gaining insight into one's working models, one is able to see their patterns firsthand and consider how they continue to be drawn into similar relationships and interactions. Through this insight, individuals are also able to understand how their childhood caregivers were able or unable to respond appropriately to their needs. With this understanding, these same individuals are able to learn to identify similar patterns in their adult relationships, including their romantic relationships.

Chapter Two

Digital Relationships

The Role of Technology and Social Media in the Formation and Maintenance of Romantic Relationships

Currently, technology and social media play a significant role in the formation and maintenance of romantic relationships. Therefore, a special section will be provided to enhance the understanding of how technology and social media impact the development of romantic relationships. This chapter will be devoted to a review of the various platforms of social media and how they contribute to the motivation to participate in romantic relationships.

FACEBOOK, TWITTER, AND INSTAGRAM

According to facebook.com, Facebook was created by Mark Zuckerberg on February 4, 2004, with a mission to "give people the power to share and make the world more open and connected." On Facebook, individuals can create a profile that provides information about themselves, including their name or nickname, gender, and relationship status (www.facebook.com). In addition, users can also add photographs to their profile. Users can post an update on their feelings, thoughts, events, or even their location. Specific to relevant posts, users can *tag* their friends by sending a link to their profile. Individuals can build their network by accepting friend requests from family, friends, and other individuals and can also send friend requests to others to consider joining their network. Facebook.com reported that in June 2015, approximately 968 million users logged onto Facebook on a daily basis. Furthermore, 844 million users utilized the mobile site on a daily basis. Twitter was also created as a tool to increase the connection and communication of friends, families, and coworkers (www.twitter.com). Twitter operates through the sharing of messages called tweets, which includes text with a maximum of 140 characters as well as photographs, videos, and links. Twitter users post messages to their profiles as well as their included network of *followers*. Followers are individuals that the user invites to be a part of their network and allow the user to subscribe to those individuals' Twitter updates. When a new message has been posted by any of the user's followers, it appears on the user's Twitter page. Users can also be followed by others and are sent an email when a new follower is identified. However, there is an option for a user to have their tweets remain protected by approving new followers. Users can also send private messages to another user, which are not accessible to public viewing. Finally, Instagram offers a service that advertises increasing connection through the sharing of photographs (www.instagram.com). Users are able to take pictures with their cellular phones and upload the pictures for friends and family to view. Users are even able to apply a filter to pictures as an added incentive. All photographs uploaded to Instagram are public; however, if users make their accounts private, they can approve any requests to follow or view their pictures.

Each of the platforms above includes the word *connection* in their company descriptions and missions. One is forced to stop and ponder about the definition of connection and how these platforms either enhance or inhibit true connection with others. Technology has continued to become a vehicle in today's society for communication, bonding, and connection. Johnson (2013) discusses the influence of technology on relationships. She describes how technology is utilized as a way to bond or connect in this society. Use of social media systems has become more popular than actual and direct modes of communication. Even though individuals describe being more connected through the use of social media, it must be still acknowledged that the connection is diluted by the internet and some type of technological device. Surveys of technology and social media use can provide a better understanding of its influence on relationship development, maintenance, and dissolution. As technology and social media use continue to rise and become the major method of communication utilized by society, it is imperative that its significance be explored as it relates to interpersonal relationships. The following data is offered to provide clarity on American technology and social media use.[1]

SOCIAL MEDIA USAGE

According to Pew research reports (Pew Research Center, 2015) in 2014, 71 percent of Americans used Facebook. The age of Facebook users has increased with older Americans' (sixty-five and older) Facebook use increasing from 35 percent in 2012 to 56 percent in 2014. Related to gender, women (77 percent) tend to use Facebook more than men (66 percent). However, the age group with the highest use of Facebook includes eighteen-to-twenty-nine-year-olds which represent 87 percent. Those thirty-to-forty-nine-year-old individuals represent 73 percent and fifty-to-sixty-four-year-olds represent 63 percent of Facebook usage. Related to ethnicity and Facebook use, 73 percent of Hispanic adults use Facebook, 71 percent of white, non-Hispanic adults use Facebook, and 67 percent of black, non-Hispanic adults use Facebook (Pew Research Center, 2015). This report was updated in 2016 and revealed an increase in Facebook usage, with 79 percent of online users reporting using Facebook (Pew Research Center, 2016). Older adults (sixty-five years old and older) also experienced an increase in usage with 62 percent of these individuals using Facebook. Women (83 percent) also reported slightly higher usage when compared to men (75 percent). Finally, similar to 2015, the age group of eighteen-to-twenty-nine-year-olds (88 percent) still represents the largest age group to use Facebook followed by thirty-to-forty-nine-year-olds (84 percent) (Pew Research Center, 2016).

When queried about friendships, Facebook users reported a median Facebook friend network of 155 *friends*. However, when asked to specify *actual* friends, this number dropped to fifty friends. Within adults' Facebook friendship networks, most adults reported being friends with family (93 percent were friends with familial relatives other than parents/children; 45 percent were friends with parents; 43 percent were friends with children). When looking at adults' Facebook friendships with friends, 91 percent reported being Facebook friends with current friends and 87 percent reported being Facebook friends with past friends from high school and college. Other Facebook friends included 58 percent being friends with work colleagues and 36 percent being friends with neighbors. Finally, 39 percent of adults reported being Facebook friends with individuals they had never met (Pew Research Center, 2015).

In 2014, 23 percent of adults used Twitter, compared to 24 percent of adults in 2016 (Pew Research Center, 2015, 2016). Twenty-one percent of users were women and 24 percent of users were men (Pew Research Center, 2015). Adult use based on ethnicity is basically similar with 27 percent of black, non-Hispanic adults; 25 percent of Hispanic adults; and 21 percent of white, non-Hispanic adults using Twitter. The age group of eighteen-to-twenty-nine-year-olds represents the largest group of Twitter users at 37 percent. Other age groups include thirty-to-forty-nine-year-olds with 25 percent, fifty-to-sixty-four-year-olds with 12 percent, and sixty-five-year-olds and older with 10 percent of Twitter use. The groups that experienced a significant increase in use from 2013 include the following populations: men, white adults, non-Hispanic adults, and sixty-five-year-olds and older adults (Pew Research Center, 2015). In 2014, 26 percent of adult users reported using Instagram. Women represented 29 percent of adult users and men were associated with a 22 percent usage rate. Black, non-Hispanic adults represented 38 percent; Hispanic adults represented 34 percent; and white, non-Hispanic adults represented 21 percent of Instagram use. Instagram use by age group included, eighteen-to-twenty-nine-year-olds (53 percent), thirty-to-forty-nine-year-olds (25 percent), fifty-to-sixty-four-year-olds (11 percent) and adults age sixty-five and older (6 percent). The groups that experienced a significant increase in use from 2013 include all demographic groups reported (Pew Research Center, 2015).

Because social media is so widely utilized, it is not surprising that 52 percent (2015) and 56 percent (2016) of adults use two or more sites, with 28 percent of users using only one social media site (Pew Research Center, 2015, 2016). Among those who only utilize one social media site, it appears that Facebook is the most used platform with 79 percent reporting usage. Facebook maintains popularity among its users; however, other sites are experiencing usage increases. In addition, many new sites continue to be created (Pew Research Center, 2015). When studying daily use of social media sites, Facebook use continues to rise with other sites maintaining stable usage. For example, 70 percent (2015) and 76 percent (2016) of users reported visiting Facebook daily, 49 percent (2015) and 51 percent (2016) of users reported visiting Instagram daily and 36 percent (2015) and 42 percent (2016) of users reported visiting Twitter daily (Pew Research Center, 2015, 2016). Not only do Facebook users represent the largest daily usage of social media sites, 45 percent of daily Facebook users utilize Facebook several times per day (Pew Research Center, 2015). Finally, daily Facebook usage is associated with a significant increase of use since 2013 from 63 percent to 70 percent in 2015 to 76 percent in 2016. Instagram usage did not experience a significant change from 2013 to 2015 or 2016. Twitter daily usage experienced a decrease in daily usage from 46 percent in 2013 to 36 percent in 2014 (Pew Research Center, 2015, 2016). One additional finding of the 2016 report revealed that 72 percent of American adults utilize messaging apps. The report, categorized into three areas and revealed evidence of 29 percent usage of general purpose apps, (i.e., WhatsApp and Kik), 24 percent usage of automatic deletion apps, (i.e., Snapchat, Wickr) and 5 percent usage of anonymous chat apps (i.e., YikYak, Whisper) (Pew Research Center, 2016).

ONLINE DATING

Online dating sites are increasing as individuals attempt to overcome the difficulties of finding potential mates through traditional means (Pew Research Center, 2013). There are currently three types of online dating applications. The first type allows users to create a profile and view the profiles of potential mates (i.e., match.com, OkCupid, Plenty of Fish). The second form involves matching potential mates using an algorithm method (i.e., eHarmony). Finally, a third form includes cell phone dating applications, (i.e., Tinder, Grindr). The advantages of these online dating sites over traditional methods of dating are that they provide (Pew Research Center, 2013):

- an ability to seek out potential mates from a wide social network
- an opportunity to communicate before initially meeting via online communication
- an ability to screen potential mates through the use of algorithmic matching programs

Online dating sites improve opportunities for certain groups of individuals to find potential mates due to limited social resources (i.e., middle-aged heterosexuals, gay and lesbian adults, African-Americans). On the other hand, online dating sites could potentially have a conflicting outcome on the stability of marriage with the possible trend of young adult men delaying or not marrying due to the increased accessibility to potential partners and decreased motivation to commitment (Pew Research Center, 2013).

Apparently, 9 percent of American adults (and 11 percent of internet users) have reported using an online dating site including match.com, OkCupid, and eHarmony. Furthermore, 3 percent of American adults (and 7 percent of cell phone app users) have reported using a cell phone dating app. This represents 38 percent of American adults who are single and looking for a partner that have used an online dating site or cell phone dating app (Pew Research Center, 2013). It appears that given the impact of the digital era on daily life in romantic relationships, many individuals in long-term relationships initially met online. Specifically, 5 percent of American adults in committed romantic relationships met each other online. Meeting a potential mate online is more common for younger individuals, with eighteen-to-twenty-nine-year-olds making up 8 percent of those married or in a committed relationship who met their romantic partner online. Meeting a mate online is less common for older adults (with thirty-to-forty-nine-year-olds making up 7 percent, fifty-to-sixty-four-year-olds making up 3 percent, and sixty-five-year-olds and older adults making up 1 percent). Relevant to online dating apps and sites, 34 percent of American adults reported using these resources to meet a potential partner with 3 percent stating that they had not used these dating sites or apps (Pew Research Center, 2013).

Two online behaviors have increased over the years (2005–2013) and include flirting and searching for past or future romantic partners. American adults reported flirting and searching for online partners in similar amounts (24 percent). Searching for past romantic partners, 22 percent of men and 26 percent of women reported engaging in researching past relationships. In addition, 27 percent of black non-Hispanic adults, 24 percent of white non-Hispanic adults, and 22 percent of Hispanic adults endorsed looking up information about past relationships. When looking at the age of adults to engage in looking up previous romantic partners, 32 percent were eighteen-to-twenty-four-year-olds, 34 percent were twenty-five-to-thirty-four-year-olds, 29 percent were thirty-five-to-forty-four-year-olds, 21 percent were forty-five-to-fifty-four-year-olds, 15 percent were fifty-five-to-sixty-four-year-olds and nine percent were sixty-five-year-olds and older (see table 1). For those American adults who reported flirting online, 27 percent were men and 21 percent were women. In addition, 32 percent of black non-Hispanic adults, 29 percent of Hispanic adults, and 22 percent of white non-Hispanic adults reported flirting online. Furthermore, 47 percent of eighteen-to-twenty-four-year-olds, 40 percent of twenty-five-to-thirty-four-year-olds, 26 percent of thirty-five-to-sixty-four-year-olds, 13 percent of forty-five-to-fifty-four-year-olds, 8 percent of fifty-five-to-sixty-four-year-olds and 6 percent of sixty-five-year-olds and older adults reported flirting online (see table 3). Further research of online searches for information about past romantic partners shows that 38 percent of single adults looking for romantic relationships, 32 percent of married or committed relationships of ten years or less, 24 percent of single individuals not looking for a relationship and 15 percent of married or committed individuals of more than ten years reported having searched online for information about someone they dated in the past (see table 2). Additionally, 51 percent of single adults looking for romantic relationships, 39 percent of married or committed relationships of ten years or less, 24 percent of single adults not looking for romantic relationships and 6 percent of married or committed adults for more than 10 years reported having flirted online (Pew Research Center, 2013) (see table 4).

Table 1. Search for Previous Romantic Partners by Gender, Ethnicity, and Age Group

Category	*Percentage*
Gender	
Women	26
Men	22
Ethnicity	
Black, Non-Hispanic	27
White, Non-Hispanic	24
Hispanic	22
Age	
18–24 year olds	32
25–34 year olds	34
35–44 year olds	29
45–54 year olds	21
55–64 year olds	15
65+ year olds	9

Note. Adapted from "Online Dating and Relationships: Part 3: The Broader Online Environment around Dating and Relationships," by A. Smith and M. Duggan, 2013, Pew Research. Copyright 2013 by the Pew Research Center.

Table 2. Search for Previous Romantic Partners by Relationship Status

Relationship Status	*Percentage*
Single adults desiring a relationship	38
Single adults not desiring a relationship	24
Married/committed couples (10 years or less)	32
Married/committed couples (10 years or more)	15

Note. Adapted from "Online Dating and Relationships: Part 3: The Broader Online Environment around Dating and Relationships," by A. Smith and M. Duggan, 2013, Pew Research. Copyright 2013 by the Pew Research Center.

Table 3. Engaging in Flirting Online by Gender, Ethnicity, and Age Group

Category	*Percentage*
Gender	
Women	21
Men	27
Ethnicity	
Black, Non-Hispanic	32
White, Non-Hispanic	22
Hispanic	29
Age	
18–24 year olds	47
25–34 year olds	40
35–44 year olds	26
45–54 year olds	13
55–64 year olds	8
65+ year olds	6

Note. Adapted from "Online Dating and Relationships: Part 3: The Broader Online Environment around Dating and Relationships," by A. Smith and M. Duggan, 2013, Pew Research. Copyright 2013 by the Pew Research Center.

Table 4. Engaging in Flirting Online by Relationship Status

Relationship Status	*Percentage*
Single adults desiring a relationship	51
Single adults not desiring a relationship	24
Married/committed couples (10 years or less)	39
Married/committed couples (10 years or more)	6

Note. Adapted from "Online Dating and Relationships: Part 3: The Broader Online Environment around Dating and Relationships," by A. Smith and M. Duggan, 2013, Pew Research. Copyright 2013 by the Pew Research Center.

When looking at American adults who have searched online about a current romantic partner or about a partner before an initial date, 29 percent of Americans have reported searching for this information, with 25 percent being men and 33 percent being women. In addition, 34 percent of eighteen-to-twenty-nine-year-olds, 29 percent of thirty-to-forty-nine-year-olds and 16 percent of fifty-to-sixty-four-year-olds endorsed looking up information about a current dating partner (see table 5). Finally, out of those who are single and looking for a romantic relationship and in a committed relationship for ten years or less, 53 percent reported using an online dating site or app and 21 percent reported not using an online dating site or app (Pew Research Center, 2013).

Table 5. Searching a Current Partner or Potential Partner before an Initial Date by Gender and Age Group (Single and Looking or in a Committed Relationship for 10 Years or Less)

Category	*Percentage*
Gender	
Women	33
Men	25
Age	
18–29 year olds	34
30–49 year olds	29
50–64 year olds	16

Note. Adapted from "Online Dating and Relationships: Part 3: The Broader Online Environment around Dating and Relationships," by A. Smith and M. Duggan, 2013, Pew Research. Copyright 2013 by the Pew Research Center.

Twenty-four percent of American adults who are single and looking for a romantic relationship or in a committed relationship for ten years or less used the internet or email to maintain a long-distance relationship with 23 percent being men and 24 percent being women. In addition, 29 percent were eighteen-to-twenty-nine-year-olds, 23 percent were thirty-to-forty-nine-year-olds, and 13 percent were fifty-to-sixty-four-year-olds (see table 6). Twenty percent of American adults who are single and looking for a romantic relationship or in a committed relationship for ten years or less, asked someone out for a first date online or by email, with 23 percent being men and 16 percent being women. In

Table 6. Internet/Email Use to Maintain a Long-Term Relationship by Gender and Age Group

Category	*Percentage*
Gender	
Women	24
Men	23
Age	
18–29 year olds	29
30–49 year olds	23
50–64 year olds	13

Note. Adapted from "Online Dating and Relationships: Part 3: The Broader Online Environment around Dating and Relationships," by A. Smith and M. Duggan, 2013, Pew Research. Copyright 2013 by the Pew Research Center.

Table 7. Internet/Email Use to Request a First Date by Gender and Age Group

Category	*Percentage*
Gender	
Women	16
Men	23
Age	
18–29 year olds	16
30–49 year olds	24
50–64 year olds	18

Note. Adapted from "Online Dating and Relationships: Part 3: The Broader Online Environment around Dating and Relationships," by A. Smith and M. Duggan, 2013, Pew Research. Copyright 2013 by the Pew Research Center.

addition, 16 percent were eighteen-to-twenty-nine-year-olds, 24 percent were thirty-to-forty-nine-year-olds and 18 percent were fifty-to-sixty-four-year-olds (Pew Research Center, 2013) (see table 7).

ROMANTIC RELATIONSHIPS AND SOCIAL NETWORKING SITES

Utilizing information gained from social networking sites (SNS), 31 percent of SNS users have utilized SNS to gain access to information related to previous romantic partners. Related to age, 48 percent of eighteen-to-twenty-nine-year-olds, 31 percent of thirty-to-forty-nine-year-olds, 16 percent of fifty-to-sixty-four-year-olds and 7 percent of sixty-five-year-olds and older adults reported using SMS to obtain information of previous romantic partners (see table 8). Online daters also use SNS to post pictures or other information related to a date, with 17 percent of online daters reporting doing this. Related to age, 31 percent of eighteen-to-twenty-nine-year-olds, 15 percent of thirty-to-forty-nine-year-olds, 4 percent of fifty-to-sixty-four-year-olds, and less than 1 percent of sixty-five-year-olds and older adults reported posting pictures and information related to their dates on SNS (Pew Research Center, 2013) (see table 9).

Table 8. Use of SNS to Gain Information to a Previous Romantic Partner by Age Group

Age	*Percentage*
18–29 year olds	48
30–49 year olds	31
50–64 year olds	16
65+ year olds	7

Note. Adapted from "Online Dating and Relationships: Part 4: Social Networking Sites, Cell Phones, Dating, and Relationships," by A. Smith and M. Duggan, 2013, Pew Research. Copyright 2013 by the Pew Research Center.

Table 9. Use of SNS to Post Pictures or Information Related to a Date by Age Group

Age	*Percentage*
18–29 year olds	31
30–49 year olds	15
50–64 year olds	4
65+ year olds	<1

Note. Adapted from "Online Dating and Relationships: Part 4: Social Networking Sites, Cell Phones, Dating, and Relationships," by A. Smith and M. Duggan, 2013, Pew Research. Copyright 2013 by the Pew Research Center.

More observations related to online dating and SNS use include 30 percent of SNS users reported obtaining information about a potential romantic partner. Also, following a friend's suggestion, 12 percent of SMS users reported deciding to friend or follow an individual on a social networking site with the potential to date that individual. Furthermore, 15 percent of SNS users reported asking an individual out on a date via a social networking site (Pew Research Center, 2013) (see table 10).

Table 10. SNS Use and Other Dating Behaviors

Category	*Percentage*
SNS Use to obtain information regarding a potential romantic partner	30
SNS Use to friend/follow a potential romantic partner	12
SNS Use to ask a potential romantic partner out on a date	15

Note. Adapted from "Online Dating and Relationships: Part 4: Social Networking Sites, Cell Phones, Dating, and Relationships," by A. Smith and M. Duggan, 2013, Pew Research. Copyright 2013 by the Pew Research Center.

Individuals also reported uncomfortable dating experiences on social networking sites and this is especially true for younger adults (Pew Research Center, 2013). Twenty-seven percent of SNS users reported having to block or unfriend someone who was flirting with them (41 percent of eighteen-to-twenty-nine-year-olds, 26 percent of thirty-to-forty-nine-year-olds, 13 percent of fifty-to-sixty-four-year-olds and 7 percent of sixty-five-year-olds and older adults) (see table 11). In addition, 22 percent of SMS users reported unfriending or blocking a previous romantic partner (36 percent of eighteen-to-twenty-nine-year-olds, 23 percent of thirty-to-forty-nine-year-olds, 5 percent of fifty-to-sixty-four-year-olds and 4 percent of sixty-five-year-olds and older adults) (see table 12); and 17 percent of SMS users reported deleting pictures of previous romantic partners (36 percent of eighteen-to-twenty-nine-year-olds, 13 percent of thirty-to-forty-nine-year-olds, 2 percent of fifty-to-sixty-four-year-olds and 1 percent of sixty-four-year-olds and older adults) (see table 13).

Table 11. Blocking/Unfriending Someone Who was Flirting with Them by Age Group

Age	Percentage
18–29 year olds	41
30–49 year olds	26
50–64 year olds	13
65+ year olds	7

Note. Adapted from "Online Dating and Relationships: Part 4: Social Networking Sites, Cell Phones, Dating, and Relationships," by A. Smith and M. Duggan, 2013, Pew Research. Copyright 2013 by the Pew Research Center.

Table 12. Blocking/Unfriending a Previous Romantic Partner by Age Group

Age	Percentage
18–29 year olds	36
30–49 year olds	23
50–64 year olds	5
65+ year olds	4

Note. Adapted from "Online Dating and Relationships: Part 4: Social Networking Sites, Cell Phones, Dating, and Relationships," by A. Smith and M. Duggan, 2013, Pew Research. Copyright 2013 by the Pew Research Center.

Table 13. Deleting Pictures of Previous Romantic Partners by Age Group

Age	Percentage
18–29 year olds	36
30–49 year olds	13
50–64 year olds	2
65+ year olds	1

Note. Adapted from "Online Dating and Relationships: Part 4: Social Networking Sites, Cell Phones, Dating, and Relationships," by A. Smith and M. Duggan, 2013, Pew Research. Copyright 2013 by the Pew Research Center.

Sixty-six percent of American adults are married (47 percent), in a committed relationship with a romantic partner but not living together (12 percent), and living with a romantic partner (6 percent). Of the 66 percent of American adults who are married or in committed relationships, 93 percent own a cell phone, 88 percent utilize the internet, and 71 percent visit/use social networking sites (SNS) (see table 14). A small group of American adults either married or in committed relationships share digital tools, with approximately 27 percent of married/committed couples sharing an email account, 11 percent of married/committed couples sharing an online calendar, and 11 percent of married/committed couples sharing a social networking site profile, on sites such as Facebook and Twitter. It appears that couples that have been in a relationship longer tend to share email addresses, account passwords, and social media profiles. Accordingly, 67 percent of married/committed couples share a password (Pew Research Center, 2013) (see table 15).

Table 14. Cell Phone, Internet and SNS Use

Category	*Percentage*
Cell Phone Use	93
Internet Use	88
SNS Use	71

Note. Adapted from "Couples, the Internet and Social Media: Main Report," by A. Lenhart and M. Duggan, 2014, Pew Research. Copyright 2014 by the Pew Research Center.

Table 15. Digital Tool Sharing

Category	*Percentage*
Email Account	27
Online Calendar	11
SNS Profile	11
Password	67

Note. Adapted from "Couples, the Internet and Social Media: Main Report," by A. Lenhart and M. Duggan, 2014, Pew Research. Copyright 2014 by the Pew Research Center.

When asked to report on the perception of the impact of the internet on their relationships, 10 percent of married and committed romantic couples acknowledged that the internet had a major impact, 17 percent stated that the internet had a minor impact, and 72 percent described the internet as having no impact at all on their relationships (see table 16). The perception of the impact of the internet on relationships varied by age. Young married and committed couples tended to report the most impact of the internet on their relationships. Specifically, 21 percent of eighteen-to-twenty-nine-year-olds reported a major impact and 24 percent of eighteen-to-twenty-nine-year-olds reported a minor impact. Also, couples who had been together for shorter durations (less than ten years) tended to perceive the internet to have more of an impact on their relationships (when compared to relationships of more than ten years). In addition, couples who owned smart phones, used social media sites, and dated online tended to perceive that the internet had more of an impact on their relationships. Even among those who perceived the internet as having a minor impact on their relationships, most reported a positive experience with 74 percent reporting a positive impact, 20 percent reporting a negative impact and 4 percent reporting a positive and negative impact (Pew Research Center, 2013).

Table 16. Internet's Impact on Married and Committed Relationships

Category	Percentage
Major Impact	10
Minor Impact	17
No Impact	72

Note. Adapted from "Couples, the Internet and Social Media: Main Report," by A. Lenhart and M. Duggan, 2014, Pew Research. Copyright 2014 by the Pew Research Center.

Although technology in many ways has increased the ways individuals (and couples) can communicate with each other, it appears that it also can bring conflict to a relationship. One source of conflict involves arguments regarding the amount of time spent online, which accounted for 8 percent of adults. Another four percent reported feeling upset regarding their partners' online activity. This conflict is more likely to be experienced by couples in shorter relationships (ten years or less) and by younger aged adults (Pew Research Center, 2013).

Related to cell phone usage, 25 percent of partners in committed romantic relationships perceived that their partners' cell phone use was distracting when together (Pew Research Center, 2013). Again, this was more common in younger couples. On the other hand, 21 percent of partners in committed relationships perceived greater emotional intimacy or connection as a result of online communication or text messaging. Furthermore, 25 percent of partners in relationships reported texting their partner while both were at home. Nine percent stated that they were able to obtain resolution to arguments through online communication and texting (see table 17). Individuals in long-term relationships (ten years or more) reported experiencing these outcomes of internet use on their relationships more than couples in shorter relationships (less than ten years). Younger adults also reported positive aspects of technology including texting their partner while at home (33 percent), feeling more connected as a result of online communication and texting (41 percent) and enhancing conflict resolution (23 percent).

Table 17. Total Outcomes of Internet/Technology Use

Category	Percentage
Arguments regarding time spent online	8
Feeling upset regarding partner's online activity	4
Finding cell phone use as distracting	25
Greater Emotional Intimacy	21
Texting a partner while both at home	25
Resolution to arguments through online communication and texting	9

Note. Adapted from "Couples, the Internet and Social Media: Main Report," by A. Lenhart and M. Duggan, 2014, Pew Research. Copyright 2014 by the Pew Research Center.

Technology has offered the opportunity for individuals to communicate with each other utilizing physically intimate images. Sexting is the act of receiving, sending, or forwarding photos or videos of a sexual nature, through cell phones. Three percent of adult cell phone users acknowledged forwarding a sext. Twenty percent of adult cell phone users have reported being the recipient of a sext and 9 percent have reported being senders of sexts and is a significant increase from 2012. Younger adults tended to be the population that participates in the activity of sexting, with 44 percent of eighteen-to-twenty-four-year-olds and 34 percent of twenty-five-to-thirty-four-year-olds receiving sexts and 15 percent of eighteen-to-twenty-four-year-olds and 22 percent of twenty-five-to-thirty-four-year-olds sending sexts (see table 18). American adults who owned a smart phone, had a greater likelihood of sexting (compared to other cell phone users) due to the ease of taking and sending photographs (Pew Research Center, 2013).

Table 18. Sext Behavior and by Age Group

Category	*Percentage*
Forwarding a Sext	3
Recipient of a Sext	20
Sending a Sext	9
Receiving Sexts:	
18–24 year olds	44
25–34 year olds	34
Sending Sexts:	
18–24 year olds	15
25–34 year olds	22

Note. Adapted from "Couples, the Internet and Social Media: Main Report," by A. Lenhart and M. Duggan, 2014, Pew Research. Copyright 2014 by the Pew Research Center.

Specifically looking at romantic relationships, American adults who are romantically dating tend to be more likely to engage in sexting, with 42 percent reporting having received a sext, 23 percent reporting having sent a sext, and 10 percent reporting having forwarded a sext (Pew Research Center, 2013) (see table 19). Online daters also tend to be more likely to engage in receiving, sending, and forwarding suggestive photos or videos, with 55 percent reporting having received a sext, 31 percent reporting having sent one, and 9 percent reporting having forwarded one (see table 20). In addition, these percentages are associated with a significant increase when compared with counterparts who do not utilize online dating. Finally, looking at American married and committed couples, it appeared that they engaged in sexting at similar rates as single adults, with 10 percent of single adults and 9 percent of adults in committed relationships engaging in sexting. However, behavioral patterns changed when it came to receiving sexts, with 25 percent of single adults and 18 percent of committed relationships reporting that they have received a sext. The duration of a relationship also influences sexting, with 32 percent of American committed couples of a shorter duration (less than ten years) reporting receiving a sext, compared to 6 percent of American committed couples in longer relationships (ten years or more). Furthermore, 17 percent of American committed adults in shorter relationships have reported sending sexts and 4 percent of these individuals reported forwarding sexts compared to the 2 percent reporting sending sexts and 1 percent reporting forwarding sexts of committed couples in longer relationships (see table 21).

Table 19. Sexting within Romantic Relationships: Single Cell Phone Users Looking for a Relationship

Category	*Percentage*
Receiving a Sext	42
Sending a Sext	23
Forwarding a Sext	10

Note. Adapted from "Couples, the Internet and Social Media: Main Report," by A. Lenhart and M. Duggan, 2014, Pew Research. Copyright 2014 by the Pew Research Center.

Table 20. Online Dating Relationships and Sexting

Category	*Percentage*
Receiving a Sext	55
Sending a Sext	31
Forwarding a Sext	9

Note. Adapted from "Couples, the Internet and Social Media: Main Report," by A. Lenhart and M. Duggan, 2014, Pew Research. Copyright 2014 by the Pew Research Center.

Table 21. Sexting Rates by Relationship Status

Relationship Status	*Percentage*
Single Adults	10
Committed Relationships	9
Receiving a Sext:	
Single Adults	25
Committed Relationships	18
Committed Relationships (less than 10 years)	32
Committed Relationships (more than 10 years)	6
Sending a Sext:	
Committed Relationships (less than 10 years)	17
Committed Relationships (more than 10 years)	2
Forwarding a Sext:	
Committed Relationships (less than 10 years)	4
Committed Relationships (less than 10 years)	1

Note. Adapted from "Couples, the Internet and Social Media: Main Report," by A. Lenhart and M. Duggan, 2014, Pew Research. Copyright 2014 by the Pew Research Center.

Since 2005, online dating has been perceived as a good way to meet people and has increased from 44 percent to 59 percent in 2013. The perception that online dating provides a more effective way to find a romantic partner has also increased from 47 percent in 2005 to 53 percent in 2013. Finally, those who perceived individuals who utilize online dating sites as being *desperate* has declined from 29 percent in 2005 to 21 percent in 2013. A new question asked of online users included agreement with the perception of whether online dating prevents individuals from settling down due to increased/continuous options for dating partners and 32 percent of respondents agreed with this perception. Actual online daters perceived online dating even more positively, with 79 percent of online daters endorsing that online dating is an effective way to meet people and 70 percent endorsing that online dating gives access to better romantic partners. However, among online daters, 13 percent endorsed that individuals who utilize online dating sites are desperate. In addition, 29 percent of online daters endorsed the perception that online dating prevents individuals from settling down (Pew Research Center, 2013). In addition to negative perceptions of online dating, online daters also reported negative experiences of online dating. Fifty-four percent of online daters reported that they experience someone else misrepresenting themselves. Twenty-eight percent of online daters reported contact by someone involved in harassment or in some way made them feel uncomfortable. Related to gender, 42 percent of women reported uncomfortable experiences related to online dating compared with 17 percent of men (Pew Research Center, 2013). Finally, other important trends related to online dating sites included observations of sites designed to match individuals on shared interests and on sites that have associated costs, as well as whether individuals utilize friends' help in creating their profiles. Forty percent of online daters reported using a dating site or app that matches individuals on similar interests. Furthermore, 33 percent of online daters reported paying for an online dating site or app. Twenty-two percent of online daters requested assistance in creating their dating profiles, with 30 percent of women and 16 percent of men reported having requested this assistance (Pew Research Center, 2013).

ONLINE RELATIONSHIP DEVELOPMENT

Romantic relationship development is being redefined in the influence of social media use. Fox and Warber (2013) conducted a study that provided valuable insight into romantic relationship development on Facebook. The study's participants identified five stages of development. The first stage involved meeting a potential partner face-to-face. The second stage included utilizing Facebook to explore the potential partner's profile and to send a friend request to the potential partner. The third stage included inquiring about the potential partner's phone number. The fourth stage involved sending and receiving texts to and from the partner and also sending invitations to the romantic partner to engage in group activities. The fifth stage included participating in posting and messaging on the romantic partner's Facebook page. After these stages, calling and dating begins.

Over the years there have been an increasing number of studies profiling internet use and its influence on dating and mate selection. One study investigated the use of the internet to search for romantic partners (Rosenfeld & Thomas, 2012). They found that relationships created online were no different in quality or security than relationships created offline. Young heterosexual individuals have a lower likelihood of meeting partners online. Although these individuals tend to be most familiar with technology they also have more available single potential romantic partners. The article identified populations that face a thin dating market, which included the lesbian, gay, bisexual and transgender (LGBT) community and middle-aged heterosexual individuals.

Another study of characteristics of Americans married between 2005 and 2012, who met through social networking sites, was conducted by Hall (2014). One characteristic that emerged was a trend involving the population's age. Those who met through social networking sites and got married were younger than those individuals who met through some other online method, than those who met offline, or met offline through friends. Besides age, another trend that emerged involved race. African-Americans tended to meet online through social networking sites as compared to white individuals. Regarding gender, a sex difference did not emerge for those who met on social networking sites and other online venues. However, men were more likely to meet online through social networking sites as compared to meeting through friends offline. Yet another study explored other modes of communication, including the interpersonal motivation involved in texting and calling (Jin & Park, 2010). They found that three particular themes of affection, inclusion, and escape were motivation for both calling and texting. The authors proposed that individuals utilized cell phones to facilitate communication, caring, and connection (Jin & Park, 2010). However, this study also showed that individuals utilize cell phones as a method of escape from a distressing event.

Romantic partners utilize various methods to maintain communication and contact in their romantic relationships. With obstacles related to geographical separation, work obligations, time constraints, and so forth, many couples turn to other options besides the traditional methods of calling and writing letters. Romantic couples utilize video chat platforms, email and instant messaging. Video chat options allow couples to execute communication within their romantic relationships with the opportunity to see each other in real time. It can provide a higher level of communication than can be provided by phone alone, which does not allow the added benefit of seeing the other person. Although not as ideal as a face-to-face and in-person method of communication, video chat allows users to talk to and interact with significant others over geographical distances.

Neustaedter and Greenberg (2011) studied intimacy experienced in long-distance relationships of couples who utilized video chat to communicate. Participants were primarily from the United States and Canada, with a minority of participants being citizens of other countries. Participants reported initiating video chat to communicate and acknowledged using this medium either before becoming separated or right after moving apart. Participants also described utilizing video chat as an emotional motivator in order to feel closer to their partner (i.e., video chat allowed users to see their partner's face, facial expression, and body language). In addition, participants stated that video chat allowed them to experience their partner's surroundings and new purchases. Video chat users also described a need to create a schedule that would mimic a couple living together. Users would attempt to schedule time to spend with each other before or after work or school, or during lunch or dinner. One obstacle to scheduling involved differing time zones. This would influence the number of hours certain partners of particular time zones could communicate with each other. Partners would exert effort to find mutually similar times of availability to communicate to compensate for differing time zones (Neustaedter & Greenberg, 2011).

Many video chat users preferred using this system to view each other engaging in everyday life tasks and also to virtually participate in shared activities. This study's participants described preferring to view their partners engaging in activities, such as house cleaning, eating and cooking meals, sleeping, and engaging in leisurely activities (i.e., reading, playing games and watching television). Most partners would occasionally check in on the other partner as they engaged in these various activities, with conversation either occurring periodically or not at all. Other activities of video chat users included simultaneously watching television or other media sources together. Partners exerted effort into achieving true simultaneous participation by orchestrating an attempt to begin television shows and movies at the exact same time. However, problems related to audio issues and feedback sound often complicated partners' entertainment experience. The purpose of this behavior reported by participants involved a desire to obtain more closeness with their partner (Neustaedter & Greenberg, 2011).

Participants described using video chat to communicate various topics. Participants disclosed discussing relationship issues and arguing over video chat platforms. However, one reported issue included difficulties in maintaining eye contact. Some users preferred not to argue over video chat due to feeling a lack of an ability to escape or a perception that its use would create distance during an argument. Other video chat users would send affectionate messages through text or instant messaging after an argument over video chat (Neustaedter & Greenberg, 2011). Intimate and sexual acts were also virtually enacted over video chat (Neustaedter & Greenberg, 2011). Many partners would simulate kissing or hugging their partner through video chat. Partners often attempted to fall asleep at the same time or watch their partners as they slept. Video chat users described using the system to engage in cybersex and masturbatory behaviors. However, users reported that they experienced feelings of awkwardness, privacy concerns, and an increased experience of missing their partner (due to not being able to actually touch them).

CONCLUDING REMARKS

To summarize, the above statistics showed that the majority of Americans use Facebook. In addition, Facebook appears to be utilized by all age groups, with older American adults increasing their utilization rates. Furthermore, it seems that women and young adults between the ages of 18 and 29 appear to be the demographic population who utilize Facebook the most. Hispanic, white non-Hispanic, and black non-Hispanic American adults tend to utilize Facebook at high and similar rates. Individuals tend to utilize Facebook to communicate with family and friends and to a smaller amount with individuals that are unknown to them. Americans also utilize Twitter and Instagram but in smaller amounts when compared to Facebook use. Slightly over half of American adults use two or more social media sites. However, when looking at adults who utilize only one site, the majority of individuals use Facebook. In addition, adults visit Facebook, Twitter, and Instagram on a daily basis, and almost half of Facebook users visit Facebook several times per day.

To increase one's dating resources, American adults are utilizing online dating applications. These applications improve dating options, especially for groups identified as having limited social resources (middle-aged heterosexual adults, gay, and lesbian adults and African-American adults). However, it was also suggested that online dating could encourage young men to delay marriage and relationship commitment due to increased accessibility. Online dating behaviors have been identified and studied, including flirting and searching for past, present, and future romantic partners. In addition, American adults also utilize internet and email to communicate and maintain a long-distance relationship. Furthermore, American adults reported using social media sites to post pictures or other information related to going on a date and utilized social media sites to ask someone out on a potential date. Uncomfortable and conflictual dating behaviors are also experienced on social networking sites including having to unfriend or block someone. Previous romantic partners were also reported to be blocked by American adults. In addition, individuals endorsed deleting pictures of previous romantic partners. Online daters also experienced negative dating experiences including harassment.

American adults tend to differ on their assessment of the impact of the internet on their relationships. The demographic populations who endorsed more of an impact included couples who have been committed for shorter durations (less than 10 years) and committed couples who own smart phones, use social media sites, and date online. Conflict from social media usage included arguments related to the amount of time spent online, concern regarding romantic partners' online activity, and distracting use of cell phones when in the presence of romantic partners. However, an almost equal amount of American adults described greater connection due to online communication and text messaging, by texting each other while both partners were in the home and by serving as an aid in conflict resolution. Americans are increasing in their perception of online dating as being a good way to meet people. Specifically, those who participated in online dating reported a positive view of online dating as an effective resource to meet dating candidates. In addition, the perception that those who utilize online dating described as desperate has decreased. Individuals reported believing that online dating prevents individuals from settling down due to increased options and accessibility.

Social media usage has provided observations of online romantic relationship development (Fox & Warber, 2013). Five stages have been identified, including meeting face-to-face, exploring profile pages and sending friend requests, requesting a phone number, exchanging text messages and inviting partners to participate in group activities, and posting and messaging partner's pages. After participating in these online behaviors, partners begin calling and dating each other. In addition to learning of ways that the internet has influenced romantic relationship development, several other observations have emerged. It is apparent that relationships created online appear to be similar to relationships created offline in terms of quality and security (Rosenfeld & Thomas, 2012). Furthermore, there seems to be some populations that have a thin dating market including the lesbian, gay, bisexual and transgender community and middle-aged heterosexuals. Finally, there are age, race, and gender trends related to online dating (Hall, 2014). Individuals who met romantic partners through social media sites tended to be younger. In addition, African-Americans, when compared to white individuals tended, to meet more romantic partners online. Finally, when compared to meeting romantic partners through friends or offline, men met more romantic partners through social media sites.

Studying the use of cell phones to facilitate communication, it was found that calling and texting were both used for affection and inclusion but also escape from a distressing event (Jin & Park, 2010). Romantic couples now utilize video chat platforms, email, and instant messaging to communicate with each other over more traditional methods of calling and writing letters (Neustaedter & Greenberg, 2011). This communication pattern especially allows romantic couples to talk to and interact with each other over geographical distances. Users of video chat were able to participate in their partner's lives without being physically close to their partner (Neustaedter & Greenberg, 2011). They were able to engage in activities that would not be possible with the use of traditional communication over the telephone or cellular phone. They were able to view their partners' living spaces or view their partners doing household chores or some other activity. In addition, they were able to participate in activities with their partner, such as eating or watching television together or sleeping with each other. Romantic couples also utilized video chats to engage in physical affection or sexual acts. However, users also discussed problems with video chat, including many issues that involve internet, use such as audio issues, feedback, or dropped signals. Other issues included difficulty maintaining eye contact. Similar to in-person communication, some users avoided video chat due to the inability to escape during conflictual discussions. Finally, privacy and comfort issues were reported when engaging in acts of intimacy. Moreover, users reported missing partners' more after participating in intimate acts.

Along with the continued advancement and popularity of technology and social media, many individuals are using social media as a method to date, choose, and research potential mates. As the advances in technology continue to grow, it will not be surprising to see the influence of technology on dating patterns grow. This influence will need to be studied as it pertains to the evolution of romantic dating practices to obtain a better understanding of the formation of relationships. It is hypothesized that the advantages of increased dating opportunities that have been provided with the existence of the internet, social media, and dating apps have increased the resources for individuals to obtain potential mates. Traditionally individuals would meet partners through family, friends, or academic institutions. With all individuals, but especially women, delaying committed unions like marriage due to professional endeavors, make it difficult to take advantage of a resource pool of potential candidates for mating. After undergraduate education, most individuals lose the highly available potential pool of candidates of which to find suitable mates. Even with social organizations and religious institutions, chances are increased but are still low due to the lowered number of available mates. In essence, the internet, social media, and dating apps allow individuals to increase networking pools and have access to a dating population that they would not ordinarily have without these options.

NOTE

1. The information and associated charts have been adapted with permission from The PEW Research Center. All inferences are those made by the author and do not necessarily reflect the opinions of PEW Research.

Chapter Three

The Relationship between Grief and Connection

GRIEF

Much research has been devoted to obtaining a better understanding of the experience and process of romantic relationship breakups and divorce. However, the experience of grief related to breakups and divorce has been less extensively studied. Most of what is known about grief related to breakups and divorce is obtained from observations of grief related to death. Any discussion of death must take into consideration the influence of culture (Parkes, Laungani, & Young, 2015). Each individual's conception of death is embedded within cultural values and is reflected by their personal cultural and religious values. Because each society's view of death is significant in its own right, there is no right or wrong way of defining, understanding, or dealing with death or grief. Rosenblatt (2011) described the importance in remembering the collective experience of grief. Although the individual is often emphasized when it comes to discussing the effects of loss, for some cultures loss can be experienced by the entire cultural community.

Death rituals include traditions such as isolation, mourning clothing, special markings, tearing clothing, not bathing, self-mutilation, avoiding contact, and shaving one's head (Rosenblatt, 2015). The course of rituals related to death can last from months to years. Death ceremonies can occur during various stages of death from *deceased* to *completely dead* or during death anniversary dates. Some death rituals include reburying the deceased. One purpose of death rituals is that they provide a definition of death and the experience of death (Rosenblatt, 2015). They provide guidelines of how to approach, carry out, and understand death. When these rituals are not followed one can experience guilt or a disruption in one's life. Societal values prove to be strong and even individuals within a society can feel compelled to carry out rituals in order to not be perceived as *bad*. Another purpose of death rituals, specifically funerals, is a method of passage of the deceased person into afterlife. Individuals engage in customs or traditions that have the goal of reducing or eliminating reminders of the loss (Rosenblatt, Walsh, & Jackson, 1976). These traditions seem to occur in many societies and include the goal of establishing a new routine of living. This includes eliminating property (i.e., destroying, giving away, or putting aside), instituting a system of not saying the name of the deceased, and moving. However, these practices could lead to negative grief reactions.

Death ceremonies and funerals are considered to be rites of passage processes (Rosenblatt, Walsh, & Jackson, 1976; Rosenblatt, 2015). This is reflected in the fact that after death many cultures perform passage ceremonies, to move the deceased from the world of living to that of the dead. In addition, those who remain living must pass from old roles to new roles. The importance of death ceremonies lies in the fact that they lead one to accept the loss. Death ceremonies in the United States result in opportunities to reconnect, redefine, and share news with friends, family, and other individuals attending the ceremony, and a chance for a public and group acceptance of the loss. In a majority of societies, *final ceremonies* are honored, which are additional ceremonies approximately ten days after the initial ceremony (Rosenblatt, Walsh, & Jackson, 1976; Rosenblatt, 2015). Although the United States often only honors initial ceremonies, there appears to be value in having final ceremonies and is reflected in the number of societies that do honor it. What is found with final ceremonies is that the experience of prolonged grief is less likely to occur. Because the United States does not typically engage in final ceremonies, it is likely that more Americans experience prolonged grief as compared to other societies that do perform final ceremonies. In America, death and funeral ceremonies are mostly viewed as private (Rosenblatt, 2015). Funerals are usually carried on in a quiet, respectful manner, without a great deal of emotional reaction. In some situations, excessive emotional reactivity can be restricted by others, including clergy. Controlled emotions during a funeral might be allowed expression once one is alone and has the privacy to experience grief reactions without judgment or control.

An American living in the United States might not receive support for participating in death rituals (Rosenblatt, 2015). Society might not encourage or accept the ritualistic behavior exhibited by some cultures, especially those the society is not familiar with or judges negatively. In addition, employers might not provide adequate time for various death rituals and mourning practices. Society can find ways to control certain rituals to conform to majority values and traditions. Uncertainty regarding appropriate bereavement symptoms leads individuals to potentially suppress their emotional experience or experience grief reactions in private (Rosenblatt, Walsh, & Jackson, 1976). It is suggested that Americans often inhibit their grief, which leads to disruption and delays in returning back to daily routines and functioning. One theory that has been offered for the reason that Americans tend to have difficulty with the reality of death is the tendency of Americans to deny death. This could potentially be a reason why Americans tend to suppress their grief reactions or only allow them in private.

Rosenblatt (1983) studied nineteenth century diary entries in North America to obtain insight into the experience of grief. The loss experienced in the diary entries included deaths and separations involving someone moving away, either temporarily or permanently. One observation found in these diary entries was that grief is experienced intermittently, with time periods of memories of the lost alternating with other times where the loss is not mentioned. Apparently, the diary entries of grief reflected the existence of elements of control and lack of control. It appears that grief is influenced by external events (i.e., situations and people) and can contribute to an individual's grief by making one's experience of grief seemingly out of one's control. At other times, through avoidance of places, people, or thoughts, one can maintain control of grief. Memories, thoughts, people, and places have the opportunity to serve as reminders of the loss and return even after one perceives that they have dealt with the grief or loss. These reminders can have either short or long-term consequences.

Observations of diary entries of those experiencing grief and loss provide insight into the course of grief (Rosenblatt, 1983). It appears that grief lessens after the first few months of experiencing loss. In addition, it appears that by the third year after experiencing a loss, grief seems to not be as intense and other parts of the individual's world enters the forefront. However, some types of losses can experience a return of intense grief reactions years after experiencing a loss. Interestingly, when looking at the data of diary entries, it was found that long-term grieving happens more frequently for separations as compared to deaths. In addition, it also appeared that separated loved ones remained in personal awareness more than deceased loved ones. Anniversary reactions are grief reactions that correspond with calendar dates following a loss. From the study of diary entries, anniversary reactions were experienced one, two and three years after a loss (Rosenblatt, 1983). Holidays and other significant dates shared with the lost individual can serve as reminders of the loss and result in grief reactions.

This study also made observations of who initiates the romantic relationship breakups and found that both leavers and the left both experience grief (Rosenblatt, 1983). Due to increased reminders, those who were left experienced more grief right after an experience of loss. To conceptualize this data in relation to romantic relationship breakups, it can be argued that the leaver potentially is focused on incorporating new elements into his or her life (i.e., new relationship, lodging, etc.). The leaver also does not have the experience of being unexpectedly broken up with, since he or she is the one who initiated the breakup. Furthermore, the leaver does not experience the same negative self-esteem issues, such as rejection that the left often experiences. Despite these hypotheses, it is still acknowledged that both the leaver and the left experience grief reactions.

Tears

Tears are viewed and judged in many different ways by the society in which one lives. Tears are a human biological response. Individuals often differ in the connotations they place on the expression of tears. In American society, tears are most often judged as a weakness and somehow an unnatural human expression. Because of this mislabeling many people are not allowed the freedom to express what is not only a biological function but also the true and valid emotion they might be experiencing at the moment (grief, happiness, etc.). The generational passing down of this disinhibition, limits one from fully processing emotions. In studying grief across cultures, crying is the behavior that is best understood. Rosenblatt, Walsh, and Jackson (1976) found that crying was a symptom of bereavement in seventy-two societies (out of seventy-three societies). Anger and aggression have also been studied and is found to occur in fifty societies. Furthermore, it was also found that the more one experiences self-anger and aggression, the more likely other-anger and aggression were present. Fear was found to be present in thirty-seven societies. Related to gender, men seem to cry less and engage in less public emotional expressivity. But it is important to note, that in thirty-two societies women and men cried at equal rates. In societies where there was unequal crying (28 societies), women were found to cry more than men.

Efran and Greene (2012) offer a two-stage theory of the existence of tears. They postulate that tears are produced when a system shift occurs, the change from sympathetic activity (when the body experiences tension and stress) to parasympathetic activity (when the body is rebalancing and recovering). A *psychological meaningful event* often stimulates this change in activity. Tears occur during the second stage of parasympathetic activity when the body is attempting to recover. Furthermore, an individual experiences relief from crying as a result of being in the recovery stage. Efran and Greene (2012) provide evidence for the evolutionary foundation of tears as a vehicle to obtain aid from caregivers. Interestingly, tears tend to occur in certain situations rather than others. Tears tend to be elicited in times of perceived safety (i.e., friendly and sympathetic gestures, voices, faces). Alternatively, tears rarely occur during crises, in the proximity of enemies or continued durations of sadness. Therapeutic crying (crying that is experienced in the context of psychotherapy) can be healing and related to hurtful psychological experiences (Glahn, 2012). Given this biochemical or neurophysiological basis for tears, it makes sense that tears are less connected to specific emotions per se but are more a byproduct or indication of an individual shift into the recovery stage.

More research on crying shows that crying had *positive* results in particular situations (Bylsma et al., 2011):

- In the presence of social support systems (i.e., having a friend close by)
- If the origin of the individual's crying had a positive nature
- If the crying led to increased understanding or insight
- If the individual cried alone or around one additional individual

On the other hand, crying had *negative* results if:

- The individual experienced shame or embarrassment when crying
- If unsupportive individuals were present
- Origin of the crying was related to witnessing suffering
- In the presence of two or more individuals

Gender research of crying shows that women tend to cry more often than men (Bylsma, et al., 2011; Collier, 2014; Nelson, 2005). It is postulated that the reason for gender issues in crying might have biological ties to hormones. Specifically, higher levels of prolactin in women could be the reason that women tend to cry more often. In addition, it is also believed that crying releases toxins or hormones associated with stress from the body (Bylsma, Vingerhoets, & Rottenberg, 2008). There are also cultural factors that play a role in crying (Collier, 2014; van Hemert, van de Vijver, & Vingerhoets, 2011). Apparently when cultures support the expression of emotion this often contributes to higher levels of crying.

The theory of attachment can also be tied to the experience of crying (Nelson, 2005). Studies on tears might provide evidence that crying communicates to others a need for support (Balsters et al., 2013). In a study conducted at Tilburg University, researchers found that individuals are more willing to provide support to another individual when they are visibly crying compared to another individual who is not crying. Secure attachment styles experience appropriate crying and feel more comfortable crying and exhibit healthier crying behaviors. On the other hand, individuals with insecure attachment styles often are more prone to easily cry and are harder to comfort when crying.

Other studies on attachment styles and crying have found particular crying profiles associated with specific attachment styles (Laan, van Assen, & Vingerhoets, 2012). Nelson (2005) further described how attachment behavior has its origins in the childhood experience of crying. Similar to childhood, crying in adulthood has the goal of connection and obtaining comfort from an attachment figure. Crying is a reaction to separation, either real or imagined and is a reflection of loss. Nelson (2005) further distinguishes two types of crying: crying *in* despair and crying *of* despair. Crying in despair or protest crying involves feelings of anguish and anger. The goal or motivation for this type of crying is to avoid the loss. Because of its demanding nature, it often puts others off and results in withdrawal or resentment. On the other hand, crying of despair is exhibited by those that understand that the loss cannot be avoided. This type of crying is associated with sadness and is perceived by others as authentic and heart wrenching. Unlike protest crying, crying of despair elicits compassion, empathy, and connection.

CONCEPTUALIZATIONS OF LOSS RELATED TO ROMANTIC RELATIONSHIP DISSOLUTION

Fromm (1956) very eloquently discussed loss and the resulting experience of shame, guilt, and anxiety. He further explained that one has an innate need to connect with others and not be alone and that the consequence of being unconnected is insanity. Freud (1917), on the other hand, conceptualized grief as being slow and emotionally demanding. Furthermore, he acknowledged the effortful energy that is put forth to manage grief reactions. He believed one needed to engage in detachment from oneself and memories in order to complete grief work. Freud described one's ego as becoming free and uninhibited. He believed that there is a point where an individual becomes free to act without the intensity of felt grief and without existing as if the lost loved one was still living.

Bowlby (1973) described a concept called *separation distress* and it is based on his observations of children's responses to unavailable caregivers. Four behavior responses are offered as outcomes of separation distress. The first emotional and behavioral response involves *anger* and *protest*. Follow-up behaviors include *clinging* and *seeking*. The third emotional response includes *depression* and *despair*. Finally, *detachment* occurs in the emotional and physical responses to separation distress. These reactions provide us with the sequence of emotional and behavioral responses to the experience of separation. Loss and separation create distress and its effects can be devastating when the individual is one's primary attachment figure.

Bowlby (1973) provided evidence that infants display anxiety, anger, protest behaviors, and yearning reactions toward unavailable attachment figures. When this absence is substantial, these infants experience grief, are unable to be consoled, and ultimately experience feelings of desperation. As suspected, there is a similar response with adults and an absent attachment figure. However, in adulthood the response is not as extreme as witnessed in childhood. When studying the effects of the experience of rejection in romantic relationships, we find that individuals tend to experience severe sadness and impairment to one's feelings of personal worth and desirability. Specifically, in romantic relationship breakups, especially ones that are unexpected, the response can be similar to the grief process. This process can include feelings of:

- Anxiety
- Sorrow
- Loneliness
- Emptiness
- Doubts about love-worthiness

Death of an attachment figure often elicits more severe reactions. It can cause impairment in functioning and lead to psychological conditions, such as depression or posttraumatic stress disorder. In addition, reactions to death of a loved one can lead to impairments to physical health. Apparently, these responses occur as a result of unmet attachment needs that were at one time being met by the absent attachment figure. The grief reactions symbolize the significance the attachment figure held for the individual. Loss and bereavement conceptualized within attachment theory, describes how during loss proximity seeking no longer works. Therefore, secondary attachment strategies must be employed. Secondary strategies activated during the bereavement process in attachment theory can have both beneficial and detrimental results. These secondary strategies serve as an adaptive response to the lack of responsiveness of attachment figures. However, if these strategies are employed and a successful consequence does not occur new responsive relationships might not be created. Not only are new, healthy relationships jeopardized but in addition an individual's mental and physical health can become impaired (Cassidy & Shaver, 2008, 2016; Mikulincer & Shaver, 2007, 2016).

The Process of Loss

During loss, individuals alternate between being present and avoiding the loss. In addition, individuals also vacillate between attaching and detaching from the emotions associated with the loss. Both are healthy ways to handle loss and allow one to deal with the loss and not become overwhelmed. However, to only stay in one modality, complete attachment or detachment, can lead to the probability that one can be overwhelmed by the emotions and not grieve properly. This vacillation between attachment and detachment can also be described using the concepts of *hyperactivation* and *deactivation* (Cassidy & Shaver, 2008, 2016; Mikulincer & Shaver, 2007, 2016). An individual must spend time in both processes in order to gain insight from the loss but also to be able to transfer or form new attachment bonds. The first process is called *hyperactivation.* When an attachment system is hyperactivated, one attempts to obtain sources of attention and care. These individuals are sensitive to identifying whether a figure is available or not. Furthermore, they intensely desire closeness and intimacy and attempt to obtain support by displaying distress. They often find themselves preoccupied by relationships with unavailable partners. In the loss or absence of the attachment partner, these individuals often succumb to depression and extreme grief. The second process is called *deactivation.* When an attachment system is deactivated the individual attempts to detach themselves from attachment needs, thoughts, and emotions. These individuals value their independence and avoid closeness with unavailable partners. Distancing is used as a protective mechanism to lower the probability of the attachment system being activated. Involved within these distancing behaviors includes avoidance of loss related emotions. In addition, the significance of the absent attachment figure is diminished. Bowlby (1982) offered the reminder that despite the individual's attempts to avoid or dismiss their emotions, they still have an effect on the person, even if the individual is unconscious of it.

Romantic Relationship Dissolution and Attachment Styles

Attachment theory provides evidence that suppression of grief reactions can prove to be harmful. Without successful resolution of grief, an individual can experience maladjustment and impairments in physical and emotional health. This outcome typically occurs when a significant attachment was formed. Outcomes are less severe when the attachment was not as strong or the emotional attachment in the relationship was low. This is particularly significant for avoidantly attached individuals. Because these individuals tend to execute dismissive and detached behaviors and attempt to maintain their independence in relationships, these individuals often lack signs of grief after the loss of a partner. This makes sense given the avoidantly attached individual's attachment process. During intimate relationships, these individuals avoid becoming emotionally invested. Therefore, once they experience loss of the relationship they appear able to maintain their functioning and not display common signs of grief following the loss. Reviewing research on romantic relationships, individuals who were anxiously attached employed more emotion-focused coping strategies after a breakup (i.e., anger, heightened sexual arousal, intense preoccupation, identity issues, school and work disruptions). Avoidantly attached individuals employed more distancing coping skills after a romantic relationship breakup (i.e., avoiding seeking support for the breakup and avoiding initiating new romantic relationships). Securely attached individuals were able to experience greater acceptance of their breakups and were able to recover faster (Cassidy & Shaver, 2008, 2016; Mikulincer & Shaver, 2007, 2016).

Because anxiously attached individuals have a large emotional investment in their romantic partners, in times of death and loss these individuals will most likely experience difficulty with the loss and become preoccupied with the loss. On the other hand, because of avoidantly attached individuals' intense self-reliance and lowered emotional investment in their romantic relationships these individuals are less likely to be affected by the loss. Securely attached individuals are able and more likely to experience the emotions associated with loss without becoming overwhelmed by the distress and are better able to adjust following loss. However, the grief process can be thwarted by too much dependence on one strategy (i.e., hyperactivation or deactivation). This is relevant based on insecure attachment bonds. Anxiously attached individuals might depend too much on hyperactivation and be unable to shift into deactivating activities. On the other hand, those who are avoidantly attached might depend too much on deactivation and not utilize the strategies that might help them grieve properly. In either situation, the grief process can be impaired. This too is another illustration of the importance of a healthy balance between hyperactivation and deactivation. However, it is important to note that there hasn't been research to establish evidence to support this balance (Cassidy & Shaver, 2008, 2016; Mikulincer & Shaver, 2007, 2016).

These behaviors are validated by the studies of Deborah Davis (Johnson, 2013). Davis utilized the internet to obtain information regarding attachment styles and behaviors during breakups. During a breakup, individuals with anxious attachment styles elicited behaviors involving obsession, anger, hostility, and destruction. In addition, they exhibited yearning and sexual desire for the former partner. Anxiously attached individuals tended to seek out new romantic relationships soon after a breakup. Individuals with an avoidant attachment style created more distance with the former partner. Some avoidantly attached individuals created this distance by initiating a geographic move. In addition, they avoided obtaining support from others. They also avoided reminders of the relationships. Sometimes avoidantly attached individuals delayed getting into a new relationship right after a breakup. Both anxiously and avoidantly attached individuals utilized alcohol and drugs as a way to manage emotions following a breakup. In addition, insecurely attached individuals had shorter romantic relationships when compared to securely attached individuals (Davis, Shaver & Vernon, 2003; Hazan & Shaver, 1987; Sprecher et al., 1998). Moreover, insecurely attached individuals experienced more adjustment issues following a romantic relationship breakup. Insecurely attached individuals also experienced depressive symptoms as well as feelings of being tense and confused (Pistole, 1996).

Research and clinical practice solidify the fact that recovery from a breakup is most effective with a secure attachment style. Securely attached individuals (especially when both individuals are securely attached) experience less anger and sadness. Securely attached individuals often do not resort to denial or suppression of their emotions following loss. They are able to address the loss without becoming disorganized. They gain understanding of the loss. They are able to invite new relationships into their lives following loss. One task that leads to successful resolution of grief reactions in attachment theory involves the formation or identification of new attachment figures that can provide safety, security, and comfort. Creating or identifying attachment figures that provide safety, security, support, and comfort and are responsive to an individual's needs promotes the opportunity to establish new connections. Research has been provided that maladjustment can occur when an individual has not accepted the loss and hasn't transferred attachment bonds to new partners. It is important for the individual to shift their actual reliance on the absent attachment figure to a symbolic reliance. Although here the loss is discussed in the case of death, it is speculated that a similar experience would occur in the case of loss of a romantic relationship.

TYPES OF LOSS

Individuals experience a multitude of emotions in the face of loss. These feelings also shift and can feel unpredictable at times. This is the natural experience of the grief process. In the literature, grief and loss have been characterized by four different terms. *Mourning* involves the cultural practices utilized to express loss and grief (Brown & Goodman, 2005). *Grief* describes the responses to loss, involving emotional, physiological, cognitive, and behavioral consequences. *Bereavement* includes the death of a loved one. Finally, *complicated grief* involves situations of atypical symptom duration and intensity (Prigerson & Jacobs, 2001). Complicated grief is a chronic yearning and preoccupation with the deceased or lost loved one. In most situations of bereavement or uncomplicated grief, the duration of symptoms lessens at approximately six months. After this time, grief might still be present but it no longer inhibits functioning. Hay and Kessler (2014) also described classifications of grief related losses that are applicable to an understanding of romantic relationship breakups. The first classification is *complicated grief* and describes grief reactions and the experience of grief when an unexpected event happens. This can be used to discuss divorce, non-reciprocally agreed breakups, or separations. The second classification is *loss in limbo* and involves anticipating a loss in the future. One might experience fear that they will be unable to survive if the loss actually occurs. This can be used to discuss relationships that experience multiple breakups or relationships where there is the constant threat of ending the relationship. The third classification is *disenfranchised grief*. This explains grief experienced regarding a loss that might be socially rejected or must be hidden in some way. This would involve breakups involving LGBT (lesbian, gay, bisexual, transgender) couples, loss experienced when individuals learn that their former partners have entered a new relationship, or a relationship was hidden due to fear of or actual disapproval of others.

Two additional categories of loss include *anticipatory grief* and *absent grief*. Anticipatory grief and mourning have historically been used to describe events of death; however, it can also be applied to other loss situations, such as the dissolution of romantic relationships (Corr, 2011a). It involves the anticipation of an upcoming loss in the form of a breakup or divorce. Even though the breakup or divorce has not occurred yet, one begins to experience loss reactions to the possibility of an upcoming dissolution. During this process of anticipatory grief and mourning one might experience acknowledgment of the loss and its significance as well as the disturbance it causes in one's life (Corr, 2011a). Viewing this process as a healthy process, one is able to obtain skills to cope with the upcoming loss as well as obtain social systems to provide support (Corr, 2011a). Absent grief has been defined as the lack of distress following the death of a loved one. It involves a lack of emotional reactions to loss and is manifested by denial and avoidance. Early bereavement studies described absent grief as pathological. Furthermore, it was assumed that absent grief led to a delayed grief response. However, empirical study of absent grief revealed that resiliency is a common occurrence as a result of loss and is not associated with delayed grief responses.

COMPLICATED GRIEF

Grief is a normal process following loss. In most situations, individuals have reactions to loss but are able to maintain overall functioning. However, there are situations of grief that can become complicated and can have emotional, cognitive, and physical consequences. *Complicated grief* is a type of grief that impacts one's functioning and can lead to the need for treatment. Much of the research related to complicated grief has been conducted by Prigerson (Prigerson, Frank, et al., 1995; Prigerson, Maciejewski, et al., 1995; Prigerson, Shear, et al., 1995; Prigerson, et al., 1996; Prigerson, Bierhals, et al., 1997; Prigerson, Shear et al., 1997; Prigerson & Jacobs, 2001). Prigerson, Frank, et al. (1995) have conducted studies of older adults experiencing symptoms of bereavement. The results from this research identified a set of emotions identifiable from symptoms of depression and anxiety. These distinct emotions formed the basis of the concept of complicated grief and included denial, shock, crying, disbelief, preoccupation, searching and yearning regarding the deceased. Symptoms of complicated grief can cause long-term issues, including grief and depressive symptoms (Prigerson, Frank, et al., 1995) as wells as impaired overall functioning, sleep, mood, and self-esteem (Prigerson, Shear, et al., 1995).

The Inventory of Complicated Grief (ICG) was created to measure the symptoms of complicated grief (Prigerson, Maciejewski, et al., 1995). Nineteen items are rated measuring the frequency of experiencing the emotional, cognitive, and behavioral symptoms of complicated grief on a Likert scale from 0 = never to 4 = always. The reliability coefficient of the Inventory of Complicated Grief is .94, with a test-retest reliability of .80. One significant outcome of the Inventory of Complicated Grief scale is the finding that three items measuring shock, distressing intrusive thoughts, and resentment distinguish the symptoms of complicated grief from uncomplicated grief. These symptoms also are symptoms that comprise the criteria for the diagnosis of posttraumatic stress disorder (APA, 2013). Additional symptoms provide support for the notion that symptoms of complicated grief are similar to symptoms of posttraumatic stress disorder and include avoidance, guilt, somatic concerns, detachment, and hallucinations. As a result of this finding, Prigerson, Maciejewski, et al. (1995) speculated that complicated grief could be a form of posttraumatic stress disorder.

Cohen et al. (2002) theorized that individuals react to loss with several types of reminders that can lead to trauma related thoughts, memories, and images. As a result, individuals will experience physiological reactions and psychological distress. To deal with trauma related stimuli following loss, an individual will potentially utilize avoidance. Symptoms of complicated grief that are similar to symptoms of posttraumatic stress disorder include thoughts, memories, and images that are intrusive and distressful, as well as avoidance and numbing (Parkes, Reif, & Couldrick, 1996). Long-term emotional consequences can occur if complicated grief is not treated (Melhem et al., 2004).

Complicated grief symptoms, when compared to symptoms of bereavement, continue to be experienced despite the passage of time and psychotropic medication treatment (Jacobs, Nelson, & Zisook, 1987; Pasternak et al., 1991; Prigerson, Frank, et al., 1995; Prigerson, 1996). Persistent complicated grief can also be associated with physical symptoms such as cancer, cardiac disorders, and other additional emotional symptoms of alcohol and tobacco use and suicidal ideation (Chen et al., 1999; Prigerson, Maciejewski, et al., 1995; Prigerson, Bierhals, 1997; Prigerson, Shear, 1997). Particular thoughts and beliefs can serve as obstacles to grief and can include self-blame, the belief of not being happy, not being able to manage the injustice of death, and feeling as if one does not have the right to be happy. In addition, other obstacles include avoidance behaviors, including an avoidance of location or tasks associated with the deceased. Optimal experiences of grief involve situations where individuals are able to pair the above behaviors with optimistic thoughts, acceptance, and realistic appraisals (Shear, 2010).

Complicated Grief and Attachment Theory

Shear (2010) acknowledged the value of attachment theory in the development of complicated grief treatment. Utilizing the concept of working models and its accompanying implicit and explicit memories, the foundation of complicated grief treatment is based on the knowledge obtained from these implicit and explicit memories that are influential in one's experience of grief. The explicit and narrative memory involves the acceptance of the death and details related to the death. Immediately after and for some time after a loved one's death, implicit information involves old rules that were relevant to the deceased loved one. After some time, one is able to integrate new expectations and develop new rules. Shear (2010) suggested that the experience of symptoms of acute grief is a reflection of an activated attachment system. Furthermore, she offered that once the death has been accepted and integrated into explicit and implicit memory, the attachment system becomes deactivated. Eventually the integration of explicit and implicit memories leads to the modification of one's working models. Looking at the influence of attachment in the process of complicated grief, it is found that individuals with insecure attachment tended to experience more distress following bereavement. The specific experience of childhood separation anxiety (i.e., abuse, neglect, parental death) was linked with the experience of complicated grief symptoms following bereavement during adulthood. Therefore, complicated grief is conceptualized as an attachment disorder. (Lobb et al., 2010; Silverman, Johnson, & Prigerson, 2001; Vanderwerker et al., 2006).

GRIEF MODELS

There are several models of grief that have been utilized to explain the process of grief. Three major models have been identified when experiencing the symptoms and behaviors associated with grief. Elisabeth Kubler-Ross (2014) offered a stage theory of grief to describe loss. Kubler-Ross studied adults with life-threatening illnesses and observed that they experienced a process of moving through stages involving denial, bargaining, anger, depression, and acceptance. Her theory continues to hold popularity because it is an easy model to understand but also provides hope for the resolution of grief (Doka, 2011). An alternative to Kubler-Ross's stage model is a task model to explain grief. It is argued that task models allow for individual expression of loss and grief. William Worden (1982, 2009) theorized a task model and provided it as an appropriate way to explain the grieving process. Worden's task model has four common tasks: acceptance of the reality of loss, emotional exploration of the pain associated with loss, adjustment after loss, and the creation of a new life while maintaining a connection with the lost individual. Kubler-Ross has received criticism due to her use of a stage model. Due to the acknowledged individuality of emotional experiences in general, but specifically related to grief and loss, stage theories do not adequately explain a universal process of grief and loss. Worden's use of a task approach allowed for more diversity of emotional experience related to grief and loss. Lacking linearity, individuals could adopt whatever task that is relevant to them during their experience of grief.

A third model of grief involves Stroebe and Schut's (1999, 2010) dual process model of coping with bereavement. They identify two categories of coping processes including a (1) loss orientation and a (2) restoration orientation. In loss orientation, individuals focus on and gain insight into the loss experienced. In this phase, there is a painful fixation on the loss. In restoration orientation, individuals attempt to redefine him or herself during the process of bereavement. One distinct element of the dual process model is a concept called oscillation, which refers to the bereaved individual vacillating between times of confrontation and times of avoidance to the loss. This regulatory process is present in both loss and restoration orientation coping processes and is considered significant in the recovery of bereavement. Furthermore, deficits in being able to engage in the oscillation process of avoidance and confrontation is linked with poor functioning as it relates to the experience of bereavement. It is hypothesized that individuals who experience complicated grief have difficulty in shifting between the processes of avoidance and confrontation. Gender seems to have an influence on the dual process model with women tending to be more loss oriented, and men more restoration oriented when experiencing bereavement. It is important to consider the influence of gender as it provides an indication of how both genders tend to grieve, but in different ways.

Changes in the duration and time spent on these coping tasks occur. Eventually there is a shift from loss orientation to restoration orientation as the need to directly focus on the loss becomes less of a priority. In addition, the time spent on both coping strategies will lessen over time. In Stroebe and Schut's (2010) discussion of the dual process model they acknowledged the question of whether the model could be applied to other types of loss. Among the various other types of loss besides death offered, the authors acknowledged the potential applicability of divorce. It is also speculated whether romantic relationship breakups can also be added to the list. However, the authors contend that research must be undertaken to empirically test the applicability of the dual process model to various types of loss, including romantic relationship dissolution.

GRIEF AND ROMANTIC RELATIONSHIP DISSOLUTION

It is hypothesized that some individuals experience symptoms of grief and loss during and following the dissolution of a romantic relationship. Based on attachment theory, strong attachments are formed as a result of romantic partners serving as individuals' main attachment figures. Important information can be gained from looking at how animals experience *grief* or the loss of a mate. Studies on virgin male and female prairie voles were conducted to investigate the experience of loss and grief in animals (Young & Alexander, 2012). When the male and female voles were placed together they formed a connection. Male voles were also split up in pairs and made to live together. These male-male pairs and male-female pairs were separated after five days and then were put through a number of behavioral tests. The males within the separated male-female vole pairs almost seemed to give up in a forced-swim test and just floated around (compared to the male-male separated pairs and the non-separated pairs who paddled around). In two more tests, a tail-suspension test and an elevated maze test, the males within the separated male-female vole pairs acted similarly. The researchers called this behavior passive stress coping. The males within the separated male-female vole pairs were found to have greater levels of corticosterone (i.e., stress chemical) in their blood. Interestingly, the males in the non-separated male-female vole pairs also had high levels of corticosterone levels in their blood. Male voles in the separated male-male vole pairs did not exhibit this passive stress coping and did not engage in *grieving*. When looking at the female voles in the separated female-female and female-male vole pairs, the separated females showed behaviors similar to grieving. To summarize, separated male voles appear to exhibit grieving behaviors only when separated from female bonds; however, separated female voles tend to grieve in both female and male bonds.

Evidence of brain activity following a romantic dissolution has been studied in several investigations. It appears that areas of the reward system (ventral tegmental area, ventral striatum, pallidum and putamen) are activated during a breakup (Cardinal & Howes, 2005; Fisher, Aron, & Brown, 2006). This results in the feeling of being uncertain of one's future when a breakup is experienced. In addition, obsessive-compulsive behaviors and anger control are evidenced by activation in the orbitofrontal cortex (Fisher, Aron, & Brown, 2006). Studying romantic couples in a later stage of relationship dissolution showed deactivation of these brain areas (Najib et al., 2004). This is most likely due to a greater level of acceptance in this stage of romantic breakup. A somewhat recent fMRI investigation provided evidence of reduced brain activity and is similar to an experience of major depression (Stoessel et al., 2011). Fisher (2004) studied the brains of humans following a romantic relationship breakup. When she viewed fMRI brain images of romantic relationship breakups that involved rejection, she found that those who experienced rejection endorsed feelings of rage, paranoia, and despair. Emotions of love and hate appear to have connections when viewing brain images. Rage is closely associated to areas of the brain that involve one's expectations of rewards. When it becomes clear that a reward may not be obtained, an experience of rage occurs.

Furthermore, Fisher (2004) witnessed a phenomenon that occurs as a result of rejection and categorized it into two different behaviors, *protest* and *resignation*. In the *protest* stage, individuals obsessively ruminate about regaining contact with the former romantic partner. They engage in behaviors that will potentially provide proximity and reconciliation. Fisher (2004) believes that behaviors of protest are a result of elevated dopamine and norepinephrine levels. These increased levels are associated with alertness, stimulation, and help-seeking behaviors. However, when these behaviors are unreciprocated or it becomes clear that reconciliation will not occur, individuals experience *resignation*. Individuals cease their efforts at reconciliation and experience feelings of despair.

An Expanded Theory of Loss

Harvey and Miller (1998) offered an expanded theory of loss that includes multiple life stressors including, among other events, divorce and romantic relationship breakups. The authors believe that a theory of loss must incorporate one's perception of the meaning of such loss. Furthermore, they contend that individuals' personal losses and the causes of their losses are connected and are a component of their personality. Multiple losses result in multiple episodes of grief. In addition, experiencing a loss can have secondary losses. Ultimately, loss can result in influencing later generations of families, such as in the case of the Holocaust. One issue that can complicate the experience of loss is when individuals feel as if they have little control over the loss event. In these circumstances, individuals must employ strategies to find meaning and understanding of the loss events. As a result, individuals find ways to integrate the loss into their identities (Harvey & Miller, 1998).

Grief and Divorce

There are several models to describe the process of divorce (Bohannan, 1968; Kaslow, 1991; Levinger, 1979; Wallerstein & Blakeslee, 2004). Other models describe relationship dissolution in general and can be applied to both married and unmarried couples (Baxter, 1984; Duck, 1982; Rollie & Duck, 2006). Many of these models allude to the experience of grief that is experienced in cases of romantic dissolution. In Kessler's (1975) model, a fifth stage of divorce is described where the process of mourning is explicitly acknowledged and refers to the time that an individual recognizes the multiple losses that are inherent in divorce. During this time, an individual can experience symptoms of anger and depression. This loss can be reinforced with continued contact with the ex-spouse. It has been offered that it might be beneficial to consider and study dissolution as an event of change instead of viewing it as an ending (Rollie & Duck, 2006). However, one problem that is inherent in the measurement and investigation regarding models of dissolution is that they fail to adequately and appropriately describe same sex couples or various cultures and ethnicities (Rollie & Duck, 2006).

Divorce has previously been considered a grief process (Crosby, Gage, & Raymond, 1983; Crosby, Lybarger & Mason, 1987). Grief related to divorce has been conceptualized to be similar to bereavement related to death, with the exception of the fact that the experience of death is final and irreversible. In addition, except for in a small number of special cases (i.e., euthanasia), divorce, as compared to death, involves a decision-making process (to sever the relationship). Crosby, Gages and Raymond (1983) offered a conceptual model related to the grief process of divorce, which includes (1) a large range in how romantic partners reach a decision, and accept and resolve the divorce; (2) there is a circular process of affective, cognitive, and behavioral manifestations; (3) the cyclical pattern of manifestations occur in an upward or downward spiral;

(4) due to one partner being the initiator of the decision to divorce, there will be one passive partner and one active partner; and (5) recovery is necessary in the areas of affect, cognition, and behavior. Crosby, Lybarger, and Mason (1987) investigated the difference between active agents (i.e., the initiator of divorce) and passive agents (i.e., the non-initiator of divorce). They found that each agent had specific ways of operating within affective, cognitive, and behavioral approaches. In stage one of the affective stage, active agents feel fear whereas passive agents feel hurt. In the second stage of the affective stage, active agents feel hope and passive agents feel hurt. In the third affective stage, both active and passive agents feel hope. In the first cognitive stage, active agents think about approaching and passive agents think about avoidance. In the second cognitive stage, active agents think about acceptance and passive agents provide no clear picture of their cognitions. In the third cognitive stage, both active and passive agents think about acceptance. Finally, in the first behavioral stage, both active and passive agents seek to approach. In the second behavioral stage, passive agents work at reconstruction and active agents work to negotiate. In the third behavioral stage, both the active and passive agents are working toward reconstruction. They also found that mutuals (i.e., couples who come to a mutual decision to divorce) feel, think, and behave similar to active agents. Because mutuals came to a mutual decision, they would look similar to active agents (i.e., who initiated decisions regarding divorce) than passive agents (i.e., who had the decision of divorce made for them).

Feeney and Monin (2008, 2016) offer an attachment based conceptualization of the experience of divorce. Using the two foundations for optimal functioning based on the tenets of attachment theory (secure base and reciprocally rewarding relationships), they propose that divorce occurs when one or two of these are missing in one or both partners of a married couple. Similar to our understanding of attachment figures as they relate to childhood healthy functioning a similar pattern exists for partners serving as attachment figures for each other. Therefore, partners who can serve as *secure bases* for each other by being trustworthy will result in more secure partners and a more secure relationship. On the other hand, when this is missing, the result will include insecure partners and an insecure relationship. In addition, unmet needs can lead to anger, resentment, and vulnerability to stress, which further contributes to the deterioration of the relationship. In order to participate as a trustworthy attachment figure and both partners expressing behaviors within a mutually rewarding relationship, each partner must be able to switch roles of being both *caretaker* and *dependent* or *receiver* and *giver*. Each must be able to embody both roles in order for the relationship to be evaluated as a mutually rewarding relationship. Furthermore, a partner's working model of attachment figures based on their childhood caretaking and other relationships, influences and contributes to the interaction between partners in a marriage. If dysfunctional behaviors, expectations, and interactions comprise partners' working models of attachment figures, it can negatively impact their experience in their marriage. The result can include the utilization of defensive behaviors, such as avoidance, excessive dependency, and dismissal, which all can ultimately lead to divorce.

Feeney and Monin (2008, 2016) discuss how divorced individuals often continue to experience feelings of attachment for their divorced partners. These feelings tend to be experienced most intensely right after a divorce and when the divorced partner initiated the divorce. Apparently, feelings of attachment often exist following a divorce no matter how long the marriage lasted. This is the case even in situations that involve feelings of emotional distress and when there is acknowledgment that the marriage should be dissolved. Feeney and Monin (2008, 2016) argue that continued feelings of attachment for a divorced partner are a result of separation anxiety and an activated attachment system. Other theories include a defensive process to avoid the pain of separation and attachment (Reibstein, 1998); and an attempt to resolve the conflict of wishing to regain the separated attachment figure; and a wish to separate in order to build new attachment relationships (Mikulincer & Florian, 1996). Contact following a divorce has mixed results. Most of the available literature suggests that contact after a divorce can be complicated and can involve anger, retaliation, and physical and verbal abuse. However, there is some evidence that some divorced individuals can maintain a relationship with their ex-partner and can result in healthy functioning.

Compared to securely attached divorced individuals, insecurely attached individuals would be more likely to experience more distress following a divorce (Feeney & Monin, 2008, 2016). Due to insecurely attached individuals working models and their reduced effective coping skills, they will tend to suffer more negative consequences following a divorce. On the other hand, securely attached divorced individuals tend to have more positive working models and more effective coping skills and support systems. Interestingly, Davila and Bradbury (2001) found that married couples with insecure attachment styles tended to express dissatisfaction in their relationships. However, these insecure married couples tended to stay married. Based on attachment theory, as a result of anxiously attached individuals' working models of themselves and others, these individuals are motivated to maintain their relationships despite dissatisfaction and dysfunction (Kirkpatrick & Davis, 1994).

Grief and Romantic Relationship Breakups

A literature review of romantic breakups showed that individuals experience symptoms of bereavement similar to losses, such as death and divorce (Field,

2011). The outcome of this review of relevant literature showed that bereaved individuals experience issues related to sleep, including insomnia, rumination, and dreaming about the lost individual. Another symptom related to sleeping issues of bereaved individuals includes intrusive thoughts. When individuals avoided negative images, it often resulted in an increase in dreams. Yet another symptom involves a syndrome called the *broken heart* syndrome and is characterized as pain in the chest or heart (Field, 2011). What often accompanies the *broken heart* syndrome is elevated norepinephrine and epinephrine. Dysfunction of the immune system has been associated with decreased vagal activity, and an increase in the following: skin conductance, stress level, heart rate, blood pressure, cortisol levels, and norepinephrine levels. Potential consequences of immune system disturbances can lead to an increased probability of developing a physical illness.

Field (2011) proposed two models that explain what occurs in romantic relationships, heartbreak, and bereavement. The first model is a *social regulator model* of loss. This model suggests that the loss of a loved one involves loss of control of social routines, tasks, and activities. The disruption caused by the loss of these various social regulators causes the bereaved individual to become disorganized. The loss of an individual in a relationship disrupts the security and co-regulation that relationships offer and as a result the bereaved individual experiences deficits in psychological and physiological body rhythms. The second model involves *psychobiological attunement* (Field, 2011). This model is based on the assumption that romantic partners stimulate each other and as a result have an influence on each other's arousal. This occurs in close relationships, where each partner is attuned to the other and is able to meet the behavioral and physiological needs of the other. When loss occurs, the relationship benefits of activating and calming stimulation is also lost. The bereaved individual vacillates between over stimulation and under stimulation, without being able to achieve desired arousal. Similar to the first model, when loss is experienced, the bereaved individual experiences negative consequences such as impairment in immune functioning and physiological disruptions.

Romantic Relationship Breakups and Attachment Styles

Securely attached individuals typically experience romantic relationship breakups with resiliency, acceptance, and emotional recovery (Madey & Jilek, 2012; Sbarra, 2006). Anxiously attached individuals react to romantic relationship breakups with emotional and physiological distress, drug and alcohol abuse, preoccupation with the ex-romantic partner, a lost sense of self, poor coping skills, rumination, and self-blame (Birnbaum et al., 1997; Burnette et al., 2009; Fagundes, 2012; Saffrey & Ehrenberg, 2007; Sbarra & Emery, 2005; Spielmann, MacDonald & Wilson, 2009; Sprecher et al., 1998). There are conflicting results when it comes to the experience of avoidantly attached individuals and romantic relationship breakups. Bowlby (1980) proposed that avoidantly attached individuals tend to experience an absence of grief when experiencing romantic relationship breakups due to their small amount of utilization of protest and despair behaviors, and their ability to quickly detach and reorganize (Bowlby, 1980). In addition, those individuals who had higher levels of avoidant attachment experienced less distress than individuals who had lower levels of avoidant attachment behavior (Simpson, 1990). On the other hand, avoidant attachment style has been associated with self-blame, alcohol and drug abuse, less motivation to begin a new relationship, and less interest in sex.

Grief and Same Sex Romantic Relationships

Loss and bereavement as it is related to same sex romantic relationships from an attachment perspective has not been extensively studied yet. However, conclusions from available research of romantic relationship breakups have not identified any difference between same sex and heterosexual romantic relationships based on what causes separations and distress experienced following loss (Kurdek, 1997; Mohr, 2008). Furthermore, an important aspect of grief and loss related to the illness and resulting death of AIDS also is relevant to the discussion of same sex romantic relationships and the experience of loss. The result can involve a risk factor of developing major depression as was found in an intensive study of gay men (Folkman et al., 1996). However, the levels of depression observed in this study matched levels found in heterosexual couples and provides additional evidence that both same sex and heterosexual romantic relationship experience similar reactions to loss. However, there have been some areas where heterosexual and same sex relationships tend to differ (Mohr, 2008). When comparing heterosexual married couples, gay couples tended to experience more autonomy and more romantic relationship breakups, but experienced fewer barriers to leaving their romantic relationships. In addition to more autonomy and relationship breakups, lesbian couples also experienced more intimacy and more equality than heterosexual married couples (Kurdek, 1998; Mohr, 2008).

Gottman et al. (2003) conducted a study on gay and lesbian relationships based on previous research on heterosexual relationships that observed that evaluations of relationship satisfaction were related to physiological reactivity (Levenson & Gottman, 1983; 1985). Utilizing three cardiovascular measures of interbeat interval, finger pulse amplitude, and pulse transit time to ear, these researchers were able to reflect connections between physiological reactivity and relationship satisfaction but were also able to make predictions regarding relationship breakups. Comparisons of both populations resulted in differences. For heterosexual couples, lower satisfaction was related to higher physiological reactivity. These individuals were also predicted to have a higher probability of relationship breakup. However, in same sex relationships the opposite was present and lower relationship satisfaction and a higher probability for a romantic relationship breakup was associated with lower physiological reactivity. The researchers theorized that the reason for this difference might be related to the existence of a connection between physiological reactions and emotional and cognitive processes that encourage an opportunity for attachment or a positive evaluation.

Additional differences within same sex relationships were also found (Gottman et al., 2003). Specific factors of relationship satisfaction were different for lesbian couples and gay couples. For lesbian relationships, affection was considered the most important factor of relationship satisfaction. On the other hand, in gay relationships validation was endorsed as the most important factor. These findings reflected the positive physiological arousal in lesbian relationships and negative relationship in gay relationships. The final point to note is that higher levels of cardiovascular arousal measures were connected with different results in same sex relationships and heterosexual relationships. For same sex relationships, this higher arousal was connected to higher levels of relationship satisfaction. On the other hand, in heterosexual relationships higher arousal was connected with lower levels of relationship satisfaction and relationship stability.

The lack of recognition of the relationship process for same sex couples has caused same sex couples to create their own relationship milestones or anniversaries. In contrast, heterosexual individuals have historically been allowed the opportunity to marry and divorce and therefore can easily use these dates to mark their anniversaries. Before marriage or legal unions were instituted for same sex couples, these couples did not have these identifiable markers to formally identify their relationships. Often these individuals would use the date of their first sexual encounter, cohabitation or commitment ceremony (Oswald & Clausell, 2006). In addition, the ending of same sex relationships was marked by the ending of sexual contact or when both partners obtained a new residence (Oswald & Clausell, 2006).

The dissolution of marital and romantic relationships of same sex individuals is a complex topic to discuss due to the historical absence of laws permitting marriage. As a result, there has also been a lack of a history of clear policy making around the legalization of relationship dissolution for same sex marriages. K. R. Allen (2007), using some case material from her own experience, utilized the theory of ambiguous loss to explain how the lack of legalized divorce for same sex individuals can complicate their emotional experience during the dissolution of the marriage. According to ambiguous loss theory, K. R. Allen (2007) posited that same sex individuals have a difficult time dealing with the loss of dissolution of the relationship due to an experience of ambiguity and a breakdown of an individual's coping strategies and resiliency to deal with the loss. She argues that without the clear defining qualities of legalized divorce for heterosexual individuals, same sex couples ending their relationships will experience confusion about the process and about family membership. Furthermore, clarity regarding child custody and visitation arrangements would help improve the loss experienced during a separation by providing a framework and protection for the members of the family. Since 2015 and the legalization of marriage for all same sex couples, these couples will now be able to utilize the process of divorce to officially end their marriages. Due to the limited research available of the dissolution processes of same sex couples, it is unclear as to the magnitude of the factors that affect emotional recovery from grief.

Grief and Romantic Relationships with Transgender Individuals

Regarding romantic relationship dissolution of trans relationships, limited studies show that half of partners transition with their romantic relationships intact (N. Brown, 2010; Devor, 1997). Trans individuals already experience a great deal of loss related to sexual prejudice, including loss of relationships in the form of family, friends, romantic partners, and religious community members, employment, and access to adequate healthcare. In addition, trans individuals experience being mislabeled or mis-gendered. Furthermore, there are multiple adjustment related tasks that a partner of a trans individual must address including utilizing new pronouns and names, negotiating changed gender roles, addressing new sexual desires, and ultimately acceptance of the partner in a different way than originally experienced (Meier, Sharps et al., 2013b). However, relationships and social support appear to buffer against stressors (Keicolt-Glaser & Newton, 2001).

One study observed the rates of romantic relationships in FtM's and found that half of the couples reported being in a romantic relationship before transitioning and half of those couples remained intact at the time that the study was conducted (Meier, Sharps et al., 2013). Specifically, the study found that the romantic relationships of trans individuals that ultimately ended were those relationships where trans individuals had been transitioning for a longer period of time. In addition, half of the relationships that ended endorsed transitioning as a reason for dissolution. An important finding from this study relates to social support, in that perceptions of the quality of the romantic relationship tended to be more important than just holding a romantic relationship status. The authors contend that romantic relationships with trans individuals can be maintained through the transition process.

Regarding the transition process, there is limited data to fully understand the implications on romantic relationship development. However, there are few conclusions that this limited study has revealed. It appears that the emotional component of a romantic relationship might take priority over sexual components in maintaining the relationship and intimacy of trans individuals in romantic relationships (Hines, 2006). It also appears that fluidity and flexibility is obtained within the transitioning process regarding gender roles and sexual practices (N. Brown, 2010; Dozier, 2005). It appears that there are various factors that couples with trans individuals must address as a consequence of the transitioning process. N. Brown's (2010) study revealed that a change in sexual practices included more limited sex initially with an increase in the flexibility and variation later in the transition process. During this time, couples engage in relearning each other's bodies and sexual needs. It also seems that having a flexible approach to sexual orientation allows for a successful outcome in romantic relationships with trans individuals (N. Brown, 2010). This is validated by N. Brown's (2010) observation that a lesbian sexual orientation that lacked flexibility had more doubts and more difficulties with arousal. In addition, N. Brown (2010) also suggested that transitional stages are important, including changes in libido as well as body dysphoria (B, Brown, 2010; Joslin-Roher & Wheeler, 2009), which has consequences on identity and also sex. Finally, one interesting factor includes the finding that the transitioning process can affect posttraumatic reactions due to a trauma history as a result of the partner's transition. Therefore, it is important to address and treat any past trauma that resurfaces as a result of the transition process.

Grief, Divorce, and Ethnicity

There is limited study of the process of divorce and romantic relationship dissolution in various ethnic groups, with the majority of studies conducted on White populations. One reason that explains the lack of useful data for African-Americans (but arguably for several non-majority racial groups) is that the family structure of African-Americans has been pathologized due to a trend of single parent female headed homes and teen pregnancy (Billingsley, 1992). Several arguments are offered for the factors that play a role in relationship dissolution for the African-American population. One argument involves the existence of racism and discrimination (Adelmann, Chadwick, & Baerger, 1996; Billingsley, 1988; Broman, 1993). Socioeconomic status and financial stress have also been shown to increase the instability of African-American couples (White, 1990; Yang & Lester, 1991). In addition, in relationships where African-American wives earn higher salaries or have more demanding jobs than their African-American husbands also can contribute to relationship disruption. Orbuch and Brown (2006) suggested that multigenerational households, connection to familial support systems (especially parents), and support systems, including the church and friendships, can serve as protective factors and lead to positive consequences during and after a divorce.

Another trend that influences African-American relationships includes the unequal gender ratios of African-American men and women, with a smaller ratio of men to women (Dixon, 2009). In addition, African-Americans experience lower availability of African-American males as potential romantic partners due to death, incarceration, and limited financial resources. In a review of African-American relationship patterns, it was found that this population is married for a shorter time when compared to White Americans. In addition, African-Americans have been found to be the least likely ethnic group to get and stay married. When African-Americans do marry, they tend to get married at an older age (Dixon, 2009).

Similar to African-Americans, there is also limited study of the relationship dissolution processes of Latin Americans. Research does suggest that the Latin American community has utilized divorce less but instead uses separation as a way to end their relationships (Umana-Taylor & Alfaro, 2006). Similar to concerns related to African-Americans, a similar trend is seen in increased Puerto Rican female headed homes due to out of wedlock pregnancies and divorce. Another trend among Puerto Ricans is that this population tends to build their relationships through the process of cohabitation, and have high probabilities of not getting married and ending in dissolution. Furthermore, Puerto Rican females reported perceiving their cohabitation as similar to being married (Landale & Fennelly, 1992). Due to the high level of religiosity in the Latin population, values related to denomination and religious practices play a role in how this population views family and romantic relationship statuses of marriage and divorce (Ellison, Wolfinger, & Ramos-Wada, 2012). Finally, immigration has also influenced relationships due to stress related to discrimination, limited financial resources, and separation due to immigration status (Umana-Taylor & Alfaro, 2006).

Observations of interracial marriages suggest that these couples differ in their risk to divorce and is dependent on specific ethnic couplings (Bratter & King, 2008). Interracial marriages that were most likely to divorce included White females and non-White males when compared to couples with both partners being White. Couples, including White men and non-White women, especially White male and Black female couples were less likely than both White female and male partners to divorce (Bratter & King, 2008). Bratter and King (2008) suggest that the historical patterns of race relations might provide insight into the vulnerability of interracial couples. For example, African-Americans enter into interracial marriages at lower rates than other minority groups (Lee & Edmonston, 2005). In addition, White individuals are least likely to marry African American individuals. However, other racial groups such as Asian-Americans and Hispanic Americans, have had less racial divide issues and therefore tend to experience higher interracial marriage rates and are similar to marriages with both partners being White (Yancey, 2003).

THE CONSEQUENCES OF GRIEF

The grief experienced as a result of loss from a divorce or romantic relationships is multifaceted. Dissolution of married and unmarried couples share many similarities related to the grief and loss that is experienced after the relationship has ended. The following section will discuss the potential consequences of grief and will be categorized in the areas of intrapersonal, interpersonal, religious, community, and societal.

Intrapersonal

Often individuals experience conflict related to separation or divorce from their romantic partner. They can experience various conflicting emotions which can potentially complicate healing. Those who experience the loss of a married partner can have emotions such as loneliness, sadness, anger, anxiety, regret, resentment, and guilt; however, they can also experience feelings of affection, longing, and a desire for reconciliation (Weiss, 1976). Other emotions experienced following the loss of a romantic relationship include anxiety, anger, depression, and detachment (Bowlby, 1973, 1979; Feeney & Monin, 2008, 2016), as well as feelings of loneliness (Gottman, 1994). Individuals experiencing the loss of a romantic relationship can experience emotional consequences at different periods and based on their particular role within the relationship (Gray & Silver, 1990; Kitson, 1982). Based on who initiated the divorce or who wanted the marriage to continue can determine when, but also how, one experiences intense distress. Better adjustment has been correlated with individuals who have initiated the relationship ending.

Partners who did not initiate the relationship breakup can experience disruptions in their self-esteem. Especially in cases where the breakup involves elements of rejection, infidelity, betrayal, and devaluation, one can experience a serious blow to one's self-esteem. This effect may be the result of what Hay and Kessler (2014) describe as being due to cognitive appraisals. They suggest that an individual's cognitive grief style explains the way that an individual will experience and react to grief. Furthermore, issues of self-esteem are most likely related to the individual's cognitive appraisal of the situation and the negative self-talk they engage in as a result of the breakup. In most situations, this is related and connected to past traumas and patterns in the individual's life that become triggered by the current breakup.

It is hypothesized that individuals who base their self-worth on being in a romantic relationship might experience the loss of relationships at a greater degree. Studies of self-worth on being in a romantic relationship have been associated with increased concerns related to appearance, an increased desire to have a romantic partner and fears of being alone (Sanchez et al., 2008; Sanchez & Kwang, 2007). Self-worth based on romantic relationships has also been linked to increased levels of emotional distress and stalking following a romantic relationship breakup (Park, Sanchez, & Brynildsen, 2011). Those who were more sensitive to rejection tended to avoid romantic partners who rejected them and were less likely to respond with stalking following a romantic relationship breakup. In addition, among women with low self-esteem, being rejected by a romantic partner led to their experience of future depressive symptoms (Katz, Beach, & Joiner, 1998). In addition, individuals with low self-esteem tended to distance themselves as a result of relationship threats initiated by themselves and by their romantic partners (Murray et al., 1998). Other individuals tended to experience depressive symptoms and respond with anger and hostility toward a romantic partner (Ayduk, Downey, & Kim, 2001). Intuitively, the same part of the brain that is activated by love is activated by rejection (Eisenberger & Lieberman, 2003). Those who experience rejection often have symptoms of depression more frequently than individuals who initiated the breakup (Ayduk, Downey, & Kim, 2001). In addition, rejection has been associated with increased levels of blood pressure and cortisol (Stroud et al., 2000) and analgesia and numbing (MacDonald, Kingsbury, & Shaw, 2005). When looking at fMRI studies, individuals experiencing rejection displayed similar signs to drug withdrawal, such as cocaine and opioids (Bartels & Zeki, 2000). In addition, to the similar symptoms of drug withdrawal, these individuals also experienced anxiety, depression, crying, loss of appetite, and irritability.

Romantic partners influence each other, especially each other's identity and self-esteem (Agnew, 2000; Aron et al., 1991). Furthermore, romantic partners experience an overlap between each partner's identity and self-concept (Agnew et al., 1998). In addition, romantic partners integrate each other's traits (Aron, Paris, & Aron, 1995) even to the point of having difficulty to differentiate between themselves and their partner (Aron et al., 1991). Slotter, Gardner, and Finkel (2010) hypothesize that romantic relationship breakups cause changes in an individual's identity. As a consequence of the loss of the romantic relationship and the loss of the romantic partner, the individual is left with the task of restructuring his or her identity. In their study of self-concept following a romantic relationship breakup, they found that participants endorsed changes in their self-concept. Furthermore, the more change that was endorsed revealed less clarity in participants' personal self-concept. As a result, participants experienced distress related to self-concept change and the lack of self-concept clarity. Another finding of the study revealed that in more committed relationships imagining the loss of a romantic partner was linked with an increase in the predicted change of self-concept. Following a romantic relationship breakup, these authors found that participants referred to themselves with terms that were smaller and lacked clarity. Interestingly, these authors also conceptualized that individuals can potentially transfer their identities formed by previous romantic relationships into new relationships, in an effort to decrease the distress experienced as a result of romantic relationship breakups (Slotter, Gardner, & Finkel, 2010).

Divorce and romantic relationship breakups change the structure of the relationship and as a result many consequences are imposed onto the individual partners. Individuals must adapt and create new roles, routines, and identities. When individuals experience a loss of a romantic relationship they are forced to obtain new roles, including finding new individuals to fulfill roles that have become empty by the former romantic partner as well as deciding on which roles to fulfill on one's own. Furthermore, individuals must experience the loss and grieve the absence of the formerly shared routine. Part of the loss of a romantic relationship involves the activities associated with the former relationship. The loss of a relationship leads individuals to seek new meaning into their identities. Much of one's identity becomes integrated into romantic relationships and in the presence of the loss of relationships individuals are forced to begin to redefine themselves. Hay and Kessler (2014) also acknowledged grief associated with an unfilled vision of one's life. A romantic relationship symbolizes a vision that one has for one's life. Once a relationship ends, one's vision of a life with the romantic partner becomes shattered. An individual is tasked with the need to begin to reconstruct a new vision that no longer includes the former romantic partner.

Hay and Kessler (2014) identified infertility and miscarriage experienced in a relationship as another type of loss that leads to feelings of grief. Infertility and miscarriage are in themselves a loss but in the case of dissolution of a romantic relationship, this loss becomes compounded by the loss of the relationship. After a relationship ends, individuals can experience the loss of infertility and miscarriage again as they grieve the relationship ending and as they return to the reality of a failed opportunity to have children with the former partner.

Another issue that needs to be considered refers to gender roles, especially in the romantic relationships of trans individuals. In a study by Moen, Kim, and Hofmeister (2001) they found that couples endorsed lower marital satisfaction when their spouse did not fit their expectation of gender roles. The authors suggest that the change in social status (i.e., LGBTQ to heterosexual status) provides understanding into the dissatisfaction experienced with gender roles. Therefore, it is proposed that individuals experience a loss related to this status change. It was noted before that there are multiple adjustment related tasks that a partner of a trans individual must address (i.e., new pronouns and names, gender roles, sexual desires) (Meier, Sharp, et al., 2013). These tasks can be associated with feelings of loss related to the change in the partner undergoing the transition process. If a romantic relationship with a trans individual ends, it is important to consider these losses in light of the loss of the romantic relationship overall.

Finally, when one experiences a loss one also experiences a shock to an idea of stability. Many cultures believe in the continuation of life after death and the communication of the dead with the living world. It is understood that when a loved one dies, a part of the person who is left behind dies as well (Rosenblatt, 2015). In addition, the person who remains living loses certain assumptions of the world, such as stability. When one experiences death, one experiences distress due to lacking a schema in order to understand it. It threatens one's perceived meaning of life. This also occurs in the existence of divorce and romantic relationship breakups. One's internal experience of the order and stability of life becomes distorted after the ending of a romantic relationship. An individual must find ways to reintegrate a sense of stability following the loss of a romantic relationship. Rosenblatt (1983) offers a theory based on an integration of the theories of development, symbolic interaction, and memory. This theory suggests that one's first experience with a major loss can cause pronounced feelings of grief. This intensity is attributed to an immaturity in emotional control and the reality of one's and others' mortality. With increased losses, one begins to build emotional control as the reality of mortality continues to increase. With the influence of symbolic interaction, one experiences distress as a result of the instability caused by loss. In addition, one also experiences instability related to self and others and this further leads to increased distress. The integration of a memory theory on loss involves the reminders that one experiences during grief. More research needs to be conducted in the area of memory in the experience of grief.

Interpersonal

Due to strong attachment feelings to previous romantic partners (Brown et al., 1980; Goode, 1956; Kitson, 1982; Weiss, 1975), individuals continued contact with a previous partner has been shown to cause additional stress on the individual (Bohannan, 1968; Duran-Aydintug, 1998; Hetherington, Cox, & Cox, 1982; Kitson & Morgan, 1990; Weiss, 1975, 1976). Right after a divorce, divorced couples often tend to have more positive emotions related to the positive qualities of the ex-spouse (Ehrlich, 2014). Divorced couples are forced to adjust their relationships and create clear boundary setting in order to improve the chances that continued contact will be successful (Reibstein 1998). Ending of the romantic relationship elicits separation anxiety and causes the attachment system to be activated (Bowlby, 1973, 1979). Once the attachment system is activated individuals seek to gain proximity to their attachment figures—their former romantic partners (Bowlby, 1982). As a result, individuals are left with the conflict of the desire to seek proximity and the need to detach from the relationship (Mikulincer & Florian, 1996). Cassidy (2008, 2016) suggests that individuals can manage this conflict by transitioning their attachment bond to an affiliative bond. How conflict was resolved in the marriage (or romantic relationship) often determines how a couple will handle the process of divorce (or breakup) (Wallerstein & Blakeslee, 2004). Therefore, it is important that ex-couples utilize (or obtain through counseling) the skills necessary to address conflict in a healthy way, post dissolution, especially in situations where children are involved.

A symbolic baby (Leonoff, 2015) is created when a couple marries and is essential to the survival of the relationship. Grief and loss are experienced as a result of divorce when the creative energy of the couple is siphoned off (Ahktar & Blue, 2017; Leonoff, 2015). The formerly shared vision of the couple no longer exists, which leads each partner to redefine their separate identities and offers a time for reflection (Leonoff, 2015). Kaslow (1991) recommended that divorce also provides an opportunity for additional tasks, including identification of ego functioning and use of defenses, as well as addressing childhood and family of origin conflict. Although this theory is discussed in terms of divorce, its utility can be considered in the case of romantic relationship breakups as well.

It can be hypothesized that romantic partners of trans individuals have experienced a type of romantic relationship dissolution. Given the many options of the transition process,[1] this would be especially true in cases where an individual undergoes a number of social and medical processes. It is speculated that romantic partners of these individuals would experience a loss of the individual with whom they initiated the relationship. Schrock and Reid (2006) acknowledged this concern when they identified that both partners have to address identity issues related to how the transition affects themselves and the romantic relationship. In situations where couples remain intact after transition and regarding the partners who do not transition, their loss might be minimized due to the fact that the trans partner remains in the relationship. However, it is assumed by the available research that there would in fact be an experience of loss related to the romantic relationship. Ellis and Erikson (2002) utilized Kubler-Ross's (1969) stage model of grief to explain the process that is associated when trans individuals disclose their transition to their family. Joslin-Roher and Wheeler (2009) acknowledged that Ellis and Erickson's (2002) process model does not account for the experiences of the partner's experience of grief related to identity and belonging although they speculate that they might fall under the reevaluation and self-discovery stages.

In the case of children, individuals' loss experiences are exacerbated by the custodial arrangements and co-parenting of children. Individuals can experience not only the loss of the structure of the marriage but also the structure of the family (Ehrlich, 2014). Learning to co-parent in a healthy way can be difficult while attempting to manage one's own emotional process. In addition, helping children grieve the loss can be difficult while simultaneously managing one's own grief. Parents can consider giving children a family possession, especially in cases where there will be a move. The family possession represents the special bond between parent and child and can instill a sense of grounding and belonging (Lewis, 1983; Westman & Cline, 1973). Specifically, in the case of same sex couples and due to the historical lack of legalized marriage and therefore divorce, same sex couples have had to negotiate custody arrangements among themselves or through the use of a mediator. However, without the benefits of legal stipulations, some same sex couples experienced the complete separation from their child(ren) if the former significant other decided to leave the geographical area.

A couple's parents often serve as support during times of conflict in a romantic relationship (Barranti, 1985; Denham & Smith, 1989; Johnson & Barer, 1987). In the face of a breakup, parents can experience feelings of grief, distress, and ambiguity (Denham & Smith, 1989; Sanders & Trygstad, 1989). When a romantic relationship ends, individuals must attempt to handle their parents and inlaws adjustment to the dissolution as well as the relationship with any grandchildren. In some cases, parents must adjust to a maintained distance or even separation of the relationship with former romantic partners and with grandchildren (Myers & Perrin, 1993). In addition, as individuals seek new romantic relationships, parents also must adjust to limited time and contact as a result of the new relationship units. During relationship dissolution, individuals might seek out their parents for emotional, financial, and logistical support. As a result, individuals can experience a resurfacing of childhood conflict. On the other hand, in an attempt to help their children during relationship dissolution, parents can experience stress as they take on financial and emotional roles. Furthermore, parents might be limited in their ability to engage in their own interests as they offer additional help and support to their children and grandchildren (Myers & Perrin, 1993). For African-Americans, having multigenerational households was found to be a positive factor during or after a divorce due to the ability to obtain emotional, financial, and logistical support (i.e., childcare). In addition, parents and their role as grandparents has been associated with multiple benefits during times of conflict (Adkins, 1999; Taylor et al., 1990; Taylor, Keith, et al. & Tucker, 1993). African-American grandmothers, in particular, have held a historical role of providing support to children and grandchildren in times of need (Taylor et al., 1997).

Dissolution not only affects the couple, but also impacts the social network of individuals. Following divorce, many divorced individuals experience social isolation (Joung et al., 1997; Marks, 1996; Mastekaasa, 1997; Peters & Leifbroer, 1997; Ross, 1995; Umberson et al., 1996). This isolation can be due to the fact that friends of individuals who experience the loss of a romantic relationship are tasked with the conflict to decide which friendship they will maintain. In other circumstances, individuals can isolate themselves from mutual friends' support as they attempt to avoid interactions with ex-partners or for fear of judgment (Morgan, Carder, & Neal, 1997). As a result, divorced individuals tend to experience a negative influence on their social networks post-divorce when the size of their previous friend and family network decreases (Terhell, Broese van Groenou, & van Tilburg, 2004). Divorced individuals tend to increase the intensity of their relationships with family and intimate friendships. In addition, divorced individuals tend to have poor adjustment when they do not obtain emotional support from others (Marks, 1996; O'Connor ete al., 1998; Ross, 1995). Alternatively, divorced spouses have better adjustment when they obtain support from family and friends (Aseltine & Kessler, 1993; Cotton, 1999; Forgatch & DeGarmo, 1999; Garvin, Kalter & Hansell, 1993; Goldberg et al., 1992; Lawson & Thompson, 1996; Thabes, 1997).

Regarding the dissolution of same sex couples, loss related to friendships can be a significant additional loss, in addition to the loss of the significant other. Gay and lesbian communities tend to have social networks that involve more friends than family members (Julien, Chartrand, & Begin, 1999). Therefore, when it comes to the interpersonal consequences of romantic relationship dissolution related to friendships, it is important to consider the impact of the loss of friends for same sex couples, which often serve as their major support system. Friendships as a social support tend to serve a major benefit to African-Americans during and after divorce. Having a close friendship during and after a divorce has been correlated with positive well-being (Keith, 1997). These close friendships provide significant emotional support in times of distress. Friendships become even more significant in cases where African-Americans are not able to obtain support from their familial relatives (Taylor et al. 1997).

Other Areas of Loss: Pets

Many have hypothesized that individuals can have an attachment with their pets (Archer, 1997; Hay & Kessler, 2014; Lago et al., 1988; Rynearson, 1978; Sable, 1995; Sable, 2000; Sable, 2013; Serpell, 1996). Melson (1989) suggests that a relationship with pets creates a bond that involves working models of attachment relationships. However, Beck and Madresh (2008) acknowledge that the working models of romantic partners and pets are different. Rynearson (1978) illustrated the attachment relationship with pets with the following statement.

> I would suggest that this basic distrust of human attachments contributes to the intense *displacement of attachment* to the pet who is consistently receptive and unconditional as a source and object of caring. Indeed, the animal which the human considers as "pet" is usually chosen for its innate capacity to display and respond to attachment. A dynamic aggregate of behaviours flow between the two, and it is the "aliveness" of the relationship that appears crucial—a vital, reciprocating balance of attachment. Because of this intense investment, separation from or loss of pet can create complicated and enduring psychiatric reactions. (551)[2]

Beck and Madresh (2008) suggest that some assessment measures inquire about components of attachment but many do not base their assessment on attachment theory. Despite this ambiguity, there are several conclusions that have been found related to the role that pets play in individuals' lives. Accordingly, pets are perceived to be members of the family (Albert & Bulcroft,

1988; Cain, 1985; Cowles, 1985; Cusak, 1988; Hay & Kessler, 2014), such as similarities with children (Carmack, 1985; Hay & Kessler, 2014; Hirsh-Pasek & Treiman, 1982; Smith, 1983; Stewart, 1983) and with parents or partners (Albert & Bulcroft, 1987). In addition, pets are associated with decreased depressive symptoms (Sable, 1989), decreased loneliness (Olmert, 2009; Sable, 1989) and general well-being (Cusak, 1988; Muschel, 1984). Furthermore, in studies of bereavement and separations, pets have been associated with decreased loneliness and isolation (McCulloch, 1981; Rynearson, 1978; Stewart, 1983). Finally, pets are associated with happiness, security, and self-worth. Although all pets are argued to have some aspect of attachment behavior associated with them, it appears that individuals report important attachment relationships with dogs and cats. Dogs have been conceptualized to have a greater attachment than other types of animals, due to the high level of interaction that occurs with dogs (i.e., walking, grooming, etc.). In addition, individuals tend to associate human thoughts and feelings to pets, which deepen the relationship with the pet. Furthermore, it is argued that there exists an unconditional relationship between individuals and their pets (Beck & Madresh, 2008; Hay & Kessler, 2014). Individuals also reported experiencing more security when describing their pets compared with their romantic partners (Beck & Madresh, 2008).

Karen Allen (2003) argues that pets can be beneficial when coping with stressful events. Albert and Bulcroft (1988) observed that attachment with pets appear to be more important during transitions or to serve as companionship (i.e., divorced individuals, widowed individuals, individuals who have never been married, newly married couples, couples with children, and empty nesters). When experiencing the loss of a pet, individuals tend to experience distress and complicated grief (Hay & Kessler, 2014; Keddie, 1977) and it has been posited that the grief experienced with death is similar to that of pets (Archer & Winchester, 1994; Gerwolls & Labott, 1994; Quackenbush, 1984; Sanders, Mauger, & Strong, 1985; Stewart, 1983). During times of grief, social networks can be a significant source of comfort and support. However, due to the tendency that social support often is present at the time of the loss but then wanes (Sable, 1991), pets can provide security and emotional support by always being present (Sable, 1995).

To summarize, what can be inferred from the available literature is that there appears to be an attachment process that occurs with pets. In addition, in the loss or death of a pet, it also seems as if these events lead to distress and grief and potentially have similarities with loss experienced with humans. Hay and Kessler (2014) categorized grief of a pet as a disenfranchised grief, a grief that others judge as less than legitimate. Judging this type of grief as not legitimate complicates the grief experienced in the event of the death or

and can lead to increased empathy to all humankind but especially those who have had similar loss (Calhoun et al., 2010). Another positive outcome of grief involves an increase in the feeling of personal strength (Calhoun et al., 2010; Janoff-Bulman, 2006). Furthermore, another positive outcome of grief reflects a greater appreciation of life and what is valued in life (Calhoun et al., 2010). It leads one to prioritize how one balances time or in which people or events to invest or participate. Grief can also lead to insight into spiritual beliefs (Calhoun et al., 2010).

Calhoun et al. (2010) describe how positive transformation occurs. They offer that unexpected losses change assumptions about the world as being predictable and lead to a process of redefinition and exploration. In addition, those losses perceived to be especially unexpected tend to be difficult in returning to a schema of stability. Calhoun et al. (2010) also utilize the theories of constructivist and narrative psychology to explain that individuals are forced to rewrite their life stories to incorporate the change to the schema of life. The term resiliency was conceptualized based on the work of George Bonanno (Bonanno et al. 2002; Bonanno, 2004; Bonanno, Wortman, & Nesse, 2004). Bonanno and colleagues conducted a prospective study of older adults who experienced the death of their loved ones. The study's participants experienced transient grief reactions and were able to maintain functioning. A result of this study showed that the majority if the participants were able to utilize coping skills to manage their grief. Furthermore, a minority of participants needed professional treatment.

Bonanno (2004) makes a distinction between recovery and resiliency. Recovery involves a duration (either rapid or up to 2 years) of maladaptive symptoms, such as depression or posttraumatic stress disorder, after which typical functioning returns to baseline levels. Resiliency includes a state of balance and homeostasis; it also involves the capacity of individuals who experience loss and trauma to maintain psychological and physical health. Transient maladaptive symptomatology might be experienced but resilient individuals are overall able to maintain healthy functioning. Bonanno (2004) believed that resilient individuals do not need therapeutic intervention. In addition, most individuals who experience trauma and loss tend to be resilient. Finally, Bonanno (2004) hypothesized that resiliency is achieved through multiple pathways (i.e., hardiness, self-enhancement, repressive coping, positive emotion, and laughter).

Marshall, Bejanyan, and Ferenczi (2013) studied the influence of attachment style on personal growth following romantic relationship breakups. They found that anxiously attached individuals as compared to avoidantly attached individuals were more prone to experience personal growth. Anxiously attached individuals and avoidantly attached individuals experienced different outcomes. Anxious attachment was linked with personal growth due to rumination and rebounding with a new romantic relationship. Despite their experience of personal growth, anxiously attached individuals reported greater romantic relationship distress. Those who were anxiously attached tended to rebound with new romantic partners when more time occurred following a breakup. Avoidantly attached individuals engaged in less rumination but also experienced romantic relationship breakup recovery due to their practice of deactivation and inhibition. The authors (Marshall, Bejanyan, & Ferenczi, 2013) suggested that the avoidantly attached individuals' lack of rumination serves as an obstacle to obtain self-understanding and insight in order to improve future relationships.

APPLICATION TO PSYCHOTHERAPY

Observations from psychotherapy might provide insight of why securely attached individuals are able to fare better when it comes to romantic relationship breakups. Securely attached individuals are better able to communicate and to deal with internal and external threats to the relationship. They are able to give and receive love and be vulnerable in an appropriate manner. In most situations, securely attached individuals end relationships in a reciprocally sensitive and respectful way. In psychotherapy, individuals who have experienced romantic relationship breakups with avoidantly attached individuals tend to have more difficulty processing their partners' reactions to the breakup. This difficulty also makes their grief experience exacerbated. This is due to the fact that these individuals who were in relationships with avoidantly attached individuals often experience emotional distress as a result of not witnessing an emotional reaction in their former partners. This sometimes leads them to believe that their former partners did not care about them and leads them to think that their relationship was somehow insignificant.

Part of what is processed in psychotherapy is psychoeducation related to the attachment processes of an avoidantly attached individual. Inherent within this attachment style is an avoidance of emotional attachment during the relationship. Once that is accepted, it is understood that the same individual would most likely lack signs of grief after the breakup. Simply put, activation of attachment processes within the relationship can lead to deep emotional attachments during that relationship. As in the case of the avoidantly attached individual, if there was no activation then there would be no need to grieve. Alternatively, securely attached individuals have less difficulty grieving and processing their former partner's reactions. This is because in most cases securely attached individuals are able to openly and honesty express their emotions, are able to end romantic relationships in healthy ways, and can communicate their needs and emotional experience.

CONCLUDING REMARKS

An overview of grief traditions and practices were investigated as they pertain to the grief experienced in the dissolution of romantic relationships. A special section on the roles of tears and crying provided additional insight into the experience of loss. Conceptualizations for grief and loss by Fromm, Freud and Bowlby were provided to explain the origin of grief experiences. Three grief models, Kubler-Ross' (1969) stage theory, Worden's (1982, 2009) task theory, and Stroebe and Schut's (2010) dual process model, have been offered to explain the process of grief. Dissolution can be a traumatic process that causes feelings of loss and grief. It is a process that does not punctuate just the event of the decision but encompasses the expansive period beginning once the decision of dissolution is considered until many years post-dissolution. There are many emotional, physical, and logistical consequences that must be addressed in the case of divorce and romantic breakups. It is only with the intentional working through of these issues that leads to better adjustment when divorce and romantic relationship dissolution occurs.

Similarities of the loss shared by both married and unmarried couples were explored. Multiple consequences experienced when romantic relationships end were provided. It is argued that these consequences fall into the areas of intrapersonal, interpersonal, religious, community, and societal. These consequences provide insight that the grief and loss of a romantic relationship is a powerful process. Grief does not always result in negative symptomatology. There are many individuals who experience a positive transformation as well as psychological or posttraumatic growth following grief. Individuals can experience increased emotional connection, personal strength, a greater appreciation in life, enhanced spirituality, and a need to prioritize what's important in one's life. Finally, resiliency is present in some individuals who are equipped with the coping skills to handle stress.

Akhtar and Blue (2017) utilized Winnicott's (1960) concept of a *good enough mother* to define a new concept called *a good enough divorce*. Five criteria of a *good enough divorce* were offered that include putting a great deal of thought into and utilizing psychotherapy before deciding to divorce, operating a time-efficient approach to terminating the marriage, protecting the children, maintaining civility during the divorce and throughout the co-parenting relationship, engaging in introspection and finding meaning of the dissolved relationship, and seeking a new healthy relationship. Extending this concept even further, one can consider the idea of a *good enough romantic relationship breakup* as well, taking into consideration the impact that grief has on unmarried romantic partners. This *good enough romantic relationship breakup* would be similar to the *good enough divorce*. However, since a marriage involves the need for a legal process in order to dissolve the marriage and romantic relationships of unmarried couples do not, there would be one change to adapt the criteria to make it relevant to romantic relationship events (although its inclusion can be considered for the *good enough divorce* as well). The additional criteria would be for the romantic couple to end the relationship in a sensitive and respectful manner, which is related to the first criteria of the *good enough divorce*. Similar to the caveat provided for the *good enough divorce* that acknowledges that the criteria reflect more likely an *ideal divorce*, the same can be said for the criteria of the *good enough romantic relationship*. Finally, similar to the note for the *good enough divorce*, if most of the criteria are met for the *good enough romantic relationship*, it is good enough (Akhtar & Blue, 2017).

NOTES

1. Transitioning involves multiple options based on an individual's preferences. Individuals can choose *social* changes which include disclosing to family and friends, changing names, pronouns, hairstyles, and attire as well as using different gendered restrooms. Individuals can also elect *medical* procedures that involve hormone replacement therapy and gender confirmation therapy, originally referred to as gender or sex reassignment therapy. Finally, individuals can initiate *legal* changes, which include behaviors to update names, social security cards, licenses, passports, birth certificates as well as other legal materials, such as diplomas and wills.
2. From "Humans and pets and attachments," by E. K. Rynearson, 1978, British Journal of Psychiatry, 133, p. 551. Reprinted with permission.

Chapter Four

Digital Relationships

The Role of Technology, Social Media, and Media on the Dissolution of Romantic Relationships

Social media can provide valuable information, not only in the realm of dating and romantic formation and maintenance, but also in the dissolution of romantic relationships. Fox, Warber, and Makstaller (2013) explored how Facebook has influenced romantic relationship development. Facebook allows individuals to obtain information without having to communicate directly with an individual or potential romantic partner. In addition, Facebook chatting and texting have replaced traditional phone calling. In today's technological world, individuals have to make decisions about making their relationship public, including identifying a relationship status, displaying photos, and exchanging posts. A relationship status label, going Facebook Official or *FBO* has emerged. It involves a public identification of relationship commitment and is perceived to confirm relationship exclusivity. However, males and females might differ on their perceptions of FBO meanings of exclusivity. Facebook use causes conflict within romantic relationships and couples find that this conflict has a negative impact on their romantic relationships offline. Furthermore, the term, "Facebook Official" is perceived differently by men and women (Fox, Warber, & Makstaller, 2013). Women were found to differ from men on three factors. Women were more likely to believe that going Facebook Official involved exclusivity of the romantic relationship, reflected longevity, and was a social decision that would have both online and offline consequences.

Papp, Danielewicz and Cayemberg (2012) compared dating partners' use of Facebook profiles. They found that romantic partners exhibited similar patterns in their use of Facebook and in their profile management. This included both partners being more likely to report being partnered and displaying their partner in a profile picture. The study's observation of relationship satisfaction had differing gender effects. In heterosexual couples, higher levels of relationship satisfaction were experienced by both males and females, when males reported being partnered on their Facebook profiles. However, female reports of a partnered status did not have an effect on males' relationship satisfaction. Furthermore, females' inclusion of their partner in a profile picture resulted in greater relationship satisfaction for themselves and their partners. However, males' inclusion of their partners in a profile picture was not linked to satisfaction. Finally, Facebook disagreements between couples resulted in lower levels of relationship satisfaction for females but were not linked to males' satisfaction.

In a study asking participants to imagine a scenario on Facebook where their partners did not have any pictures of them on their partners' Facebook page or had their pictures set to private, heterosexual women experienced more feelings of jealousy, anger, and hurt when compared to heterosexual males (Muscanell et al., 2013). Authors argue that the scenarios caused feelings of jealousy, anger, and hurt because they were perceived to reflect a lack of acknowledgment or hiding of the romantic relationship. Another study (Elphinston & Noller, 2011) found that individuals who participated in higher levels of usage on Facebook also experienced higher levels of jealousy and dissatisfaction. This study found that individuals' use of Facebook exhibited an addictive behavioral pattern, which negatively influenced romantic relationships.

Darvell, Walsh, and White (2011) made observations of which individual characteristics would result in a higher probability of partner monitoring. They found that those who tended to engage in partner monitoring were those individuals that had a positive view toward frequent partner monitoring on Facebook and also experienced social pressure to engage in this activity. Furthermore, the more an individual found their romantic partner to be untrustworthy, the more likely that individual would monitor their romantic partner. In addition, the shorter the relationship, the more likely it was for individuals to engage in partner monitoring. Also, the more time spent on Facebook (frequent logins) also increased the likelihood that an individual would engage in partner monitoring. Studies of Facebook surveillance or Facebook stalking have been connected with an experience of more distress, sexual desire, and a lowered opportunity for personal growth (Marshall, 2012). In addition, studies of social media behavior after a romantic relationship breakup reveals that individuals spend a great amount of time attempting to find answers as to the reason for their breakup and can lead to jealousy (Nitzburg & Farber, 2013).

One study provides evidence that individuals who utilize Facebook to track an ex-partner following a breakup may experience delayed emotional recovery and growth (Marshall, 2012). In a study of undergraduates in England, those individuals who spent a great deal of time tracking their ex-romantic partners' Facebook page experienced increased levels of distress, negative feelings, and longing. In addition, these individuals were found to have decreased levels of personal growth. Marshall (2012) found that individuals who continued to have exposure to a former romantic partner through the use of Facebook, experienced an impact on their subsequent recovery and growth following the breakup. Those individuals who remained Facebook friends with a former romantic partner experienced lowered negative feelings, sexual desire, and longing for their former partners when compared to individuals who did not maintain a Facebook friendship. The author suggested that maintaining a Facebook friendship after a relationship breakup might have a positive influence (Marshall, 2012). However, although these individuals might have experienced better recovery from a relationship breakup, they experienced lower levels of personal growth. Marshall (2012) proposed that similar to previous research, recovery and growth most likely involve two different processes and therefore culminates in two different responses following a breakup and online contact with a former partner through Facebook. Finally, having weak-tie contact (i.e., contact that is infrequent and nonreciprocal) resulted in the poorest functioning following a breakup. This was evident when compared to strong-tie contact (i.e., communication that is frequent and reciprocal). The author proposed that weak-tie contact potentially provides information that might not be obtained through strong-tie contact and can include information that might increase negative emotions (i.e., learning that a former partner has initiated a new relationship).

Tong (2013) observed surveillance behaviors on Facebook during a breakup. After a breakup, individuals who were broken up with tended to seek information regarding the former romantic partner more than those who initiated the breakup. Most often the information sought involved the former partner's new love interests. In this study, social approval or disapproval influenced the participants' use of the surveillance of former partners. Individuals either communicated directly with their former romantic partners or did not communicate at all. Privacy influenced whether an individual engaged in surveillance behaviors. For example, the more private an individual was, the less likely they were to desire direct communication with a former romantic partner. These individuals would either utilize covert means of communication or choose not to communicate at all.

TECHNOLOGY USE AND ATTACHMENT STYLES

Weisskirch and Delevi (2012) studied romantic relationship breakups among college students. They found that romantic relationship breakups through the use of technology (text messaging, email, and social networking sites) usually affected those individuals who were anxiously and avoidantly attached. Anxiously attached individuals tended to be broken up with through the use of technology. Avoidantly attached individuals tended to initiate relationship breakups by using technology. These outcomes reflect the specific attachment behaviors associated with these attachment styles. Avoidantly attached individuals, in an attempt to avoid conflict, would most likely utilize a medium that would allow them the least amount of contact and communication. Also, anxiously attached individuals are often paired with avoidantly attached individuals and would be vulnerable to being broken up with by avoidantly attached individuals through technology.

It appears that attachment styles might provide some insight into romantic relationship breakups through social networking sites (Weisskirch & Delevi, 2012). Compared to those who identified themselves being in a romantic relationship, those who self-identified as being single had higher scores on attachment anxiety and avoidance. In addition, anxiously and avoidantly attached individuals identified the utilization of technology as a means to break up as acceptable. More specifically, the study found that being anxiously attached predicted being broken up with through technology and a willingness to use technology to break up with romantic partners. Furthermore, having a more traditional view of women's gender roles and being avoidantly attached predicted that individuals would find breaking up with a partner through technology as acceptable. Fox and Warber (2014) also observed attachment styles and the influence on relationship uncertainty and interpersonal electronic surveillance on Facebook. The attachment styles that tended to have the highest relationship uncertainty and utilized the most surveillance behaviors were preoccupied and fearfully attached individuals. It is important to continue to explore the influence of attachment styles on social media behaviors and other technological behaviors. Because technology has become so embedded in today's society and will most likely increase in priority in the future, it would be beneficial to have a better idea about how social media behavior is connected to one's attachment style. In addition, because a large part of romantic relationships encompasses social media activity it is also important to consider the implications of attachment style behavior in this area.

EFFECT OF TECHNOLOGY ON RELATIONSHIPS: APPLICATION TO PSYCHOTHERAPY

In psychotherapy, many individuals describe complications related to the influence of technology on their most intimate relationships. One of the major issues brought up in psychotherapy focuses on a romantic partner's Facebook status or the extent that a romantic partner overtly expresses being in a romantic relationship (i.e., amount of pictures posted). The Facebook practice of identifying a relationship status in many ways marks an individual's intentional decision to acknowledge (or not acknowledge) a romantic relationship. Whether an individual chooses to do this or not often becomes a source of emphasis for the individual's romantic partner. When not identified or acknowledged, individuals typically experience questions and doubt as to the meaning placed onto the romantic relationship and the romantic partner's intentions. Similar to this also involves an individual's choice in posting pictures of the couple or making it known that the individual is in a committed relationship. Again, this can be thought of as being an issue of being acknowledged and the absence of it leads to feelings of doubt and insecurity. It is important to remember that the title of one's status designation or the quantity of pictures an individual has posted about their relationship are both surface level concerns. The deeper and more meaningful issue that these behaviors represent are a need to be regarded (and the romantic relationship regarded) as significant. This is witnessed in a range of ages and might reflect a universal need to be acknowledged but also deemed significant.

CLINICAL CASE EXAMPLE

An example from psychotherapy involves a female patient in a 3-year committed romantic relationship. She initiated treatment to work through her emotions related to her boyfriend's difficulty with changing his Facebook status and posting pictures illustrating their relationship. Through psychotherapy and after receiving psychoeducation of attachment style related behavior, the patient gained insight into her boyfriend's avoidant behavior, which was being expressed through social media. In her sessions, she began to understand how their respective attachment styles played out in all dimensions of their lives, even within social media. The patient's boyfriend's avoidant attachment style would presumably inhibit him from completely opening up to the female patient by allowing her *space* on his Facebook page and openly acknowledging her. This led to the patient feeling insignificant within the romantic relationship but also suspicious of his romantic commitment to her.

Utilizing the case above, if the boyfriend were in treatment, he could obtain psychoeducation regarding his attachment style. Once he understood his attachment style and how it influences his thoughts and behaviors it would probably be important to review his history related to his childhood attachment and gain some insight into the origin of his attachment related behaviors. Once this has been explored and processed, the patient's boyfriend could move to his romantic relationship with the patient and see how his thoughts and behaviors are related to his attachment style that originated in his childhood attachment interactions, and is being played out in his current romantic relationship. As he gains better understanding of how this becomes played out in his romantic relationship, he can learn how his thoughts and behaviors are even being played out in his behavior on social media. Once he sees how his attachment style behavior is evident in his social media behavior, he can gain understanding of how it influences his romantic relationship, but more importantly how it makes his girlfriend feel unvalued.

In the case above, one can consider how the influence of attachment behavior can be evidenced even within social media behavior. Although social media engines allow one to increase connections on a superficial level, there can be deeper implications hidden in its behavior. Even if one were to argue that they experience deep connections on social media sites, it is speculative how deep these relationships prove to be when the interaction is viewed through an intermediary device, such as a smartphone. One can presume that if two individuals discuss some information or interaction initially viewed on social media that it could *lead* to a deep connection. However, this situation can only occur if individuals are able to access their thoughts and emotions and be vulnerable enough to express these thoughts and emotions to one another. As more healthy attachment relationships are formed, it will improve the attachment related behavior expressed through social media platforms.

GRIEF AND ONLINE ROMANTIC RELATIONSHIPS

Public data from Twitter has been analyzed to investigate romantic relationship breakups (Garimella, Weber, & Cin, 2014). The authors defined breakups as one individual removing the identification of another individual from their profile description. In addition to removing individuals from profile descriptions after a breakup it also appears that there is also a change in the language individuals use. Specifically, following a breakup, the following themes emerge: self-centeredness, focus on religion/spirituality, and cursing life. When looking at the change in language with a romantic partner from before and after a breakup it seems that loving statements turn to "public fighting and insulting" (i.e., changes from "I love you so . . ." to "I hate when you . . .") Changes also occur within the communication patterns between romantic couples during breakups, including a decrease in the number of messages to the romantic partner, the increase of messages to other individuals, and the decrease of original tweets (i.e., tweets that are not retweeted). Following a breakup, individuals also tend to drop followers and friends. It is difficult to identify who is actually dropped but it is hypothesized that they are mutual friends of the romantic partner.

Unlike previous research on the link between romantic relationship breakups on Facebook and changes to privacy settings (LeFebvre, Blackburn, & Brody, 2015), this current study involving breakups failed to show an influence on privacy settings. Evidence for the experience of depressive symptoms was assessed by using a category of words including, sad, anger, and anxious. When compared to couples who were not broken up, those individuals who experienced break ups had a higher level of words in this depressed category which increased over time. Those that were broken up with experienced more depressive symptoms than those that initiated the breakup. Couples who eventually broke up experienced more stonewalling (i.e., only one individual is doing all of the talking) than relationships that stayed together. For those couples who participated in more communication and interaction previous to the breakup, these same couples tended to stay in touch after the breakup (Garimella, Weber, & Cin, 2014).

LeFebvre, Blackburn, and Brady (2015) studied Facebook behaviors during and after a romantic relationship breakup. The results from their study are invaluable in terms of providing insightful observations of online behavior during and after relationship dissolution. The study revealed many similar behaviors both during and after a breakup. The top two online behaviors exhibited during and after a breakup included *relational cleansing*, which involves changing or removing one's Facebook relationship status and *minimal use or lack of Facebook use*, where individuals limit or refrain from Facebook activity. Other similar behaviors of both during and after a breakup included *surveillance*, tracking of a partner's and mutual friends' pages; *self-regulation*, not viewing a partner's page or profile, postings but also taking a "break" from Facebook; *normative Facebook activities*, engaging in tagging, posting, commenting, and sending private messages; *virtual mourning*, engaging in emotional commenting of an ex-partner; *withdrawing access*, engaging in defriending, deleting or blocking behaviors; *impression management*, posting about positive experiences and adding new pictures and *virtual reconciliation*, attempts to re-friend an ex-partner and sending apologies. The one different behavior witnessed during romantic relationship dissolution was *new relationship interest*, when individuals search through new partner's picture albums and seek evidence of previous relationships. The different behaviors observed after a romantic relationship breakup included *account modification*, changing privacy settings or deleting accounts; *off-social network communication*, increases in communication off of social networks, including calls, texts and skyping; *social network support*, seeking and obtaining social support; and *relational transgression*, including hacking into an ex-partner's page, disclosing infidelity and exposing other information relevant to the relationship and breakup.

Clayton, Nagurney, and Smith (2013) studied the influence of Facebook on infidelity, breakups, and divorce. They found that an increased use of Facebook was associated with higher levels of conflict, cheating, and relationship dissolution, especially in relationships of three years or less. This might be related to issues of neglect related to high levels of Internet and Facebook use, and communication with former romantic partners, or the potential for temptation of communicating or cheating with former romantic partners. In a study by Lyndon, Bonds-Raacke, and Cratty (2011), it was found that more than half of the study's participants reported that they made contact with their former romantic partner on Facebook. The majority of participants communicated with their former romantic partners in a passive method, and a small percentage engaged in public harassment of their romantic partners or vented about their former romantic partners. The study's authors also investigated two themes related to Facebook behavior, cyber obsessional pursuit (COP) and obsessive relational intrusion (ORI). Cyber obsessional pursuit involved pursuing someone through an electronic source with the goal of obtaining intimacy. However, this behavior is one-sided in that one individual is pursuing intimacy with another individual that does not desire an intimate relationship. Obsessive relational intrusion measured the level in which one individual participated in undesired pursuit of an ex-partner. Results of this study showed that engaging in cyber obsessional pursuits and obsessional relational intrusions were associated with venting about a partner (i.e., writing inappropriate things), harassment (i.e., posting of embarrassing photographs or creating fake Facebook pages) and provocation (i.e., looking for photographs of ex's new partner).

CONCLUDING RESULTS

Grief as a result of the dissolution of romantic relationships is not well studied based on online dating and the use of social media platforms. The research provided above gives a glimpse of the experience of grief for those experiencing grief reactions and how it is manifested on social media platforms and through online dating. At least with one study utilizing Twitter, it appears that individuals can experience what could be considered grief reactions in the form of depressive symptoms, self-centeredness, a focus on religion/spirituality, cursing life, and dropping followers and friends (Garimella, Weber, & Cin, 2014). LeFebvre, Blackburn, and Brady (2015) provided insight that following a romantic relationship breakup, individuals engage in multiple behaviors during and after romantic relationship dissolution: relational cleansing, minimal use or lack of Facebook use, surveillance, self-regulation, normative Facebook activities, virtual mourning, withdrawing access, impression management, virtual reconciliation, new relationship interest, account modification, off-social network communication, social network support, and relational transgression. The top two behaviors for both during and after a relationship breakup include relational cleansing and minimal use or lack of Facebook use. Relevant to online observations of a breakup, individuals will change, remove, or update their relationship status, engage in tagging or deleting, and limit or refrain from Facebook use. Finally, it appears that Facebook use during and after a breakup disrupts adjustment. Those individuals who limited or refrained from Facebook use during a breakup endorsed having a better adjustment post breakup.

Nitzburh and Farber (2013) found that after a breakup, individuals have the tendency to seek answers as to the reason for their breakup and as a result can experience feelings of jealousy. In addition, Tong (2013) found that individuals will utilize Facebook to seek information about a former partner's new love interest. Marshall's (2012) study of Facebook use after a breakup revealed that tracking an ex-partner led to feelings of disrupted emotional recovery and growth, as well as an increase in distress, negative feelings and longing. Lyndon, Bonds-Raacke, and Cratty (2011) observed that communication with former partners included both passivity but also included venting and harassment. Clayton, Nagurney, and Smith (2013) found that Facebook use in itself was associated with conflict, cheating, and romantic relationship dissolution.

Interestingly, a study involving oxytocin and the relationships between mothers and their daughters might have insight on the influence of technology on relationships (Johnson, 2013). To induce anxiety, young girls were given math and language tests. Communication between mothers and their daughters were observed through direct, face-to-face contact, phone, text, and no communication. Both oxytocin and cortisol were measured in the daughters' urine and saliva. High levels of oxytocin and low levels of cortisol were found in the urine and saliva of the daughters who communicated with their mothers in direct and face-to-face contact. Both daughters and mothers who communicated through text or did not communicate at all had no change in their oxytocin levels and higher levels of cortisol. Even though this study explores mother/child relationships, it provides information to make speculations related to romantic relationships. It provided data that reflects the associations between oxytocin, connection, and technological usage. What this study also suggests is that levels of connection appear to be higher in situations of direct and face-to-face contact and lower in situations of texting or no communication. It would be beneficial to replicate this type of experiment in romantic relationships in order to investigate its influence in these unique relationships.

Despite the limited study of the impact of online dating and social media platforms on the experience of grief following romantic relationship dissolution, several additional hypotheses can be considered regarding its existence. Social media has had a significant influence on society and its impact on grief, especially related to romantic relationship breakups. With the widespread accessibility of technology and social media websites, individuals have the capability to access and witness excessive amounts of information that would not be available without these resources. Historically, after a breakup an individual was able to experience the loss of a romantic relationship (for the most part) in solidarity. Now, with the availability of social media individuals experience similar lives to celebrities in the sense that society is able to obtain intimate details of their romantic relationship and resulting grief and loss. Presently, it is possible that others can know of the relationship breakup instantaneously often without both partners' consent (in the case where one partner discloses the breakup via social media). Another behavior that often causes emotional distress is the popular relationship status of Facebook where an individual can identify (or not identify) his or her relationship status. Given the research on Facebook profiles and affective responses to Facebook relationship status and profile pictures during a romantic relationship, one can speculate how these behaviors post breakup would contribute to grief reactions (Fox & Warber, 2013; Muscanell et al., 2013). Another current option that was not possible in the past is to view a partner's whereabouts after the breakup. The existence of social media platforms such as Facebook allows individuals intimate details of others' daily thoughts and actions. With Facebook, one can view whether a partner has begun dating again and whether he or she has *moved on* (whether it is accurate or not). As was shown with the studies on Facebook surveillance or Facebook stalking, this behavior can elicit much distress after a romantic relationship breakup (Clayton, Nagurney, & Smith, 2013; Lyndon, Bonds-Raacke, & Cratty, 2011; Marshall, 2012; Nitzburh & Farber, 2013; Tong, 2013).

Completely detaching after a romantic relationship might be complicated with the availability of technology and social media. In the past, the most common materials to dispose of were hard copy photographs and gifts. Presently, with technology there are often digital pictures, text messages, emails, instant messaging logs, and Facebook conversations. This can amount to a great deal of reminders that need to be disposed of or managed. An online presence often makes it difficult to avoid an individual. Without social media, an individual can attempt to avoid the partner due to knowledge of their daily routines. However, with an online presence one can often be reminded of the partner (even after going to great lengths to remove that individual from one's life). Luckily, psychologists are currently working with technology companies to create programs to organize information associated with a particular relationship that will lessen the complications of managing this information after the relationship ends. In addition, other ideas include options that would allow one to lock the Facebook page of his or her ex to provide time before being able to view it and a wastebasket system to contain reminders so that they are not destroyed impulsively (Miller, 2014). Clearly there needs to be additional study into the grief associated with romantic dissolution in the area of online dating and the utilization of social media platforms. The previous section provided the limited available research but also offered additional potential conclusions about how these symptoms might manifest or resemble grief reactions. In the next section, parasocial relationships, or relationships with media characters can provide additional observations about attachment relationships and how the ending of these relationships can lead to feelings of grief.

THE ROLE OF MULTIMEDIA: PARASOCIAL RELATIONSHIPS

Horton and Wohl (1956) first postulated that individuals have a relationship with media characters and named them parasocial relationships (PSRs). However, this interpersonal interaction between viewers and media characters is one-sided. The parasocial relationship is voluntary and is under the viewer's control to be ended at any time at the viewer's discretion. Parasocial interaction with television characters appear to be complementary (Kanazawa, 2002; Perse & Rubin, 1990; Tsao, 1996) and serve as a form of companionship and social activity. Parasocial relationships are deemed as pathological when viewers rely on these relationships as their only source of social interaction and participation (Horton & Wohl, 1956). Several characteristics exist regarding parasocial relationships (Schiappa, Allen, & Gregg, 2007). The more viewers watch television the more they reported having higher levels of parasocial relationships. Viewers were more likely to develop parasocial relationships if they had higher levels of desire to watch television. Perceptions of media characters as real, attractive, and similar to viewers were associated with the development of parasocial relationships.

Many types of media formats have been utilized to study parasocial relationships. Soap operas are one format used to observe parasocial relationships (Perse & Rubin, 1989). They are a valid option due to soap operas detailed plot stories and character creation. In addition, lighting, music, and camera techniques enhance the viewer's experience. Perse and Rubin (1989) studied parasocial relationships on soap operas and found that viewers utilize and expand their construct system of interpersonal relationships to increase their understanding of media characters. This interpersonal construct system is used to make conclusions about the attitudes, feelings, and behaviors of media characters. Film and television involve different relationships than soap operas (Houston, 1984). Television creates more powerful relationships for viewers with media stars due to its continuous and recurring viewing. Furthermore, Koenig and Lessan (1985) observed that viewers endorsed television show characters to be less close than friends, but closer than acquaintances. Parasocial relationships have also been witnessed in news programs with news reporters (Levy, 1979; Palmgreen, Wenner, & Rayburn, 1980). Qualities, such as being friendly, being a companion, and being real were elements that enhanced these parasocial relationships. The identity of the newscaster is developed in order to encourage familiarity with the viewer (Matusow, 1983) and personality, style, attractiveness, and audience appeal are often sought after in the hiring of newscasters (Bogart, 1980; Powers, 1978). Rubin, Perse, and Powell (1985) studied television news viewing and found that viewers tended to utilize television to obtain information as well as to obtain exciting entertainment. In addition, viewers who watched television news as a ritualized activity to pass time resulted in more general television viewing but less news viewing.

Stever (2009) created a classification system of media fans within a study of parasocial interaction with celebrities. The classification system included key motivations for parasocial interaction: task attraction (celebrity's talents and capabilities), romantic attraction, identificatory attachment a (the viewer desires to be like the celebrity), identificatory attachment b (the viewer perceives the celebrity to be similar to him or herself), filial attachment (viewer desires a friendship or familial relationship with the celebrity), coworker attachment (viewer desires to work with the celebrity in some capacity), hero worship (viewer views the celebrity as being extraordinary), infantile attachment (viewer depends on celebrity to meet personal needs), and parental attachment (viewer experiences nurturing feelings toward celebrity). The author recommends that this classification can be utilized to describe and identify the experience of fans. In addition, the system allows observations of how fans progress in their relationships with celebrities and their particular motivations at each stage of their relationships (Stever, 2009).

Apparently, media relationships are processed in similar ways that real social relationships are experienced (Kanazawa, 2002; Reeves & Nass, 1996). Parasocial relationships involve feelings toward media characters that allow viewers to relate and identify with them. In fact, the perceptions of television events as real and media characters as attractive were associated with parasocial relationships (Rubin & Perse, 1987; Rubin, Perse, & Powell, 1985; Rubin & McHugh, 1987; Schiappa, Allen, & Gregg, 2007). Caughey (1978,

1984, 1988) provided evidence that celebrities influence viewers' self-value and identity. Viewers reported admiring media characters' qualities and traits and were motivated to modify their own images (appearance, abilities, skills) in order to be more similar to these media characters. In addition, Boon and Lomore's (2001) research suggests that a relational orientation is significant in understanding the underpinnings of the influence of celebrity media characters on viewer self-development. Furthermore, there also appears to be gender differences as it relates to the identification with parasocial relationships and media characters (Greenwood, Pietromonaco, & Long, 2008). Women with preoccupied attachment styles tended to be linked with idealization of a favored female media character's behavior and physical appearance. It was also observed that women who chose thin media characters as their favorite media character endorsed the desire to look similarly to these characters. Finally, for women who chose media characters with an average weight endorsed perceived similarity with these characters.

The feelings experienced within parasocial relationships are continuous and are built upon through ongoing episodes. Parasocial relationships are developed through the accumulation of episodes and exposure to media characters. Having parallels to building and nurturing relationships with actual real world social relationships, parasocial relationships with media characters are built and the emotional connection deepened. In addition, due to the longevity of certain tv series (i.e., spanning over many years), one's relationship with media characters can develop into a strong long-term relationship. Newton and Buck (1985) even refer to parasocial relationships as a *significant other* and reflects the social value that television and other media outlets have in one's life. This intimate attachment also appears to occur in parasocial relationships with celebrities. The severity of one's emotional attachment and response to celebrities and other influential individuals can reflect the level in which parasocial relationships influence those who perceive a special relationship with them. In fact, Meyrowitz (1994) studied individual emotional responses to celebrities' (i.e., Elvis Presley) deaths. Even though individuals did not share an actual real world social relationship with these celebrities they still experienced an attachment to them and ultimately had an emotional reaction to their deaths.

Interestingly, relationships with media celebrities activate attachment systems in television viewers (Cohen, 1997, 2004; Cole & Leets, 1999). In addition, there might be an element of the attachment behavior played out in close relationships that is also evident in the relationships formed with media stars. Furthermore, the television viewers' attachment styles predict the intensity of the relationship between viewers and media stars. Studying attachment styles and relationships with media stars, it was found that for dating males, insecure attachment behavior (anxious attachment) was linked with strong parasocial relationships, whereas for dating females, secure attachment behavior was linked with strong parasocial relationships (Cohen, 1997). However, Cole and Leets (1999) found links for males and females with secure and anxious attachment behavior and strong parasocial relationships, whereas avoidant attachment behavior was linked with weak parasocial relationships. Given that the study's demographic population involved Jewish Israeli adults, it must be kept in mind the study's generalizability to other cultures and ethnicities. However, the study's value lies in its implications that attachment behavior influences relationships with media interactions, including film and television. More research needs to be completed in this area in order to measure the impact of media on attachment behavior.

Studying intimacy with media characters and real life social relationships, viewers selected their favorite parasocial relationships in order of preference, movie or television stars, singers and media personalities (Greenwood & Long, 2011). In addition, viewers ranked their intimacy levels for both media characters and real life social relationships, in order of preference, romantic partners (endorsed by individuals currently in a relationship), gender media characters of the opposite gender, same sex gender friends, and same sex media characters. Opposite sex media characters were associated with greater levels of intimacy when compared to same sex media characters. Looking at gender effects, women compared to men, endorsed higher levels of intimacy with same sex media characters. Differences were also found with viewers who were currently in a romantic relationship and those who were not (Greenwood & Long, 2011). Specifically, those viewers who were not identified as being in a romantic relationship were linked with higher levels of intimacy for opposite sex media characters. In addition, single viewers reported an association between the need to belong and imagined intimacy with an opposite sex media character. Related to attachment behavior, anxious attachment was associated with higher imagined intimacy with same sex media characters. The authors suggested that same sex media characters may serve a complementary role to real social relationships. In addition, they speculated that opposite sex media characters might serve a compensatory role and potentially meets one's unmet needs in romantic relationship intimacy.

Cohen (2003) described a concept called parasocial breakups (PSBs) which refers to the ending of a parasocial relationship, due to a television episode ending, a media character being taken off of the series, or some other event occurring to the media character. Consequently, viewers will choose to either not continue watching the series or tv show, or lose loyalty in the media character. Communication in real life social interpersonal relationships is how individuals lessen uncertainty. Due to the one-sided nature of parasocial relationships, viewers lower uncertainty by gaining information from viewing media characters on a television episode (passive uncertainty reduction strategies) or by discussing media characters with others (active uncertainty reduction strategies). Apparently, individuals utilize television to lessen uncertainty perceived in interpersonal relationships (L. Rubin, 1983; Perse & Rubin, 1989).

Cohen (2003, 2004) studied parasocial breakups and found parallels with breakups in close relationships. Results showed that levels of distress were associated with parasocial relationship intensity. However, although similar to distress experienced in close relationships, the level of distress in parasocial dissolution seem to be less distressful than close relationship breakups. Eyal and Cohen (2006) suggested several reasons for this finding:

- Although parasocial relationships can involve a level of closeness, they do not tend to be as intimate as close relationships (i.e., friendships) (Koenig & Lessan, 1985).
- Viewers who have parasocial relationships often have time to prepare for an episode ending (due to advertising and marketing providing details of a series ending).
- Viewers who have parasocial relationships and experience dissolution have a shared community of mourners.
- Viewers have the potential opportunity to maintain a parasocial relationship through reruns and DVD episode collections.

Finally, additional predictors that were associated with parasocial breakups included the viewer's commitment and affinity to the television show, viewer's perception of the character's popularity, as well as the viewer's experience of loneliness.

CONCLUDING REMARKS

This chapter reflects the complexity of relationship development. The influence of technology and social media impacts how all relationships, but specifically romantic relationships, have been traditionally built. Transitioning from a primarily in-person method of meeting and building relationships, what now seems to exist are relationships initiated and built in the digital world. In addition, research on parasocial relationships reveals that relationships can be built with media characters and tv story lines. Furthermore, it is apparent that there is an affective response to media interactions. With a presumed attachment to these media relationships, grief reactions occur when media personalities' story lines end or a tv show ends or is discontinued.

Individuals obtain companionship from their parasocial relationships; however, the reliance on parasocial relationships can become maladaptive when individuals utilize these relationships as their only source of social interaction (Horton & Wohl, 1956). It appears that media relationships are processed in similar ways that real social relationships are experienced (Kanazawa, 2002; Reeves & Nass, 1996) and involve feelings toward media characters that allow viewers to relate and identify with them. In addition, it seems that media celebrities have an impact on individuals' identity and self-esteem (Caughey 1978, 1984, 1988) so much so that they would engage in methods to modify themselves to be more similar to them. Parasocial relationships are continuous and are built upon through additional episodes and can develop into long-term relationships. Koenig and Lessan (1985) found that individuals endorsed television show characters to be less close than friends, but closer than acquaintances. Newton and Buck's (1985) reference to parasocial relationships as a significant other is another reminder of the significance that television and other media outlets can have on individuals' lives.

Individuals utilize television to lessen uncertainty perceived in interpersonal relationships (L. Rubin, 1983; Perse & Rubin, 1989). Individuals experience intimacy in their parasocial relationships and individuals not in a romantic relationship endorsed higher levels of intimacy when compared to individuals in a committed relationship (Greenwood & Long, 2011). Furthermore, attachment behavior can be witnessed in the process of parasocial relationship development (Cohen, 1997, 2004; Cole & Leets, 1999; Greenwood & Long, 2011). Cohen's (2003) concept of parasocial breakups and the ending of parasocial relationships results in individuals choosing to either discontinue watching the series or tv show or lose loyalty in the media character. In addition, individuals experience a special relationship with celebrities and media characters and even have an emotional reaction to their deaths (Meyrowitz, 1994). Cohen found that although similar to distress experienced in the breakups of close relationships, the level of distress in parasocial dissolution seems to be less distressful than close relationship breakups (Cohen, 2003, 2004). One helpful outcome of parasocial relationship endings as opposed to romantic relationships breakups is that viewers have a shared community of mourners (Eyal & Cohen, 2006). This provides a social network system that is not always available in the endings of close relationships.

Chapter Five

Diagnosis and Treatment

DIAGNOSTIC CRITERIA FOR BEREAVEMENT AND COMPLICATED GRIEF

Beginning in October 2015, the use of the diagnostic codes of the International Classification of Diseases, Tenth Edition, Clinical Modification, Classification of Mental and Behavioral Disorders were required in the United States for the billing and record keeping of psychiatric treatment. *The Diagnostic and Statistical Manual of Mental Disorders* (5th ed.; DSM-5; American Psychiatric Association, 2013) is a resource manual of the classification of mental disorders and is used for diagnosis and treatment. Currently, diagnoses of bereavement and complicated grief relate to situations of death. There is not a diagnostic label for experiences of grief specifically as a consequence of romantic relationship breakups. The inclusion of complicated grief only occurred in the latest version of DSM-5 which became available in 2013. The timing of the diagnosis of complicated grief to be recognized in the DSM-5 reflects the journey that the study and process of grief has taken. It is assumed that eventually grief related to other losses, including romantic breakups will one day be recognized. As society and the psychiatric community better understand the many facets of grief and more empirical study provides symptomatic evidence to the existence of grief as a result of losses besides death, grief related to romantic relationship breakups will also be recognized for its significance.

A diagnosis of persistent complex bereavement disorder, 309.89 (F43.8), formerly named complicated grief disorder, was added to the DSM-5 (APA, 2013). This diagnosis is consumed under the category of posttraumatic stress disorder and receives an *other specified* designation and also includes adjustment-like disorders. The category is provided to address symptoms that are criteria of a trauma and stress related disorder and leads to distress or impairment in functioning. Associated features of persistent complex bereavement disorder include the presence of auditory or visual hallucinations related to the perception of the deceased's presence. Risk factors include increased dependency on the deceased prior to death, death of a child and female gender. Clinicians are instructed to consider the influence of culture on the experience of persistent complex bereavement disorder. In addition, safety risk should be assessed due to the fact that many individuals who experience symptoms of persistent complex bereavement disorder also tend to report suicidal ideation (APA, 2013).

Differential diagnoses for persistent complex bereavement disorder include normal grief, depressive disorders, posttraumatic stress disorder, and separation anxiety disorder (APA, 2013). Common comorbid disorders with persistent complex bereavement disorder include major depressive disorder, posttraumatic stress disorder, and substance use disorders. Finally, other subtypes that fall under other specified trauma- and stressor-related disorders include, symptoms of an adjustment disorder that occur more than three months after the occurrence of a stressor, and symptoms of an adjustment disorder that last longer than six months. Other diagnoses have similar symptomatology as complicated grief but none of the other differential diagnoses fully encompass the symptomatology of complicated grief. For example, complicated grief and depression have mutual symptoms including the experience of sadness, crying, sleep disruption, and suicidal ideation. In addition, complicated grief and posttraumatic stress disorder both involve the experience of a traumatic event, intrusive thoughts, images, memories, avoidance, estrangement, sleep disruption, and difficulty concentrating. Shear et al. (2011) further distinguishes complicated grief and PTSD by clarifying that the foundational symptoms of complicated grief involve sadness and yearning, whereas in PTSD the significant symptom is fear.

In the DSM-IV-TR, clinicians were restricted in diagnosing an individual who experienced the loss of a loved one with major depression within two months after the death as part of a *bereavement exclusion* (APA, 2000). In the DSM-5, the bereavement exclusion was removed and clinicians are advised to distinguish between grief and the presence of a mental disorder. Although both grief and depressive disorders share symptoms of sadness and withdrawal behaviors, the DSM-5 differentiates grief and depression in the following ways. In a natural process of grief, an individual might experience painful transient emotions but also has positive memories of the loved one. In addition, the predominant feelings involve loss and emptiness. Also, with grief one's self-esteem remains intact. On the other hand, in major depressive disorders an individual typically experiences a constant depressed mood and has feelings of worthlessness and self-loathing. Clinicians are cautioned not to diagnose major depressive disorder when an individual is experiencing the normal symptoms of bereavement.

The V code of Uncomplicated Bereavement, V62.82 (Z63.4), applies to the normal reaction to the death of a loved one (APA, 2013). The criteria offered to represent the Uncomplicated Bereavement V code involves the following: (1) close relationship with the deceased individual, and (2) at least one of four symptoms on the majority of days of the week, causes distress and lasts 12 months after the death (adults) and 6 months after the death (children), (a) yearning or longing for the deceased, (b) sorrow and emotional pain, (c) preoccupation with thoughts of the deceased and (d) preoccupation with the details and circumstances of the death and (3) following the death, at least six of the following twelve symptoms are experienced on the majority of days of the week, causes distress and lasts 12 (adults) and 6 (children) months after the death (a) difficulty in acceptance of death, (b) emotional loss and disbelief (c) difficulty with positive reminiscing, (d) bitterness or anger, (e) self-blame, (f) avoidance of loss reminders, (g) a desire to die to join the deceased, (h) difficulty trusting others, (i) feeling alone or detached, (j) feeling empty or unable to function, (k) role confusion or diminished identity, (l) difficulty or reluctance to plan for the future or engage in activities or interests (4) the symptoms cause distress and impairment in functioning (5) the symptoms are not normal based on cultural, religious or age appropriate norms. An additional specifier of traumatic bereavement applies to symptoms of bereavement following deaths that are the result of a homicide or suicide. The symptoms involve distress related to preoccupations of the traumatic circumstances of the death.

Until grief from a romantic relationship is fully recognized as a diagnosis, the following diagnoses can be considered. The influence of divorce has been recognized and is associated with a V code, Disruption of Family by Separation or Divorce, V61.03 (Z63.5) and involves situations of separation and divorce. The DSM-5 defines adjustment disorders as symptoms that occur as a result of a stressor within three months of the stressor's occurrence and involve distress manifested by impairment in several areas including relationships and work. When diagnosing an adjustment disorder, the symptoms cannot be better explained by a normal process of bereavement. In addition, symptoms do not persist for more than 6 months after the stressor occurs. There are six subtypes of adjustment disorders and are differentiated by physical and emotional manifestations. An adjustment disorder that involves disturbance of a depressed mood (309.0, F43.21), disturbance of an anxious mood (309.24, F43.22), disturbance of both depressed and anxious moods (309.23, F43.23), disturbance of conduct (309.3, F43.24) and a disturbance of depression, anxiety and conduct (309.4 (F43.25) can be used to diagnose the relevant accompanying moods and behaviors. A final subtype includes 309.9 (F43.20) which involves symptoms that do not fit into one of the other subtypes.

TREATMENT

Psychotherapy

Bereavement is a healthy and normal process following the experience of loss of a significant individual or loved one. In most circumstances, individuals experience bereavement reactions and are able to maintain functioning and do not require the need for professional treatment. Other individuals with more complicated symptoms of bereavement could benefit from grief related treatment. A literature review of bereavement counseling revealed that grief interventions had a positive and enduring response for bereaved individuals who were self-referred for treatment or were referred by health professionals (Schut et al., 2001). A meta-analysis studying the effectiveness of psychotherapy for bereavement only found a small positive effect when compared to the lack of treatment following the experience of loss (Currier, Neimeyer, & Berman, 2008). Follow-up studies of up to seventy-two weeks did not reveal any definite effects. One study (Shear et al., 2005) observed the effectiveness of interpersonal psychotherapy in the treatment of complicated grief and was based on the dual process model of Streobe and Schut (1999, 2010). Compared to a treatment group for depression, the complicated grief treatment participants showed improved adjustment and lower rates of depression and grief. Another study, Boelen et al. (2007), compared the treatment of complicated grief with supportive counseling and cognitive behavioral therapy. Compared to supportive therapy, cognitive behavioral treatment resulted in greater improvement of symptomatology. From the study of the effectiveness of grief treatment, it appears that Streobe and Schut's (1999, 2010) dual process model is effective in addressing problems with loss and restoration back to life (Gamino, 2011). In addition, exposure therapy seems to be relevant when addressing the pain experienced as a result of loss (Gamino, 2011).

Complicated grief treatment (CGT) is one treatment option to address symptoms of complicated grief. Complicated grief therapy focuses on trauma related symptoms and utilizes cognitive behavioral techniques (CBT) and interpersonal therapy (IPT). In a randomized control trial comparing both complicated grief treatment and interpersonal therapy, complicated grief treatment had faster response times and higher success rates (Shear et al., 2005). Cognitive behavioral therapy (CBT) has also been used to treat grief and loss (Boelen et al. 2007; De Groot et al., 2007; Mathews & Marwit, 2004) and addresses maladaptive cognitions and behaviors. In addition, interpersonal therapy (IPT) has been utilized in the treatment of grief and loss (Shear et al., 2005). The complicated grief treatment (CGT) model includes sixteen sessions that occur over 4 months (Shear, 2010). In addition, CGT encompasses interventions from interpersonal psychotherapy (IPT), cognitive behavioral PTSD treatment (CBT) and motivational interviewing (MI). The treatment model involves an explanation regarding grief, complicated grief and complicated grief treatment, the utilization of a grief monitoring diary, the involvement of a significant other in the treatment, encouragement of improved interpersonal behaviors, focus on personal goals and self-care activities, exploration of the story of the death, along with consequences and implications, exploration of avoided locations and activities, focus on memories of the loved one and an imaginal discussion with the deceased loved one. A cognitive behavioral theory and treatment model of complicated grief involves a difficulty in the incorporation of the trauma or loss (i.e., death) into one's autobiographical memory. In addition, one experiences negative thoughts of self-blame. Similar to a general cognitive behavioral therapy, one focused on grief also addresses one's emotions and behaviors, as well as the cognitive evaluations one makes about self, the world, and the future (Beck, 1976).

An additional psychotherapeutic intervention to consider is attachment therapy. Successful psychotherapy can repair insecure attachment behaviors (Cassidy & Shaver, 2008, 2016; Mikulincer & Shaver, 2007, 2016). Bowlby offers five tasks that are involved in revising attachment style behaviors and interactions:

- Provision of a safe haven and secure base.
- Insight about the individual's attachment style behaviors, cognitive appraisals, and working models.
- Exploration of the therapeutic relationship between client/patient and therapist. It is assumed that the patient's working models and attachment behaviors will be played out within the therapeutic context.
- Insight into the individual's working models of self and others and its connection with childhood attachment with parental figures or caregivers.
- Insight into how working models are dysfunctional in their current interactions and relationships.

Bowlby (1988) draws similarities between therapists and mothers. He discussed how therapists can provide a secure base for individuals to therapeutically work on attachment related memories and experiences. Bowlby emphasizes the importance for therapists to offer a therapeutic space that involves safety, comfort, and unconditional positive regard. Similar to a parent, Bowlby suggests that the therapist serve as a source of safety and support but also provide the coping skills to encourage independence. Eventually, as a result of successful and appropriate psychotherapy, the therapist will become an attachment figure for the individual. Within the therapeutic relationship, therapists can help individuals deal with any attachment relevant material that arises during the course of psychotherapy, even attachment interactions that are acted out with the therapist. Utilizing these opportunities, therapists can help individuals have insight into their attachment related behavior and ultimately create a corrective emotional experience. It is important to remember the differences that are present when thinking of a therapist like a parent, such as the amount of emotional involvement, boundaries (emotional, financial, physical, and ethical) and availability. Because therapists can serve as attachment figures within psychotherapy and because individuals often enact their attachment related behaviors and working models within the therapeutic relationship, attachment enactments will need to be addressed within the therapeutic process (Cassidy & Shaver, 2008, 2016; Mikulincer & Shaver, 2007, 2016).

Mary Main and her colleagues (1985) created the Adult Attachment Interview (AAI). This interview is a rating and classification tool measuring adolescent and adult thoughts and feelings about childhood attachment relationships (Steele & Steele, 2008). Interview questions request the interviewee to identify five adjectives that would illustrate his or her relationships with both mother and father during childhood. Interviewees are also asked to provide memories to supplement the list of descriptive adjectives. Other items inquire about loss, trauma, distress, conflict, illness, and separation. One purpose of the interview is to activate the attachment system. An interviewee must self-regulate their affect when triggering original attachment behavior and relationships and provide responses that reflect their memories of these relationships. There is an assumption of unconscious factors that play a part in recalling attachment behaviors and relationships. These factors reflect the influence that these early memories have on behaviors and emotions but are a large part beyond the awareness of the individual. The goal of the AAI is to classify an individual's childhood attachment style and current adult attachment style (Steele & Steele, 2008).

The Adult Attachment Interview can be very beneficial in psychotherapy. With information that can be gained from the AAI, therapists can provide a safe space to enable individuals to explore their memories and attachments formed in childhood. Therapists can also make any thoughts and feelings that are unconscious become within the awareness of the individual. Seeing whether an individual is able to provide a coherent and organized recount of childhood events or whether there are substantial deviations will provide the therapist with focus areas to address within psychotherapy. This information will also increase the therapist's understanding of the individual's past and current attachment style behavior and also provide valuable clues to the origin of transference and countertransference interactions.

Utilizing these therapeutic guidelines, treatment models have emerged to focus on couples and families with the goal of addressing attachment behavior. *Emotionally focused couples therapy* focuses on attachment behavior with couples and *corrective attachment therapy* and *attachment-based family therapy* are models utilized with families. These models of therapy affirm that working models of self and others can be revised and attachment behavior can be modified. However, any psychotherapy intervention that has either a cognitive or dynamic focus can be beneficial in changing one's maladaptive working models. Having changes in both beliefs and interpersonal interactions can be therapeutically successful (Cassidy & Shaver, 2008, 2016; Mikulincer & Shaver, 2007, 2016).

There are multiple theories and treatment models within the area of marital and couples counseling. These theories describe the process of romantic relationships and provide interventions of how to repair issues that arise within these relationships. The purpose of this current text is to provide theoretical interventions specifically targeting grief that is experienced as a result of the loss of romantic attachment relationships. Related to psychotherapeutic interventions, it is assumed that most individuals will utilize individual (or group) psychotherapy to address any grief experienced by the ending of a romantic relationship. It is hoped that many couples will utilize couples therapy to repair and strengthen their relationships and potentially avoid dissolution. However, the following section will focus on one particular theoretical model, Emotionally Focused Couples Therapy, a treatment model that incorporates attachment theory as a basis for the understanding and treatment of couples' and marital conflict.

Emotionally Focused Couples Therapy, also referred to as EFT, was developed in the 1980's by Les Greenberg and Sue M. Johnson (Johnson, 2004). This theory and set of interventions emphasize the significance of emotion and communication in interactional patterns of close relationships. It involves both intrapsychic processes that incorporate the attachment behavior of the individual experience and interpersonal dynamics including the cyclical patterns of romantic partners. Furthermore, it encompasses the intuitive nature of how the intrapersonal and interpersonal processes influence each other. EFT is an experiential approach and places significance on the present experiences of romantic partners. EFT embodies attachment behavior concepts. The goals of treatment involve re-creating a secure base between romantic partners. Emotion plays a critical role in EFT as it is seen as a major influence of attachment behaviors and communication within romantic relationships. Within the romantic dyad, each partner's needs, desires, and behaviors are assumed to be healthy. Dysfunction arises when a partner's emotional behaviors are employed in times of vulnerability and danger. Partners become stuck in patterns of behavior that are self-reinforcing, within their intrapsychic experiences as well as within their interpersonal interactions (Johnson, 2004).

EFT usually culminates in 8–20 sessions. This therapy has the most positive prognosis with couples who desire to nurture their relationship but have engaged in negative behavior patterns. This therapy is not appropriate for couples who are violent or separated. EFT couples therapy has three stages and nine steps. The first stage, the de-escalation stage, involves three steps of modifying negative cycles of behavior. The first step includes building a therapeutic alliance between therapist and couple and identifying the couple's core conflict. The second step includes the identification of the negative interactional cycle. The third step includes the assessment of the emotions accompanying the negative interactional cycle. The fourth step of the first stage includes a new understanding of the conflict as part of the negative cycle, with individual emotions and needs (Johnson, 2004). The second stage, the changing interactional positions stage, involves three steps of changing the relationship structure of the couple. The first step includes identifying attachment emotions and needs and then incorporating them into the interactional pattern of the couple. The second step is integrating the couple's new behaviors. The third step is supporting the couple's needs and desires as well as creating new opportunities for emotional connection (Johnson, 2004). The third stage, the consolidation and integration stage, involves two steps. The first step includes the maintenance of new behavior patterns. The second step includes supporting and maintaining new patterns of attachment behavior interactional patterns (Johnson, 2004).

EFT is based on an attachment conceptualization of interpersonal relating. It encompasses attachment theory's contention that close relationships are categorized by attachment behaviors and emotional experiences. Similar to attachment theory, EFT views health as involving interdependency. EFT shares attachment theory's belief that connected attachments create both a secure base and safe haven to aid in exploration and prevent the consequences of stress and uncertainty. In addition, security within attached relationships involves emotional accessibility and responsiveness. Certain situations, such as those that invoke fear and uncertainty, can become detrimental to romantic relationships. When a connection is lost, separation distress occurs. Insecure attachment can be activated in manners of responsiveness, anxiety, avoidance, or disorganization. Working models of self and others are created that involve expectations, beliefs, and emotions about the process of relationships. Finally, EFT shares the idea of attachment theory that loss and abandonment by attachment figures is viewed as a trauma. Ultimately, EFT posits that relationship distress results from the deprivation of responsive attachment interactions. One of the major goals of couples therapy and of EFT is increasing the attachment security within romantic relationships (Johnson, 2004).

Johnson (2013) created an educational program, *Hold Me Tight: Conversations for Connections*, that can be helpful for individuals to gain more effective skills in communication. Also, as being part of the program, one can learn how to better regulate their affect and also navigate both connection and disconnection that are inherent in every relationship. This educational program was created using the principles of Emotionally Focused Therapy or EFT. Johnson's (2013) studies of EFT with couples have revealed an increase in satisfaction and secure attachment. What is significant regarding her research was her ability to empirically show that reparation of attachment bonds is indeed possible. This is truly a promising program in the field of attachment focused therapies.

The preceding section was offered as an option to help build and repair the attachment relationships with married and unmarried romantic partners. Its utility lies in the fact that it specifically focuses on attachment and trauma theories in relation to loss. Other marriage and couples' theories have the similar goal of repairing relationships but might not specifically focus on the areas of attachment, loss, and trauma. The ultimate goal and rationale for the inclusion of this particular theory, *Emotionally Focused Couples Theory*, is to potentially provide couples with the skills to avoid a divorce or romantic relationship breakup. Addressing the grief experienced during or after divorce and romantic relationship breakups, it is assumed that individuals will most likely enter treatment seeking individual psychotherapy. In this case, many of the psychological theoretical orientations of psychodynamic, interpersonal, and cognitive behavioral therapy can be considered. Complicated grief therapy, offered earlier in the section was not originally created in the use of divorce and romantic relationship breakups but was created to manage loss experienced through death. However, it will be important to see how this theory can be applied to loss related to the dissolution of married and unmarried partners. Although it is assumed that most individuals will seek individual therapy to manage their process of grief, it would be beneficial for the couple to consider using couples therapy to jointly obtain treatment to handle the grief process. Much could be gained from both partners acknowledging the loss that is inevitable whenever an attachment is broken. Finally, attachment theory is an excellent option to consider as an intervention. Because of its inherent focus on attachment and loss, it is perfectly suited for addressing the experience of grief of a breakup of a romantic relationship. In addition, one can obtain information related to the attachment dynamic in the previous relationship to gain insight into how it influenced the life of the relationship. Not only can additional insight be gained about one's childhood attachment with parents and its connection with the individual's attachment behavior but also its significance in the previous romantic relationship.

Additional Interventions

One study (McKiernan et al., 2017) observed the benefits of an online discussion forum for youth experiencing a romantic relationship breakup. Trained moderators facilitated the discussion forum and had additional training in suicide intervention skills. The authors concluded that the discussion forum provided a safe environment for youth to express themselves in relation to a romantic relationship breakup. Users of the forum requested stories and opinions in order to gain support for their emotional responses to their breakups. Given that this study was conducted on sixteen-to-twenty-five-year-olds in Ireland, it is important to consider its generalizability. However, it would be beneficial to consider the feasibility of this intervention with multiple age groups, ethnicities, and geographical regions. Based on the mounting popularity and usage of online interventions, it would be useful to examine this option as a method to provide social support and therapeutic benefit to those experiencing a breakup or a divorce. Based on the fact that support groups provide benefits in helping individuals manage the grief reactions associated with breakups and divorce, it seems clear that both online and offline support group interventions would be advantageous.

THE IMPORTANCE OF CULTURE

It is important for health care professionals to be aware of the cultural background and beliefs of the individual experiencing grief. Without this knowledge, it is difficult to assess whether the individual's grief reactions and expressions are within typical limits. An exploration of the individual's unique cultural beliefs related to grief as well as the individual's perceptions of the greater society's beliefs of grief will provide invaluable information to that individual's experience and symptomatology of grief. To extend the idea of the significance of culture further, it is important to be aware of language. Some cultures have words that define grief that do not correspond to English translations (Rosenblatt, 2011). Inadequate attempts at translation and mis-assumptions about the true meaning of one's verbal expression of grief can complicate the assessment, diagnosis, and treatment of that individual.

OTHER CLINICAL THEMES BENEFICIAL IN PSYCHOTHERAPY

The following clinical themes do not fall into a particular theory. However, the exploration of these themes in psychotherapy can be beneficial. Clinical vignettes are provided to illustrate the use of these clinical themes during the treatment process.

Identification of Self-Talk

Negative self-talk is very powerful and can have damaging effects on one's self-esteem. In the case of romantic relationship breakups, negative self-talk can be detrimental to the healthy resolution of grief over the breakup and can have negative implications on future relationships. Negative self-talk is the speech utilized when referring to one's self. It is the voice inside one's head and the repetitive messages one makes to one's self.

Examples of negative self-talk can include statements, such as:

- "I am unlovable."
- "I will never find someone who will love me."
- "Something is wrong with me."
- "Someone will always find someone better than me."
- "Why would anyone want to be with me?"

It can be imagined that over time these messages repeated over and over again can have a negative consequence on one's self-esteem. Hay and Kessler (2014) recommend the use of positive affirmations in improving one's cognitive appraisal of their grief in a romantic relationship breakup.

THE CASE OF TIFFANY

Consider the following clinical example. Tiffany was in a three-year relationship with a male and was unexpectedly broken up with through an email.

Her ex-boyfriend told her (via email) that he had always been in love with someone else. Tiffany and her ex-boyfriend had been planning to get married within the year. Tiffany's ex-boyfriend did not give her the respect of having an honest and direct conversation about the breakup or provide his reasons for breaking up. Tiffany was left with many unanswered questions and struggled with finding confidence that her relationship was real while it lasted. Tiffany also had similar patterns in her personal background that made it difficult for her to separate the hurt and rejection that she experienced with this relationship. Tiffany experienced a series of relationships including one with her father that made it hard for her to feel adequate. Her ex-boyfriend's decision to end their relationship due to loving another triggered her already present fears. This feeling was compounded by the way in which her ex-boyfriend broke up with her (i.e., via email).

This is a list of Tiffany's negative self-talk:

- "I am not good enough."
- "No man will ever love me."
- "How can I expect a man to love me when my father didn't?"
- "I don't deserve a loving relationship."
- "I don't even deserve an appropriate good-bye in my relationship."

Tiffany initiated psychotherapy to deal with the feelings elicited by her breakup. She eventually explored her relationship with her father and gained insight into her feelings of not feeling adequate. She began to see the similarities with her romantic partners and their inability to be emotionally expressive. She began to see how these relationships contributed to her feeling inadequate. Once Tiffany found insight into her patterns she began to see how her negative self-talk was a consequence of her experiences and not necessarily a true reflection of herself. After some time in psychotherapy, Tiffany began to see that her negative self-talk was impairing her self-esteem and affecting her ability to have a healthy relationship.

Tiffany changed her negative self-talk to positive self-talk by creating the following affirmations:

- "I am good enough."
- "I am lovable and I will find a man to love me."
- "My father was unable to appropriately express his love for me. That does not mean that I will not find romantic love."
- "I deserve a loving relationship as much as anyone else."
- "I deserved an appropriate ending to my relationship. The fact that my ex-boyfriend couldn't give me one is a reflection on him."

As is seen in this example, Tiffany was able to shift her internal dialogue from a negative to a positive one. Through her insight in psychotherapy she recognized how her mate selection process influenced the mates she chose and also how their behaviors influenced how she felt about herself. Tiffany's goal would be to begin selecting mates that would validate and reinforce her positive self-talk.

An Exploration of Past Loss

Past loss is an important factor in the experience of loss. An individual's particular loss history is often experienced as a compounded loss experience, especially in light of the current loss. In the case that past losses are not effectively processed, it can often make the experience of the current loss more difficult. By reviewing one's history of loss, one can begin to see patterns of how they have dealt with the loss and how they feel about themselves. Without taking a deep analysis of one's past losses will increase the probability that one will continue potentially maladaptive patterns. Also, past losses can combine with current losses and reinforce what could be unhealthy working models and self-appraisals. Kubler-Ross and Kessler (2005) suggest that past ungrieved losses do not disappear. Avoidance or repression does not eradicate loss. Each loss is internalized and remains until future losses occur. With each new loss, old losses are re-experienced and integrated within the current loss.

Mourning of Old Visions and the Creation of New Visions

Experiencing a loss often disrupts an individual's beliefs about the vision of his or her life (Kubler-Ross & Kessler, 2005). This disruption can be very significant and can lead to a crisis to one's identity. Again, in light of a loss, it is not only important for one to mourn the loss but also to mourn the loss of any beliefs that one might have held about the visions for their life. It is important for those experiencing a relationship breakup not to overlook the significance of their beliefs and assumptions and to be intentional about processing the emotions that are associated with the loss. Life beliefs are related to the fantasies one creates about his or her life. Because fantasies are often connected to life's beliefs it is often difficult to begin to let go or modify any fantasies. Fantasies can also be experienced as opportunities of being stuck in the idea that one could have changed the outcome of the loss. Being engaged in the fantasy allows individuals to remain connected to the loss and allows the loved one to stay alive in one's mind, even though the relationship has ended.

Often in loss, individuals can idealize the past relationship. Often what is remembered are the positive aspects of the relationship with an avoidance or denial of the negative aspects. This often maintains the created fantasy and makes it difficult for individuals to proceed in the healing process. Hay and Kessler (2014) discuss the grief that results from the idea of one's ideal mate. They describe how one can experience sadness and depression due to not obtaining that mate. The individual needs to grieve not obtaining this idea of an ideal mate and this life that they have envisioned. Hay and Kessler (2014) suggested that when one can fully grieve his or her idea of what one's life should have been, one can begin to live in the moment and begin living for oneself. The power of this loss is often underestimated and even dismissed by others when one experiences a romantic relationship loss. It is often difficult for others to understand the depth of one's vision for their life and the grief that can follow when that vision does not become reality. But because a vision focused on a romantic relationship is often viewed as superficial or insignificant (i.e., as opposed to a career vision), one can often feel unsupported in their grief regarding unfulfilled vision. If others can acknowledge and be supportive of one's vision for his or her life and grief over the unfulfilled vision, it will aid in healthy grieving and will provide additional support in helping one begin to live for oneself.

The Influence of Control

Control can be employed in the experience of loss in the desire to stabilize events, especially in situations of unexpected loss (Kubler-Ross & Kessler, 2005). Control tricks one into believing that everything will be safe. It can give one the false sense that one is holding everything together. Especially in situations where the loss is unexpected, one can be tempted to employ control in order to feel more secure. This makes sense given that the unexpected loss has taken away one's ability to feel safe and secure. Control provides the illusion that one is safe and secure. The best method to deal with an unexpected loss is for one to acknowledge the loss of safety and security. Once that loss is dealt with, one can then begin to rebuild their own personal sense of safety and security.

The Power of Regret

Regret is often an emotion that is inherent in loss (Kubler-Ross & Kessler, 2005). It is important to take an inventory of any feelings of regret because left unattended they can develop into unhealthy behaviors and feelings. When experiencing the loss of a romantic relationship loss, one is often left with many regrets about wishes of things said or done.

THE CASE OF TRACEY

Consider the following example of how one patient handled her experience of regret regarding the conflict she was having in her marital relationship. Tracey began psychotherapy during a time that she and her husband were participating in couples counseling. As they made the decision to get divorced, Tracey described several regrets that she discussed in her individual psychotherapy. She identified the following regrets as being deterrents for her ability to obtain closure from her relationship:

- I wish I had worked harder in the marriage.
- I wish I was better looking.
- I wish I was smarter and had gone back to school to obtain my master's degree.
- I wish I had cooked dinner for my husband that time I had the flu.
- I wish I had worked harder to get his mother to like me.

Tracey went through each regret and considered which she thought were significant and which she thought she could discard. For example, she was able to discard the regrets of wishing she had cooked for her husband when she had the flu. During her marriage, she always had done the majority of the cooking. However, her husband made her feel guilty for not cooking despite her having the flu and a fever. After exploring each of her regrets she found that accompanying these regrets was extreme pain. Once Tracey dealt with the pain resulting from her regrets and was able to work through them, Tracey thought about making a symbolic expiration of her regrets. Tracey selected the option of writing her regrets down on different sheets of paper. She described her practice of going into the woods behind her house to meditate every day. She mentioned an old trash can that was near where she liked to sit and meditate. She made the decision to have a private ceremony where she would take her regrets and burn them in the trash can. The next session Tracey came in and discussed her experience. She described great relief and after completing her ceremony she no longer had her previous regrets. Tracey then took an additional step with her list of regrets. She took the old regrets and described loving statements that she could utilize in her next relationship. This is what Tracey created:

- I gave all I had to my marriage. The next time I enter a relationship I will find someone who can appreciate me.
- I am attractive and any man would be lucky to have me.

- I am smart and if I decide to return to school it will be because it's my decision and not to keep my husband.

Tracey took these statements and printed them in her journal and posted them around her house so she could have a daily reminder of them.

Reestablishment of Roles

When a relationship ends, the roles that the partner fulfilled are now empty (Kubler-Ross & Kessler, 2005). Individuals are forced to make a choice about how to fill the void left when the relationship has ended. During this decision-making process, individuals can experience grief related to not only the loss of the relationship but also the additional loss of the fulfillment of particular roles in the relationship. Part of this process involves choosing whether to adopt the open role. This can be difficult for some especially if the role is one that the individual does not feel expertise in or if one dislikes the role. Other roles are often assigned to others in the individual's life or others might be drawn in to take these roles on. Grief can often be re-experienced when reassigning roles. It is a reminder of the lost relationship and the need to have roles and tasks to be fulfilled by someone else. However, in the end some roles remain unfulfilled and can provide yet another source of grief.

Acknowledgment of Loss Anniversaries

Anniversaries, associated with the loss can be difficult. They punctuate special events in the history of the loss and trigger memories of the relationship (Kubler-Ross & Kessler, 2005). The first year of anniversaries is especially difficult in the experience of a loss. Even in the situation of loss of romantic relationships it can still be important to honor the loss and the memories associated with the anniversary. This can be utilized only if needed in experiences of painful breakups.

THE CASES OF CAROLINE AND TIFFANY

Consider the next two individuals and how they chose to handle the anniversaries of their relationship breakups. Caroline lit candles on the date of her anniversary. She held a private ceremony of honoring her relationship and inviting in new memories and relationships in her life. Alternatively, Tiffany made the decision to take a trip. She stated that she wanted to create new experiences and memories to be associated with her anniversary date.

Related to anniversary dates, holidays can also trigger memories of the loss. Especially since holidays often involve other family members and friends, they can introduce additional feelings of loss as one reflects on the memories created with others in their lives. In addition, one can experience not only the loss of a loved one but also the loss of the loved one's family and friends. Individuals can find ways to make holidays more manageable for them. Whether the loss is through death or romantic relationship breakup, individuals can consider modifying holidays to suit their needs.

The following are several modifications to consider:

- Changing the structure of the holiday
- Deciding not to host or cook one year
- Having another event (going to the movies or going bowling)
- Having a special ceremony for a loved one or a moment of silence
- Changing the tradition to honor oneself

Redefining Closure

Closure is a term often utilized to represent the integrative resolution of feelings surrounding an event. However, the idea of closure is often difficult to achieve. Resolution is hard to obtain due to multiple factors and it is uncertain whether anyone is able to receive complete closure. Despite the inadequacy of this word it is continuously used when describing loss. It is important to consider a word to embody the recovery from grief. A word that represents the ongoing process of healing would be helpful. Utilizing a word that encompasses this ongoing process would hopefully decrease the assumption that one should experience grief in a particular way or in a particular time period.

Retelling the Story

One ritual often experienced during grief situations is the retelling of the story (Kubler-Ross & Kessler, 2005). This practice of telling one's story is an essential component of the healing process of the loss. It serves the role of aiding in comprehension of the loss. There is an inherent desire to understand the loss and story retelling is used as a vehicle to attempt to obtain insight. Especially in times of unexpected loss, the mind searches for a way to gain clarity of the loss itself and often why the loss occurred. Retelling of the story creates a necessary structure and establishes a foundation for understanding loss. It is important to tell one's story often and in detail. It serves to lessen the pain of loss and is an integral intervention in the grief process. During the story retelling ritual, the focus of the story often changes over time. At different stages of the loss, different aspects of the story take priority. Despite this need to retell the story and in light of its benefits in the grief process, individuals often experience that others in their lives become tired of hearing their stories. This is unfortunate because it could inhibit others in feeling safe enough to continue to tell their story and they might not obtain the healing effects of its practice. In addition, others can be helpful in the story retelling ritual in helping individuals gain insight into their loss that they might not obtain in the absence of external input and feedback.

An individual's need to tell the story is often experienced in psychotherapy. Similar, as to with friends, not only do individuals recount the story multiple times in an attempt to process the trauma and loss of the break-up but also to gain insight into the loss. Individuals often apologize for repeating their stories in psychotherapy, presumably because in their outside world they receive explicit and implicit messages that others are tired of hearing their story. Thankfully, in appropriate psychotherapy settings, individuals are allowed the safety and space to retell the story as much as needed or as much as helpful. Mental health professionals can identify when individuals become stuck in their stories. Mental health professionals have the skills to be able to challenge individuals in a way that can move them to another level of insight—the most important is the origin of why the individual might be stuck.

Dreams

Dreams can be thought of as representations of what is experienced internally. In grief, dreams can represent the lack of control in the experience of loss (Kubler-Ross & Kessler, 2005). Dreams can also serve the role of a distraction from the pain felt as a result of a loss or can be an opportunity to work out psychological issues experienced with loss. Dreams can operate as a way to obtain reassurance or be a vehicle of communication. This can be especially helpful in situations where one feels a lack of closure from the relationship. It can provide a method of bringing completion to a relationship that has unexpectedly ended.

Journaling

The study of actual diary entries provides insight into the utility and value of journaling as an intervention of one's grief work. Rosenblatt (1983) suggested that diaries can be both beneficial and detrimental to successful grief work. If one is able to limit loss experiences via diary entries there would be less stimulating memories to disengage from and would be beneficial. However, if one's use of a diary increases the experience of stimulating memories, it can result in more intense grieving.

Research related to the benefits of journaling to address the loss of a romantic relationship appears to suggest that it can be beneficial (Lepore & Greenberg, 2002; Lewandowski, 2009; Slotter & Ward, 2014). Specifically, journaling of adults experiencing relationship dissolution reported less distress after four days (Slotter & Ward, 2014). Another study of the effects of journaling, found that when comparing negative and neutral journal writing, journal writing that had a positive focus resulted in positive emotions (Lewandowski, 2009). Finally, Lepore and Greenberg (2002) found that individuals who participated in an expressive writing exercise lowered their probability of developing an upper respiratory illness, tension, and fatigue. The expressive writing exercise appeared to be a protective factor against stress symptoms, in this case higher levels of intrusive thoughts and avoidance.

It needs to be noted that the assessment of diary keeping during the process of grief work is based on diary keeping without the clinical guidance of a mental health professional. Although there has been limited published literature on the benefits of journaling in grief work and especially as it relates to the breakups of romantic relationships, it can be assumed that for some individuals journaling can be beneficial in conjunction with psychotherapy. Within the context of psychotherapy an individual can engage in targeted journaling where their journal keeping can be clinically monitored. If grief reactions intensified they can be addressed through clinical interventions and the journal keeping can be adjusted, if needed.

A grief monitoring diary is a component of complicated grief treatment (Shear, 2010). The diary activity of this treatment is based off a cognitive behavioral therapy intervention. Individuals are asked to rate their highest and lowest levels of grief on a daily basis. In addition, individuals are asked to rate average daily levels of grief as well as logging descriptions of situational contexts related to the individuals' experience of grief. The treatment's goals for this particular intervention include psychoeducation to treatment participants of the fluctuating levels of grief as well as to provide insight into the types of situations that trigger grief (i.e., high and low levels of grief recordings). A final goal of this intervention is to provide an assessment of participants' response to treatment by providing baseline grief levels (i.e., daily average grief ratings). Evidence of this treatment's efficacy has been supported and was discussed earlier as it relates to the treatment of complicated grief. Basing speculations off of the entire treatment's success, it is hypothesized that the journaling component provides a valuable addition to the treatment and reflects the benefits of monitored journaling as a part of grief work.

Loss Ceremonies and Funerals

Funerals can be helpful traditions in the honoring of those who have passed away. In many ways, it serves the symbolic function of completion. It allows individuals to celebrate the life of their loved one and also marks finality in a sense. It is often a known and predictable end point that one can identify and plan as an event that marks the end of the process. In situations of divorce, Lewis (1983) illustrated a *Dissolution of a Marriage*, an example of a religious ceremony of a divorcing couple. Bach and Bernard (1971) also described *Unwedding Rituals* and *exit ceremonies* as ways to address the ending of marriages. Kaslow (1991) suggested that divorce ceremonies can encompass religious and spiritual aspects of the union and can serve as an event to honor the relationship. These types of ceremonies provide an opportunity of forgiveness and release. The practice of these ceremonies is understood as a psycho-social transition (Lewis, 1983) that helps one grieve during the divorce process. These ceremonies can provide resolution to the marital relationship and can address the experience of loss that occurs with divorce. In addition, these ceremonies can be healing for children to witness and can address their feelings of anger and guilt (Bach & Bernard, 1971). Hight (1977) suggests having a *contractual, working separation*, which is a separation contract that is employed before a divorce occurs. It serves as a rehearsal of divorce and allows the couple the opportunity to begin to experience the emotional components of the upcoming divorce. It also includes living arrangements and financial concerns as well as other decisions that need to be made during the legal divorce process.

It is unfortunate in many ways that there is not a similar tradition for the end of romantic relationships. Without the symbolic ceremony of a funeral it allows others to underestimate the impact of the event on someone's life. Without a funeral or loss ceremony, the act of healing has to be obtained in solidarity without a public validation of this ending. Another reason that a funeral could be helpful in romantic relationship endings is that it allows the individual to have an event to express their emotions in an environment that supports mourning of the loss. In addition, it allows for the public to be present and provide mass support for the individual who is enduring the loss. It can validate the individual's sense of loss in ways that might not occur if something such as a funeral was not to occur.

Funerals celebrating lives that have died do not occur in breakups. This public acknowledgment of loss is not present. In some ways, the ceremonial expression validates the death and provides support. The lack of this experience in the case of breakups forces the individual to grieve alone without support and without the confirmation that their emotions are valid. If our society had a tradition of a ceremony or funeral for romantic relationship endings perhaps individuals and society as a whole would view these grief events differently. Potentially others would gain more respect and compassion for this type of grief and loss.

CONCLUDING THOUGHTS

Related to diagnosis, the DSM-5 offers persistent complex bereavement disorder to describe grief related to the death of a loved one. In addition, a V code of uncomplicated bereavement is utilized in situations where functioning is not severely impacted following the death of a loved one. When considering the influence of divorce on symptomatology one can use the V code, disruption of family by separation or divorce. Until there are specific diagnoses for romantic relationship breakups, clinicians can continue to utilize the various diagnoses for adjustment disorders. Regarding treatment, complicated grief treatment was examined and offered as a method for treating the loss through death of a loved one. When considering utilizing individual psychotherapy, clinicians can consider using attachment theory, psychodynamic, interpersonal, and cognitive behavioral interventions. Although all marriage and couples psychotherapy models can be utilized to address relational concerns, Emotionally Focused Couples Therapy was provided due to its emphasis on attachment based concepts. Furthermore, additional interventions were explained including the benefits of support groups and online resources. Finally, clinicians were reminded to assess how culture plays a role in the experience of grief.

The remainder of the chapter was devoted to other concepts related to grief that can be explored within treatment. Concepts such as self-talk, exploring previous losses, mourning old visions, and creating new ones, reestablishing roles and acknowledging loss anniversaries and retelling the story were explored to examine the role that they play in the experience of grief. In addition, the roles of control, regret, and closure were also investigated. Dreams were briefly discussed as it pertains to grief reactions and journaling as a method to manage grief reactions was also offered. Finally, relevant case material was provided throughout the section to illustrate applicable ways to introduce these concepts into psychotherapy.

Chapter Six

Romantic Relationship Grief in Psychotherapy

Kubler-Ross described her grief theory as different categories besides stages, such as reactions, defenses, and adaptations. Her theory has been adopted because it is an easy one to understand and apply to situations of grief (Corr, 2011b). In addition, it offers structure to a process that is perceived to be outside one's control (Doka, 2011). Kubler-Ross's theory has received criticism due to not fully explaining the experience of grief. One major criticism of her theory is that it does not explicitly take into consideration cultural influences on the experience of grief. Other concerns of her theory involve the lack of empirical validation, the inadequacy of the five emotional reactions and the language of the grief process as a stage theory as opposed to a set of reactions. One final concern related to the theory includes its generalizability, given that Kubler-Ross postulated her theory based on two and a half years of interviews conducted with adult patients with a terminal illness (Corr, 2011b; Doka, 2011).

In the previous chapter, Kubler-Ross's theory was presented as a stage theory, just as she conceptualized it. However, given the criticism discussed here, one could consider the concepts as more accurately a set of potential reactions of grief first conceptualized to describe dying but offered here to explain grief related to romantic relationship breakups. Kubler-Ross acknowledged that everyone has a unique experience with grief and that her theory might have limitations (Kubler-Ross & Kessler, 2005). Despite the criticism that exists related to Kubler-Ross's grief theory it remains an easy and understandable model to discuss grief and by no means serves as the only model to explain grief reactions.

This chapter will provide a description of the stages of grief, conceptualized by Kubler-Ross. Although originally created to discuss the experience of grief related to death, it is now becoming clear that they prove utility in also discussing grief related to breakups of romantic relationships. An overview of these stages will be offered as they potentially relate to romantic breakups and could be useful in better explaining the process of grief of these breakups. Clinical case vignettes will illustrate experiences of grief in romantic relationships and the influence of attachment related behaviors will be explored as well.

DENIAL

The first stage Kubler-Ross identified in her stage theory of grief reactions is *denial* (Kubler-Ross & Kessler, 2005). This stage is often characterized by shock and numbness. Kubler-Ross provided reassurance that this stage helps one deal with and ultimately survive the loss. In addition, it allows one to not become overwhelmed by the loss and allows one to pace the emotional experience surrounding the loss. It is often during this stage that individuals repeat the story of their loss over and over again. This is a healthy reaction of the mind attempting to deal with the trauma of the loss. At the end of this stage as denial fades, reality of the loss replaces the denial.

The Case of Tina

To illustrate this stage of grief, consider Tina. She had been dating her boyfriend for five years. She had gone on a trip and when she returned home she was confronted with an empty house. Her boyfriend had moved out while she was away. The only explanation she received was a note on the bed they shared that read, "I can't do this anymore." He never called or attempted to contact her. The shock of arriving home to an empty house and the lack of control that the situation produced stayed with Tina for several months. Throughout the early months in treatment she would continuously repeat, "This can't be happening. It isn't true. He's just confused. He's going to come back. We are going to get back together." Tina and her ex-boyfriend did not get back together but this was Tina's way of dealing with the shock of arriving home and being unexpectedly abandoned. Her mind could not make sense of what had happened and she was aware of the lack of control of the breakup (i.e., when it happened, how it happened, where it happened, etc.). Although it would have probably been healthier for her ex-boyfriend to break up with her in a different way (i.e., doing it in person, providing some explanation of his changed feelings, not removing his things until she returned, etc.), his lack of doing so allowed Tina to remain in this stage of denial longer than usual. Without details, Tina was allowed to create the scenario that there was still the possibility of getting back together. This duration of denial allowed Tina the time to process the loss and not become overwhelmed by it.

Within psychotherapy, Tina was able to gain understanding regarding her stage of grief and her experience of denial. Her desire for details related to her ex-boyfriend's experience was validated. Tina began to understand that although these details might have been valuable in her ability to understand and gain insight, she also recognized that she would not be able to obtain these details due to her ex-boyfriend's inability to effectively communicate his feelings or experience. Eventually, Tina understood why she needed to participate in denial as a part of her grief process. From an attachment perspective, Tina can be categorized as securely attached and her ex-boyfriend is most likely identified as being avoidantly attached. Her ex-boyfriend's method of leaving the relationship is a hallmark representation of an avoidantly attached individual. However, when Tina was able to further investigate her relationship with her ex-boyfriend she noticed other characteristics of his avoidant attachment style. Tina remembered how uncomfortable her ex-boyfriend would become during disagreements. He would often leave their apartment during an argument and would stay out all night. When he would return, he would do so without acknowledging their argument or his whereabouts after leaving their apartment.

By understanding her ex-boyfriend's avoidant attachment style, she began to gain insight into their romantic relationship, but also their attachment behaviors. Tina began to understand that her ex-boyfriend was not a good match for her and due to his attachment style behavior, he would not be able to meet her attachment needs. Tina, through psychotherapy, understood that a good romantic attachment figure for her would be someone who is securely attached. She realized that her ex-boyfriend's choice of ending their relationship was related to his attachment style. She considered her own attachment needs and realized that these needs would be best met by another securely attached individual. Tina was able to grieve the fact that she had been in a romantic relationship with a mate that was unable to meet her needs. She was able to personalize her ex-boyfriend's behaviors less because she understood the origin of his attachment style. Tina challenged herself to better select romantic partners that could meet her needs.

The Case of Sandy

Sandy experienced a breakup with her girlfriend of seven years. She described not being surprised because she and her girlfriend had been experiencing trouble in their relationship for almost a year. They had been arguing and it was becoming harder to live together. Much like their usual arguments Sandy and her girlfriend broke up during a heated disagreement. The two of them were yelling at each other and Sandy's girlfriend yelled, "Fine, let's just end this then." As soon as Sandy's girlfriend yelled those words, they both fell silent. They didn't speak to each other for several days. A month later after understanding that they needed to discuss living arrangements, they made plans to begin looking for alternative living. But until that conversation and until they each found a new place to live, Sandy and her girlfriend lived together almost as roommates. Sandy moved into the guest room. They came and went, not speaking to each other, sometimes staying out all night and not coming home for several days. During this time Sandy lived in the stage of denial and she kept thinking to herself "this isn't happening. We will get back together. We are just going through a rough patch." Even after having the conversation about moving and after they both moved, Sandy still held onto the idea that they would get back together.

Similar to Tina, Sandy needed this stage of denial. She needed the denial to deal with the shock of the loss of her relationship. Otherwise, she would have been overwhelmed with the emotions that accompanied her loss. A few months after Sandy moved out she began to see the denial slip away and she was ready to move into another stage of her grief. In addition, to obtaining a better understanding of her experience of denial, Sandy also began to have more insight into other aspects of her relationship. Sandy explored the communication and the constant arguing that she had with her ex-girlfriend. She hypothesized that their inability to truly communicate about what was really going on in their relationship and their inability to immediately separate after breaking up were also forms of denial. In addition, they reinforced her belief that they would get back together. Sandy needed to acknowledge this existence of denial to not only grieve the relationship but also gain true insight into her romantic relationship dynamics.

According to attachment theory, both Sandy and her girlfriend can be described as avoidantly attached. They both would avoid communicating during times of conflict. They would either deflect any attempts at communication or would avoid conversations by leaving. Even their decision to maintain living together but not communicating reflects avoidant behavior. When Sandy and her ex-girlfriend would communicate, they often avoided the underlying issues and would discuss superficial conflicts that would never truly resolve their concerns. Through therapy, Sandy began to understand how their similar methods of avoidance and lack of communication were detrimental to their relationships. If they had not broken up when they did, they most likely would have done so at some point as a result of their relevant attachment styles. Sandy began to understand her attachment style in psychotherapy by being provided with feedback of how her attachment behaviors were manifesting within treatment. Through the safety of the therapeutic relationship, she was able to see how her avoidant patterns influenced her interpersonal interactions.

ANGER

A second stage of grief in Kubler-Ross' theory is *anger* (Kubler-Ross & Kessler, 2005). Kubler-Ross described that anger occurs when the individual realizes that survival is possible. She stressed the importance of experiencing anger and not repressing it.

The Case of Robyn

Robyn was overcome with anger. She and her significant other had been trying to work on their relationship after multiple previous breakups. Robyn had suspected infidelity on her boyfriend's part but it was confirmed when she learned that she was positive with HIV. Before learning of her medical status, Robyn and her boyfriend decided to separate. One day before Robyn's doctor's appointment when she learned the news of her HIV status, she and her boyfriend decided to break up for good. Now on top of the grief of the loss of her relationship Robyn was also struggling with the loss and anger associated with her new medical concerns and adjustment to her lifestyle. She also experienced anger related to her children's future related to her health situation. She now was left with concerns for a medically regimented lifestyle and the limitations to witnessing milestones in her children's lives when she felt ill. Robyn's anger resurfaced multiple times (as she had to take her HIV medication, as she contracted pneumonia due to her compromised immune system, and when she was unable to attend her daughter's recital because she was too tired). Eventually, through treatment, Robyn was able to work through her emotions of anger. She still experienced bouts of anger but she began to accept her reality regarding her medical condition and all the consequences that came with it. This allowed her space to process her feelings regarding the loss of the relationship which had gotten misplaced as she dealt with the priority of her physical health.

According to attachment dynamics, Robyn is classified as being securely attached and her significant other was most likely anxiously attached. During the relationship, he would express to Robyn his fears that she would leave him. He also would verbalize that Robyn was not being as intimate as he was and that she would eventually fall in love with another man. Better educated about his attachment style, Robyn was able to understand their interpersonal interactions and why they occurred. It also eliminated some of her anger because she began to understand that his behavior was a product of his attachment style. Within psychotherapy, Robyn was able to explore and express her emotions in a safe environment. Robyn also attended a group therapy process group that was focused on relationships. Within her group therapy format,

Robyn received validation of her anger related to her breakup and her medical status. Because she was able to appropriately and safely experience her anger in the safe and therapeutic setting of psychotherapy, she was able to grieve her loss and avoid becoming consumed by anger.

The Case of Robert

Robert experienced anger about one year after his breakup. He was not able or ready to access his anger before then. He had experienced other emotions of loss (i.e., depression, denial) but had not yet gotten in touch with his anger. Robert was cleaning out his house one year after the breakup with his girlfriend of ten years. Robert had not cleaned out the house earlier than that because it hurt too much to go through his ex-girlfriend's things. However, he decided it was time and on this particular day he had been cleaning out the attic. Not long into his task he came upon a diary of his ex-girlfriend's. Robert struggled about whether to look in the diary. Despite their breakup he still held a sense of loyalty to her privacy. However, Robert felt an overwhelming urge to obtain answers regarding their relationship. Robert read his ex-girlfriend's diary and in it he learned how his girlfriend described her emotional and sexual affair with another man. Robert experienced extreme anger at the added betrayal that the facts of his ex-girlfriend's diary provided. The diary allowed Robert the opportunity to access his anger and deal with his emotions related to his loss.

In this situation, Robert is identified as securely attached and his ex-girlfriend was most likely anxiously attached. Robert's ex-girlfriend was similar to Robyn's ex-boyfriend. His ex-girlfriend voiced constant fears that he didn't love her and that she loved him more than he loved her. She also would express concern that Robert would leave her for another woman. Learning more about her attachment style allowed Robert to have additional insight into their entire relationship. He was able to better accept her infidelity as he had more clarity into her attachment needs. It was important for Robert to adequately explore his experience of betrayal. The feeling of being betrayed in a romantic relationship is often a difficult experience and can result in multiple conflictual feelings. Robert thoroughly explored his feelings of pain, rejection, and deception. What made Robert's situation more complicated in one sense was that he found out about his ex-girlfriend's infidelity after the relationship ended. He was unable to communicate with his ex-girlfriend regarding his emotional experience and therefore needed to process his emotions without being able to communicate with her. In some ways, Robert was re-traumatized and propelled into another experience of grief when he found the diary. Robert began to realize the benefits of exploring a new experience of grief related to his feelings of betrayal.

BARGAINING

Another stage of grief that Kubler-Ross offers in explaining the experience of loss is *bargaining* (Kubler-Ross & Kessler, 2005). Bargaining describes the stage of grief where one attempts to escape the pain of the loss. This is the stage where one entertains negotiations to avoid the pain and the loss one is experiencing. In a lot of ways, it is a distraction from reality. Furthermore, it can trick one into believing that one has the power to change the events that have occurred and take away the pain one is experiencing.

The Case of Jason

Jason and his girlfriend broke up last week. Immediately Jason entered the bargaining stage. He started negotiating in an attempt to get his relationship back. He would say things like, "If I do something nice for someone than maybe she will come back to me." Three months after the breakup, Jason realized his negotiations were a way for him to feel like he had power in a situation where he felt powerless. However, none of the negotiations allowed him to get what he truly wanted—to get his girlfriend back.

In this scenario, Jason is identified as being anxiously attached and his ex-girlfriend is most likely securely attached. Jason entered psychotherapy and learned more about his attachment style behavior. He gained insight into the origin of his attachment style and childhood attachment experience with his mother. He found evidence of how his attachment needs played out in his romantic relationships and influenced whether he could get his needs met or not. He reflected back on his romantic relationship and was able to fully understand the feedback his ex-girlfriend was attempting to give him. He saw how his concerns regarding his ex-girlfriend's feelings for him were related to his attachment style and might have played a role in their eventual breakup. In psychotherapy, Jason explored how his practice of bargaining tricked him into feeling a sense of power. He was able to safely explore his feelings of powerlessness following the breakup. Once he was able to honestly express his powerlessness he was able to appropriately grieve the breakup of his romantic relationship. Jason eventually understood that his bargaining behavior would not bring his ex-girlfriend back and held no power in their reconciliation.

DEPRESSION

The fourth stage that is a part of Kubler-Ross's theory of grief stages includes *depression* (Kubler-Ross & Kessler, 2005). She described this stage as a protective mechanism for the nervous system. By shutting it down, it allows one to adapt to events and emotions that are experienced as overwhelming. As with all of the stages, depression is a healthy reaction and is necessary for the healing of the loss. Depression allows one to experience loss at its deepest level, which is necessary for the experience of loss and grief. Kubler-Ross described thinking about the depressive experience of this stage as a visitor. Thinking about depression in this way, as visiting, allows one to receive the relief that it is not permanent. However, like a human visitor the depression might return and stay awhile but will in time leave again.

The Case of Brenda

Brenda found the metaphor of depression being like a human visitor very helpful in her experience of loss of her breakup with her significant other of fifteen years. She would often come to therapy and mention that her depression was back and planned to stay for a while. During depression's *visit,* she would allow herself to be sad, sleep more often, and cry when needed. She didn't judge herself or tell herself she should be over it. She welcomed it as a natural part of the process and she knew she needed to go through it in order to heal. Because Brenda thought of her depression in this way she was able to move through this stage uncomplicated by issues of self-judgment and punishment. Her use of the metaphor, likening her depression to a visitor, allowed her to normalize her experience so that when it occurred she was able to manage it without being consumed by it. In this current case, both Brenda and her significant other can be classified as securely attached. She was able to reflect on and grieve the relationship in a healthy way. She was able to accept the relationship for what it was and what it brought her and was not consumed with questions about her ex-romantic partner's love for her. Because Brenda was able to trust in the love that existed in her romantic relationship she was able to deal with the grief of her loss in a healthy way.

ACCEPTANCE

The fifth stage of the grief theory is *acceptance* (Kubler-Ross & Kessler, 2005). Like its name implies, it is the stage where one realistically accepts the end of the relationship. It involves the stage where one begins to reassign roles that the partner once took on. Individuals either choose to take these roles on themselves or employ others to take them on. This is also the time of reintegration, where Kubler-Ross and Kessler (2005) describe as a time to put back the pieces.

The Case of Tracey

Tracey had been in treatment for two years to address her feelings regarding a previous breakup. Tracey utilized psychotherapy to help her cycle through the stages of grief. She was able to challenge herself to actively explore her grief with minimal self-judgment. She was able to realistically accept her breakup about a year and a half into treatment. This was the point that Tracey needed to approach acceptance and she was only able to do this after she was able to appropriately grieve her breakup. As a part of her process of acceptance she began to consider the various roles that existed in her previous relationship. Tracey adopted most of the roles herself, and her family and friends were able to adopt other roles that were left vacant by her former romantic partner. For example, her brother volunteered to help Tracey move into her new condo. Tracey also utilized her new move and accomplishment of purchasing her condo on her own to start anew. She didn't avoid or deny her past but ushered in new energy. She redirected energy toward herself and focused on her interests and passions.

Chapter Seven

The Case of Shana and Jared

This chapter will solely be focused on one clinical case vignette with the purpose of illustrating the process of grief experienced through all five stages of grief. In addition, the unique attachment related behaviors of the case will be explored as they relate to the case and additional insight into the grief stages will be provided. Shana had been in a committed romantic relationship with Jared for three years. Shana and Jared grew up in the same city but met as adults through mutual friends. They began a long-distance relationship due to Jared's employment several states away. Shana and Jared experienced several brief separations during their dating relationship due to Jared's uncertainty regarding the relationship (which always left Shana feeling *not good enough*). However, Jared had begun discussing marriage with Shana and they both began making plans to prepare for additional commitments in their relationship. However, after an enjoyable holiday together Jared returned home only to break up with Shana over the telephone. Jared provided no rationale for his decision to end the relationship but only mentioned he "couldn't do it anymore." Shana reached out to Jared several times after the breakup to receive closure and feedback regarding the breakup but Jared initiated no communication or explanation for the breakup.

DENIAL

Shana experienced denial immediately after the breakup. The breakup had occurred right after a major holiday where Shana and Jared spent mutual time with both of their families. Shana also was shocked by the fact that they had recently discussed increasing the commitment in their relationship. Shana entertained the idea that Jared possibly was just confused and would initiate communication and a renewed commitment to their relationship. Shana did not spend a great deal of time in this stage of denial. Although she continued to experience shock in the way the breakup occurred she was clear about the reality of the breakup. Therefore, Shana's time in denial was short and she next moved into a stage of bargaining.

BARGAINING

Shana began to bargain when she thought about her relationship with Jared. She made comments to herself including, "What if I had moved to where he lived?" Shana fully explored these bargaining thoughts and ultimately accepted that she would value her role in their relationship. Shana's experience of bargaining involved a reassessment of certain components within her relationship. Moving had been a topic discussed by both Shana and Jared. Although, Shana's job was not exactly mobile, she had verbalized intent to move to live with Jared in order to make their relationship stronger and to increase the commitment within their relationship. At the time of their breakup, Shana offered the move again as an option to see if removing the geographical separation would address Jared's intention to end the relationship. However, Jared dismissed the idea and notified Shana that he did not want to take any steps in trying to make the relationship work.

ANGER

Shana experienced anger several times after the breakup with Jared. Several months after the breakup Jared alluded to the fact that one of the reasons that he initiated the breakup was because he was not sexually satisfied. Shana was extremely hurt by this rationale given by Jared. Due to Shana being a virgin, Jared was her first sexual partner. She was hurt that the first and only man she had shared herself physically with would throw what she considered to be her most intimate gift in her face. Furthermore, throughout the relationship Shana had initiated communication about their sexual relationship and ways they could improve it. Upon reflection of the relationship Shana was able to understand that Jared was not as sexually experienced as he portrayed himself. She also obtained insight that Jared himself was very anxious about his own sexual experiences with Shana, which did not allow her to experience herself in a sexually safe way. One thing that made Shana the angriest was the fact that Jared left Shana with this feeling and failed to ever communicate his responsibility in their sexual relationship or validate the gift of sharing herself sexually with him.

Within psychotherapy it was clear that Shana did not fully explore her experience of anger. When she processed her emotions, she found that most of her energy was self-directed and resulted in more of an experience of depression than anger. This experience is further supported by the amount of time Shana spent in the stage of depression and how severely she experienced feelings of depression related to the breakup. This is most likely due to the fact that the relationship really impacted Shana's self-esteem. For her, Jared's lack of sensitivity and respect left her feeling *less than* and *not good enough*. Shana also sacrificed much more in the relationship than Jared did, which made her feel like he was not really committed to the relationship or to her. The sexual rejection only exacerbated what was already a fragile experience. Although Shana was able to return back to her strong self-esteem after the breakup, it was still apparent that she was deeply impacted by his behaviors. However, also within psychotherapy Shana was able to obtain insight that her experience of rejection and self-esteem issues were projected onto her by Jared, who struggled with strong issues of self-judgment and low self-esteem. Because Shana got caught up in Jared's issues of self-reproach she found it difficult to stay grounded due to the added component of Jared's avoidant attachment behaviors (which exacerbated her feelings of rejection).

DEPRESSION

Shana experienced depression right after her experience of denial. She came to grips with the reality that the relationship she thought was going to materialize was quickly and unexpectedly ended. Her depression was exacerbated when Jared told her months later that he had initiated a relationship with his ex-girlfriend (two months after his breakup with Shana). In addition, he notified Shana that the reason he was so uncertain during their relationship was because he thought his ex-girlfriend was *the one* and that Shana was not. This came as a complete shock to Shana because Shana asked consistently during their relationship if Jared's uncertainty was due to an actual person and each time Jared denied it. Unfortunately, Shana left the relationship believing that Jared never truly loved her or was fully in the relationship.

Once again, the theme of rejection is highlighted. Jared created a triangle with Shana and his ex/current girlfriend. By telling Shana that she was *not the one* and his current girlfriend was *the one* and by failing to validate the relationship he experienced with Shana, he contributed to Shana's feeling of not being *good enough*. Luckily, Shana was able to explore this theme more intently within psychotherapy. She considered how the dynamics of the relationship influenced her concerns and she identified that she was being triggered by a history of romantic relationships and a relationship with her father where she also struggled with feeling *good enough*. Shana, with insight, began to understand that it was the partners she was selecting that continued to reinforce her feelings of rejection. Until Shana could begin to select partners who could validate her, she would most likely continue to experience similar emotions and interpersonal interactions in future relationships.

ACCEPTANCE

Shana grieved the loss of her relationship with Jared and with the possibility of a life with him. She also grieved the loss of Jared's family whom she became very close to during the relationship. She accepted the fact that despite how it happened that it needed to happen. In addition, she also accepted that Jared did not love and accept her. Most importantly, Shana accepted that the relationship was not authentic to who she was. Shana knew that she needed someone that could love and accept her for who she was and that person was not Jared. This understanding allowed the space for her to open her heart to allow in someone to love her in a way that would provide her with validation and appreciation.

Once Shana fully processed her grief related to her romantic relationship she explored important details related to the interpersonal dynamic she participated in with Jared. This provided a valuable lesson into factors that played an important role into their relationship. Part of Shana's insight involved Shana learning important lessons of her attachment relationship with Jared. What is interesting about Shana's case is that she is usually identified as a securely attached individual. She seeks loving and warm relationships and she enjoys intimacy within her relationships. In addition, she is able to effectively communicate her needs and feelings and is also skilled at understanding and responding to her partner's needs and feelings. She is able to be open and communicate her achievements and difficulties while also being able to be available to her partner when needed. However, being in a relationship with Jared, who can be characterized as avoidantly attached, Shana took on a role of responding in an anxiously attached manner. Because of Jared's emotional distance, Shana would feel that Jared did not wish to be as close as Shana desired in the relationship. She became hypervigilant and sensitive to Jared's emotional experience. Due to Jared's inability to communicate,

Shana began to take Jared's behavior personally. On the other hand, Jared would most likely be described as avoidantly attached. He prefers autonomy over intimacy in relationships. He most likely desires closeness but becomes uncomfortable when too much intimacy is expressed and as a result would keep Shana at an emotional and physical distance. Jared did not tend to open up to Shana and withdrew when he perceived conflict.

Because Shana entered the relationship with a securely attached mindset she desired intimacy and security in the relationship. Jared, due to his avoidant attachment style desired independence and autonomy. He would consistently create distance in the relationship. Early in their relationship, Jared would walk out of the house in the middle of Shana's attempts to communicate her feelings in the relationship. Other times, he would not call her back or gave her the silent treatment when Shana would try to communicate with him. In addition, he would initiate breaks in the relationship where he would cut off communication with Shana. He would tell her that the goal of the breaks was to figure out what he wanted. Again, due to Jared's poor communication skills, his breaks caused distance in the relationship and represented to Shana that he was not committed to her or the relationship.

Jared exhibited what Levine and Heller (2010) offer as hallmark signs of avoidantly attached individuals:

- Jared sent Shana mixed messages. He would consistently ask for breaks in the relationship and would tell her he was unsure about being in the relationship. On the other hand, he would initiate conversations about them moving to live together and even getting married. In addition, he verbalized to Shana the desire to increase their commitment by getting married and then broke up with her shortly thereafter without an explanation as to why.
- Jared would describe a desire to be in what he considered an ideal relationship. However, his constant verbal and behavioral displays of uncertainty provided hints to Shana that she was not the object of this ideal relationship.
- Jared consistently described an idea of *the one*. However, due to Shana learning that Jared began dating his ex-girlfriend and his disclosure that his ex-girlfriend was the one, Shana realized that Jared was not honest with her throughout their relationship.
- When Shana would communicate her emotional needs to Jared he would minimize her feelings, disregard them or ignore them. In addition, he would tell Shana that she was overreacting. Shana began to feel as if her feelings were not important and were being dismissed by Jared and ultimately Shana began to second guess herself.

- When Shana would initiate conversations that involved emotions and Jared was not in the mood to participate, he would refuse to respond to her or would change the subject.
- In order to avoid emotional intimacy Jared would resort to logic and objectivity. He refused to take Shana's feelings into account and made her feel like her feelings were insignificant.
- Finally, despite Shana's attempts to communicate and to make Jared feel comfortable discussing emotional matters, Jared would ignore, withdraw, or appear to not take it seriously.

These behaviors contributed to the emotional distance that Shana and Jared experienced in their relationship. Given the geographical distance between them, the added emotional distance made it difficult for the couple to survive. On one of Shana's trips to visit Jared out of town, they had an argument. Jared shut down the conversation and gave Shana the silent treatment and shortly after left for work. Shana, in an attempt to repair the relationship, sent a text trying to communicate about the issue. Jared did not respond to the text or Shana's attempt to communicate. While Jared was at work, Shana decided to cook dinner and clean the house. She also prepared for a romantic night by lighting candles and putting on lingerie. Despite receiving Shana's text while at work and, when Jared arrived home, noticing all of the things Shana prepared, he continued to give her the silent treatment and shut her out. When Shana attempted to continue to discuss their concerns with a hope of enjoying the rest of the night, Jared further shut her out by stating that he did not want to talk about it. Shana was scheduled to return home the next day and when she awoke the next morning, Jared continued to give her the silent treatment. Only shortly before Jared was going to take Shana to the airport, he broke his silent treatment, not to discuss their concerns or what occurred the day before, but to initiate a sexual encounter. This memory reflects Shana's attempts to effectively communicate within the relationship and Jared's multiple attempts to withdraw, shut out or punish Shana.

At some point in the relationship, Jared requested a key to Shana's home, however, he failed to provide a key to his own home to Shana. When Shana inquired about it, Jared reported that he felt that she did not need one or could borrow his key. This is an example of Jared's attempts to maintain his level of independence within their relationship. Shana also discussed her attempts to be available for Jared and make efforts to support him when requested or needed. Shana remembers a time that she made arrangements to visit Jared when he was asked to deliver an important speech. Shana identifies this as a significant event in their relationship because for her it reflected how insignificant she felt within their relationship. In addition to getting out of several obligations in order to join Jared at his special event, she also secretly obtained information to the location of the speech and ordered flowers for the podium in honor of Jared. At the speech, in Jared's opening line, he verbally thanked everyone who attended to support him, everyone except Shana. Shana videotaped the entire speech because she predicted that Jared would want to keep it as a memory of the event. However, the whole time, she thought about the fact that Jared did not acknowledge her, or did not even realize that he did not recognize her. Only when Shana brought it up to him in the car, did he react to it. However, his reaction was very defensive. To Shana this was one of many times she felt like she did not factor a large part into Jared's life.

Also related to the above example, Shana also felt like Jared did not make an effort to involve himself into her life. Shana remembers inviting Jared to an event hosted by one of her professional organizations. She was being honored within her field and she asked Jared if he would attend. Jared notified her that he was unable to attend. However, he also made no other efforts to acknowledge her accomplishment, such as calling her to find out how the night went, or sending her flowers or a gift to express his feelings of not being able to be present. Jared did attend one event for Shana when she was initiated into a social organization. However, Shana believes he only attended for personal reasons and not as a celebration for Shana. She felt as though he attended only to say he did because the social organization was an elite organization. Jared often was concerned with factors related to status and that most likely played more of a factor into his decision to attend versus attending to support Shana.

Shana, although usually secure in her relationships, began to become activated by Jared's behaviors and began to initiate activating strategies in an attempt to obtain closeness to Jared. She began to resemble an anxiously attached individual and became preoccupied in the relationship. As Jared would pull away Shana would ultimately desire more closeness, which would result in causing Jared to withdraw even more and leave Shana feeling alone and rejected. This cycle continued in their relationship and Shana began feeling not good enough in the relationship. This feeling became exacerbated every time Jared withdrew, walked out, dismissed her, or needed a break from the relationship. Somehow Jared continued to increase Shana's feelings of rejection during and after the breakup. Breaking up with her over the phone, never initiating an apology or explanation for the breakup, telling her that his ex-girlfriend was the one, minimizing the significance of her virginity, all increased Shana's feelings that she was not *good enough* and not important to Jared.

It is possible that romantic partners feel inferior or not good enough as a result of dating an avoidantly attached individual because of the avoidantly attached individual's attachment style and relevant working models. Avoidantly attached individuals tend to experience unhappiness and less satisfaction in their relationships. They often blame this unhappiness on not meeting the right person or only finding partners who are needy. As is clear with this statement avoidantly attached individuals look outside themselves and blame others for not being happy or meeting their needs. They are unable to be introspective and evaluate their own behavior in an attempt to find insight about their behaviors or interpersonal reactions. It is difficult to observe change in the behaviors of an avoidantly attached individual unless there is introspection or therapy. Interestingly, when avoidantly attached individuals' defenses break down, they begin to exhibit behaviors similar to those that are anxiously attached. It was important for Shana to understand that avoidantly attached individuals desire closeness but will always exhibit emotional distance and also maintain an escape route in their romantic relationships.

Levine and Heller (2010) describe deactivating strategies that an avoidantly attached individual will engage in to suppress their needs for closeness in romantic relationships. The following deactivating strategies were ones that Jared employed in their relationship:

- Jared would verbalize but also show through his actions (i.e., initiating multiple breaks within the relationships) that he was not ready to commit to the relationship. He also displayed this behavior in the romantic relationship before Shana. In both relationships, Jared remained in the relationship for years, despite feeling that he was unable to commit.
- Jared would focus on small issues within the romantic relationship. He would not make any effort to initiate change related to those issues and would also not entertain Shana's attempts to initiate change regarding these issues. Jared would allow these issues to greatly influence his romantic feelings.
- Jared would continue to hold feelings for his ex-girlfriend. He continued to keep up pictures of his ex-girlfriend and other momentos long into his relationship with Shana. It was only after Shana communicated her feelings about the items did Jared put them away. In addition, Jared told Shana how he had attempted to win his ex-girlfriend back after their break-up. Jared told Shana this after their own breakup, when he did not engage in any of these winning techniques with Shana. Whether it was accurate or not, it was another way that Jared made Shana feel as if their relationship was not as significant as the relationship with his ex-girlfriend.
- Jared would hold back from giving Shana compliments. Often times, months later he would give her a compliment. On one occasion, several

months after they went on a vacation together he commented that he liked an outfit she wore.

- Jared needed alone time during couple activities, such as birthday vacations or family reunions. On one birthday vacation for Jared, Shana went to lunch alone when they arrived at their destination. Although she requested that Jared come along with her, he declined. On that same trip, after Shana went through a great deal of trouble to create a special birthday celebration for Jared, he spent the entire day with a friend. Instead of being invited by Jared to attend, Shana spent the day by herself touring the city.
- Jared would often praise others' independence by making Shana's valid desires for closeness appear *needy*. Jared's behavior reflected his attachment style in that he valued independence and autonomy. In addition, the avoidantly attached individual's strong adherence to self-reliance has been found to be connected to less comfort with closeness, self-disclosure, intimacy, and seeking help from others. However, his comments to Shana only created more emotional distance in their relationship and made Shana feel as if her needs were invalid.
- Shana would notice that Jared would often become more distant after they had spent time together, such as after a vacation, holiday or a weekend visiting each other. He would react by not calling for days after seeing Shana or being emotionally distant when they would communicate on the phone.
- Shana would continuously experience frustration in the relationship related to Jared's secrets. She would request information from Jared and was often left confused as to why Jared appeared to withhold information from her. Keeping secrets is another deactivating strategy and allowed Jared to maintain his autonomy and independence.

Although, Jared would engage in these deactivating strategies to maintain his autonomy and independence, it also caused a conflict in his goal to obtain closeness. His behavior caused the opposite effect. His behavior did not create closeness in the relationship. In fact, it caused both emotional and physical distance. In addition, this caused Jared to experience less happiness and less satisfaction in his relationship.

During the duration of the romantic relationship, Jared and Shana would often experience conflict. One reason involved the fact that Shana, due to her secure attachment, would often want to communicate in order to bring the relationship to a closer or more intimate place. Jared, on the other hand, (although he desired closeness) would avoid closeness because of the discomfort it brought him. In order to avoid the relationship gaining more intimacy, Jared would become more distant and more hostile when communicating with Shana. Jared would avoid taking accountability of his own behavior and would even project his own behavior onto Shana by describing her as cold. What often occurs when an avoidantly attached individual dates a securely attached individual is that the avoidantly attached individual becomes closer to being secure. Utilizing the case of Jared and Shana, Jared became more secure by dating Shana. Because Shana was able to provide a secure base, Jared was able to grow emotionally and interpersonally. However, due to a lack of introspection and psychotherapy, Jared was unable to maintain the relationship or his own personal emotional growth. Ultimately his avoidant attachment style and corresponding working model resulted in his overall unhappiness in himself and the romantic relationship. Furthermore, Jared's unhappiness with himself was projected onto Shana. Shana, in turn, began to experience Jared's projected feelings of unhappiness and as a result began to feel not *good enough*. In the end, due to Shana's secure attachment style she was able to regain her positive self-esteem once she broke up with Jared and was able to appropriately grieve the relationship.

With the insight that came from therapy, Shana began to recognize the importance of finding a romantic partner that is securely attached. A securely attached individual would match Shana's desire for intimacy and security. She also needed to find a mate who was able and willing to engage in effective communication and emotional expressivity. With a securely attached partner, Shana would feel fulfilled and feel like her needs were being met. Naturally, as a part of Shana's treatment, it was important to explore her attachment with her parents. Shana reported having a very close relationship with her mother. It is most likely Shana's relationship with her mother that allowed her to have a secure attachment style and working model of others. Shana was able to easily recall and describe experiences of being comforted and shown love from her mother. On the other hand, Shana had a different relationship with her father. She exhibited anxious attachment behavior with her father with whom she desired a closer relationship than he was able to give her. Her father behaved in an avoidant attachment style with Shana. He was unable to manage his affect during conflictual situations and Shana often found him to be emotionally unavailable. Shana's father also abused alcohol for much of Shana's childhood. During her father's alcohol abuse and for most of Shana's life, Shana found him to be undependable, inconsistent, and unavailable. Shana reacted to her unpredictable upbringing by exhibiting behaviors similar to Adult Children of Alcoholics (ACOA's) by adopting a responsible, dependable, nurturing and accommodating personality.

Luckily, Shana participated in psychotherapy before and during her relationship with Jared and so she had good insight into her attachment relationships with men. She understood that she was drawn to men who played out a similar attachment relationship as the one she shared with her father. Shana tended to select men that were avoidantly attached and she would vacillate between operating in both secure and anxious attachment styles in her romantic relationships. Shana received evidence in her romantic relationships and friendships with individuals with avoidant attachment styles that her needs would never be met. In a similar way, Shana became thankful for her breakup (albeit painful) because she ultimately understood that her ex-romantic partner would never be able to meet her needs or to provide her with a secure and loving relationship.

Shana was able to utilize the insight gained in her psychotherapy following her breakup with Jared to become more intentional in mate selection. She began to look for clues earlier in her relationships for her partners to be able to have secure and loving relationships, as well as be dependable and consistent. Once Shana was able to choose more carefully she was able to participate in more healthy and secure romantic relationships. Once she was able to participate in more secure romantic relationships she began to receive the validation that is inherent within more secure romantic relationships. This allowed Shana to modify her attachment experiences with men and also her working models of romantic partners. In Shana's secure relationships, she was able to experience what Levine and Heller (2010) define as being characteristics of secure romantic relationships:

- Shana and her romantic partners avoid conflict escalation by effectively discussing issues without resorting to defensiveness or punishing each other.
- Shana and her romantic partners are able to react to constructive feedback and to modify their actions and/or beliefs, if needed.
- Shana and her romantic partners are able to effectively communicate their thoughts and feelings. They can be understanding to each other's needs and respond appropriately to those needs.
- Shana and her romantic partners do not need to engage in playing games because of their mutual goals of closeness and intimacy.
- Shana and her romantic partners are comfortable with their level of emotional and physical intimacy.
- Shana and her romantic partners believe each other's intentions are for each other's better well-being. As a result, they are able to easily forgive each other.
- Shana and her romantic partners understand emotional and sexual intimacy to be one in the same. They are comfortable with both aspects of intimacy.
- Shana and her romantic partners treat each other with love and respect.
- Shana and her romantic partners believe they are able to improve their relationship and initiate the effort needed to make their relationships better.

- Shana and her romantic partners understand their responsibility in each other's well-being. They take this very seriously and are able to accurately respond to each other's needs.

Furthermore, Shana embodies the qualities needed to create a secure base for her romantic partners. Levine and Heller (2010) suggest that to provide a secure base one must be available, one must not interfere, and one must encourage. Shana often is available in her relationships. She is able to provide comfort and extend support when needed. She also provides support without disempowering others. She allows others to feel the support needed to overcome their obstacles without taking over or undermining others. Finally, she offers encouragement and is accepting of others' strengths and flaws. She is particularly skilled in making others feel good about themselves and helping others to feel more confident. By providing these qualities and behaviors in a relationship, Shana is providing similar behaviors that a secure mother provides to her infant. These behaviors provide the elements for a securely attached relationship and will increase the chances that Shana will experience a loving and caring relationship with an individual that is available and dependable.

Shana was able to utilize the strategies that Levine and Heller (2010) recommend are needed in order to seek out secure romantic partners:

- She was able to be more intentional regarding her romantic relationships. She began to be clear about what she wanted in relationships and what would be the best types of relationships for her. She was able to identify what types of partners were aligned with her needs and to weed out anyone who wasn't.
- She continued to be able to effectively communicate her needs. If she found that others were not able to respect her needs, she took it as a sign that they were not the right partner for her and she moved on to the next potential partner.
- She stopped taking responsibility for others' hurtful behavior. Instead of personalizing it she attributed the behavior to the rightful owner. If Shana received hurtful behavior, she reevaluated the relationship and made decisions of whether to remain in the relationship or not. If she communicated the behavior, and her partner was able to acknowledge the behavior and how it affected Shana, and was able to modify his behavior, then Shana made a decision to continue on in the relationship. If Shana communicated the behavior and her partner was unable to acknowledge and modify his behavior, then Shana made a decision to end the relationship.

In hindsight, it can be argued that Jared and Shana were not the most ideal match for a romantic relationship. Shana, as a result of her own secure attachment style, most likely needed a partner who was also securely attached. From this standpoint, it would have been very difficult for Jared to meet Shana's personal and relationship needs. With a more securely attached partner Shana would have received validation of her worthiness and might not have been triggered with concerns of rejection. Because Shana was also self-sacrificing and loving she often placed her needs to the side and prioritized Jared's. This part actually made the two of them a good match. Jared had anxious personal and romantic needs within the relationship that he needed to be fulfilled. Due to his lack of introspection and empathy, he was unable to participate in a reciprocal sharing of meeting and fulfilling his partner's needs. Again, because Shana tended to be nurturing and self-sacrificing she often rushed to meet the needs of others and often was left with unfulfilled needs. As stated before, Shana would have benefited from a partner who had a secure attachment style who would be able to provide her with validation and appreciation.

Shana needed to experience a secure base in order to feel stable and secure in the relationship. Due to Jared's consistent uncertainty he did not provide dependability or security in the relationship. As a result, Shana never experienced stability in their romantic relationship. For Shana, Jared served as an attachment figure that triggered her attachment behaviors with her father. Jared's difficulties with emotional connection and communication and his lack of dependability felt familiar to Shana and as a result her attachment system was activated, which allowed her to stay in the relationship longer than was healthy for her. We can hypothesize that Shana provided a secure base for Jared in that she was dependable, consistent, nurturing, and provided effective communication in the romantic relationship. This resulted in Jared increasing a level of security in the relationship; however, not enough that he was able to change his avoidant behaviors. But it appears that Jared's attachment system might not have been activated by Shana. Jared would most likely be activated by someone that reflects his own issues of self-confidence. Instead of reflecting them, Shana attempted to be nurturing, encouraging, accepting, and empowering. Jared would most likely be triggered by a partner who is nurturing but also critical and judgmental. In this type of relationship, Jared would potentially experience intense romantic feelings as a result of his attachment system being activated. Because, as Pines's (2005) states, intense feelings in a romantic relationship occur as a result of childhood traumatic injury and similarities with a romantic partner with an attachment figure that caused the injury.

Shana most likely experienced the hypothesized sixth stage of Kubler-Ross's original grief stage theory. In time, Shana was able to find meaning after acceptance. She obtained greater understanding of her attachment style and her attachment behavior in relationships. As a result, she was able to understand how her choice in romantic partners was not allowing her to feel secure in her relationship and she began to understand who would be the necessary attachment figure to seek out who would more effectively meet her needs.

Chapter Eight

Media Depictions of Love and Grief

Sex and the City: The Movie is a scripted dramatic movie that debuted in 2008 (King et al., 2008). It was based on the Golden Globe and Emmy winning series, *Sex and the City*, that ran from 1998–2004. The series, created by Darren Star, portrayed the lives of four women who were best friends and was based on a book written by Candace Bushnell. The series and book followed the lives of these four women living in New York and explored significant themes of femininity and sexuality based on women during the 1990's. The character of Carrie Bradshaw is played by Sarah Jessica Parker, who is a writer of a column discussing sex and love. The series is often narrated from the point of Carrie who analyzed and pondered modern views of female sexuality. The series also highlighted and witnessed the romantic and sexual relationships of Carrie and her best friends. Also, starring in the series included the characters of Samantha Jones played by Kim Cattrall, Charlotte York played by Kristin Davis, and Miranda Hobbes played by Cynthia Nixon.

The series chronicled Carrie's multiple romantic relationships, with her most significant romantic story line involving her on and off again relationship with a character she affectionately calls *Mr. Big*, played by Chris North. The highs and lows of Carrie's and Mr. Big's relationship are highlighted as the audience follows the emotional experience of Carrie as she navigates through their romantic relationship. The series culminates with Carrie moving to Paris with her current romantic partner. She arrives in Paris and begins to find that she is not happy in her romantic relationship. At the same time Mr. Big travels to Paris to find Carrie to confess his love to her. He finds Carrie on the night she decides to leave her romantic partner. Carrie and Mr. Big proclaim their love for each other and the story line satisfies the audience's need for the conflictual relationship to end in romantic bliss. *The Movie* is a continuation of the series and focuses on Carrie's and Mr. Big's relationship.

The movie begins with Carrie and Mr. Big deciding to purchase a home together and ultimately to get married. Unfortunately, Mr. Big has "cold feet" and leaves Carrie at the alter on their wedding day. A conceptualization of Carrie's emotional experience is provided below highlighting her evident loss and grief reactions as she attempts to heal from their breakup.

DENIAL

As Carrie arrives at the wedding venue late due to traffic, she is notified that Mr. Big is not present. When she calls him, he tells her, "I was out front. I just left. I can't do this."

Immediately after Mr. Big leaves Carrie at the alter she enters into a stage of denial. She appears numb from the shock of Mr. Big's actions. As she discusses the day's events with her best friends that evening, her experience of grief is evident in their conversation.

> Carrie: "I thought I would still be in extreme pain. I feel nothing. I'd like some more nothing (referring to alcohol). Yes, I'm still jilted."
>
> Carrie: "Now I have nowhere to live."
>
> Charlotte: "You'll stay here."
>
> Carrie: "forever."
>
> Carrie: "Oh my clothes. I can never go back there again. How am I going to get my clothes?"
>
> Samantha: "Oh, honey, I can hire someone to do that. Anything you need."
>
> Carrie: "A hitman?"
>
> Carrie: "I have nothing to wear but a wedding gown."
>
> Charlotte: "You have your honeymoon clothes here."
>
> Carrie: "Well there's the silver lining. A honeymoon at a romantic Mexican resort that's prepaid on my credit card because I wanted to surprise the man who jilted me."
>
> Samantha: "I can get you out of that. Worse comes to worse I will say there was a death or something."
>
> Carrie: "Wasn't there?"

The movie successfully illustrates the similarities of the experience of a romantic relationship breakup to a death. The loss of an attachment figure causes strong emotions and feelings of grief as a result of the absence of that attachment relationship. Carrie described her loss as a death because it represents the detachment she feels from not only her attachment figure, Mr. Big, but also from the vision she had of sharing a life with Mr. Big.

ANGER

Carrie expresses anger immediately after learning that Mr. Big is not coming to the wedding site. Their cars meet on the street (as Carrie is leaving and as Mr. Big changes his mind and returns) and Carrie jumps out of her limo and hits Mr. Big with her bouquet of flowers. She screams at him, "I knew you would do this. I am humiliated." There is another short scene while Carrie is at dinner with her friends at what would have been her honeymoon with Mr. Big. She comments, "He couldn't get out of the car. After ten years of what he already put me through he couldn't make the effort and get out of the car. I made the effort. I put a bird on my head" (referring to her decorative head piece as part of her wedding attire).

Additionally, she states:

"He's a bad guy. Always was. Bad guys do bad things."

"After everything I know. After twenty years of everything we've learned. I threw it all away for the thrill of putting his name on the honeymoon suite. If I met me now I wouldn't know me."

We can speculate that Carrie potentially projected some of her anger toward Mr. Big onto her friend Miranda. Miranda made a comment to Mr. Big at the rehearsal dinner the night before the wedding. Miranda was going through her own conflict in her marriage after learning that her husband had been unfaithful. After having an emotional conversation with her husband, Miranda said to Mr. Big, "You two are crazy to get married. Marriage ruins everything." After hearing Miranda's comment, Mr. Big appears negatively influenced by what she said and even calls Carrie later that night to obtain reassurance. It takes Miranda awhile to admit to Carrie what she said to Mr. Big and how it potentially had an influence on his ambivalence in getting married the next day. Carrie is understandably angry with Miranda due to her lack of honesty and feeling of betrayal. However, some of her anger might have also been a reflection of her feelings of betrayal from Mr. Big, which she was unable to communicate with due to their lack of contact.

BARGAINING

It is hypothesized that Carrie did not experience the bargaining stage of grief as it was not reflected in the movie.

DEPRESSION

Carrie's best friends attempt to release Carrie of her financial responsibility of the honeymoon but are unable to do so and the four friends decide to go on the trip instead. As they arrive in Mexico, Carrie's demeanor clearly expresses that she is experiencing a stage of depression. She arrives with sunglasses on and when she removes them her eyes are red and swollen as if she has been crying a great deal. She denies her friends' encouragement to eat and drink and one scene even depicts Samantha feeding her a meal. Carrie's friends check in on her as she sleeps the first day(s) on the trip.

When she wakes up the next morning she asks Miranda, "did I dream it?" reflecting an experience of denial.

As she joins her friends for a meal, she further illustrates her grief by saying:

"Will I ever laugh again?" Miranda answers, "Yes?" Carrie asks, "When?"
Miranda answers, "When something is really, really funny."

ACCEPTANCE

Carrie returns home from Mexico and begins the process of readjusting her life. Her friends are able to negotiate buying back her condo. As she moves back in she begins to make changes in her life. She hires an assistant, changes her hair color and remodels her condo. Carrie focuses on her work and the writing of a new book. She also hosts a baby shower for Charlotte. Carrie allowed herself to experience the stages of grief related to her romantic relationship breakup. It is this allowance that provided an opportunity for Carrie to heal from the loss of her breakup.

As illustrated above, *Sex and the City: The Movie* provides an appropriate media example of the various stages that can be experienced following a romantic breakup. Utilizing the character of Carrie, her subsequent process of grief related to her loss was depicted. Her process was further analyzed and hypotheses were provided to describe her potential feelings and emotional experience. As described earlier in this text, *Sex and the City: The Movie* was selected due to the assumption that many individuals would have experienced a parasocial relationship with the characters due to the episode's and corresponding movie's high viewer ratings. In addition, due to the longevity of the series' run, the extensive fan base associated with the TV episode, and the DVDs as well as collectible packages including books and DVD collector sets, this movie was identified to be an appropriate option to review. It is further surmised that given the assumed strong parasocial relationships viewers held for *Sex and the City* characters, it is also proposed that viewers experienced a strong reaction and connection to Carrie as she experienced romantic relationship dissolution. Although there is no empirical evidence to support the existence of this, it is further questioned whether viewers who held a strong parasocial relationship with Carrie's character could also potentially identify with Carrie's emotional experience enough that it could cause some level of secondary traumatization. In other words, could a viewer connect with Carrie's character to the level of being impacted by the viewer's own experience of loss, which could lead to a re-experiencing of loss for the viewer?

To study the loss of parasocial relationships, Cohen (2004) observed viewers imagining that their favorite character was taken off air. It was hypothesized that the distress related to the loss of parasocial relationships would be similar to the process of romantic relationship breakups (Cohen, 2003, 2004). Results showed a positive association between parasocial relationship interaction and breakup distress. In addition, viewers with anxious attachment styles had the highest intensity involved in their parasocial relationships and also were most preoccupied with the loss and breakups of parasocial relationships. Securely and avoidantly attached viewers had the lowest intensity interaction with parasocial relationships as well as low levels of experienced distress related to breakups. Schiappa, Allen, and Gregg (2007) acknowledged the loss of relationship when television series are canceled or ended. In addition, they described the availability of replacements of media characters. Even when series are canceled or ended, there is the opportunity for new parasocial relationships with new media characters in upcoming seasons or alternative television programming. Another aspect of the ending of television series and parasocial breakups, refers to how the endings are scripted (Schiappa, Allen, & Gregg, 2007). It is interesting, as Schiappa, Allen, & Gregg (2007) pointed out, whether a series ending allows an ending to an ongoing plot focus or whether the series ends without a true resolution or closure. It would be beneficial to study the effects of these different endings and what influence they have on the experience and potential distress of parasocial breakups. For example, does a viewer experience less distress and more resolution to the parasocial relationship ending if a conclusion is provided during the series ending? Furthermore, does the type of scripted conclusion have different outcomes? If the conclusion is affectively understandable to viewers, would they experience more resolution than a conclusion that viewers do not agree with or desire? Finally, in the situation of scripted conclusions that do not provide resolution, what is the resulting affective experience for viewers? Speculating from evidence of real social relationship breakups, do parasocial breakups that do not provide understanding or resolution for the breakup result in more conflict and distress for viewers? It would be valuable to have more research in this area in order to provide insight to these questions. Schippa, Allen, and Gregg (2007) adds that additional research would be beneficial in the areas of studying reruns and its influence on parasocial relationships as well as seeking information regarding loyalty of television series and behavioral processes related to continuing to watch a television series or changing to another one.

Eyal and Cohen (2006) used the television series, *Friends*, specifically the series' final episode, to study the response to parasocial breakups. Using the parasocial interaction theory, the *Friends* series provided viewers with an opportunity to connect with a group of young and single adults who shared a friendship. Due to the shift away from episodes based on family members or coworkers, *Friends* targeted a series based on friendship. Using humor and interpersonal interactions, the *Friends* series was able to invite viewers to identify with its mediated characters. It is suggested that it is this identification and attractiveness that allowed viewers to participate in the parasocial friendship created by the *Friends* series. In addition, the audience was able to build a relationship with the characters through the information provided by the tv series (Schiappa, Allen, & Gregg, 2007). The final series of *Friends* aired in 2004. Given the popularity that the series elicited it is assumed that the series itself, but especially the series ending, is meaningful in that it produced an emotional response in its viewers. Despite an ability to continue to view reruns in maintaining continuity with parasocial relationships, viewers still lost an element of the relationship due to not being able to advance the story of the episode. Eyal and Cohen (2006) likened the use of reruns and DVD's to photographs and videos of close relationships. Therefore, in the dissolution of close relationships, individuals lose the opportunity to have continued memories with the loved one or advancing the story of the relationship.

In exploring the process of grief in imaginal media characters, it is also important to consider the significance of the ending of the series, *Sex and the City* and its associated movies. Two movies were created to continue the story line of these media characters and provided additional opportunities to audience members to share in the lives of these individuals as well as obtain additional details regarding the relationship outcomes of the various media characters. Audience members were able to obtain an additional ending that was not provided with the finale episode and were able to live on in the lives of the media characters. It can be assumed due to the show's popularity that viewers experienced parasocial breakups related to the episode and movie endings. As commented above, as a result of the strong parasocial relationships formed with the characters in the television episodes and the movies it can be reasonable that viewers had strong reactions to the endings. The movies, presumably to address and satisfy the viewers' desire to have a happy ending, allowed both movies, *Sex and the City: The Movie* and *Sex and the City: The Movie Part Two* to allow Carrie to end up with a happy outcome with Mr. Big. The movies allowed viewers to close out the TV show, the two movies and the parasocial relationship with Carrie in a way that reasonably elicited a positive and satisfying ending for viewers. It is questioned how viewers' experiences might have been different if Carrie's ending was different. It can be hypothesized that viewers would have a difficult and conflictual affective ending to the show, movies, and parasocial relationship with Carrie if she had not ended up happily united with Mr. Big.

A BRIEF NOTE REGARDING REALITY SHOWS

A recent format of television series includes the existence of reality television shows that observe individuals' daily private lives. Television is proliferated with multiple reality focused episodes highlighting not only celebrities but also everyday individuals. Due to the sheer magnitude of reality shows in existence currently, it is important to consider the influence it plays on society as well as individual affective and behavioral outcomes. As Cohen and Weimann (2008) stated, reality shows offer a forum of exposure of one's life that is viewed by a public audience. Hill (2005) acknowledged that viewers of reality shows are to some level comfortable with the lack of privacy due to their participation in viewing and sharing the often private details of others. The other concerns related to the existence of reality shows include the reinforcement of perverse behavior and the labeling of celebrity by engaging in disruptive behaviors and waiving rights to private life events (Cohen & Weimann, 2008).

Cohen and Weimann's (2008) study of the effects of viewing reality shows showed that perceptions of the influence of media, and specifically reality shows, involves an attitudinal element in Israeli adults. In addition, higher amounts of reality show viewing were associated with an increase in perceiving reality shows to have an influence and in censoring reality shows. However, higher viewing rates of reality shows was not associated with an increase in being critical of reality shows or being concerned of the impact of reality shows. It is suggested that viewing might reinforce influence and censorship but lack influence in the area of being critical and being concerned. Viewers endorsed several criticisms and concerns which resulted in motivation to censor reality shows in particular areas including the perception that reality shows are fake, voyeuristic, and exploitative as well as having misogynistic, violent, and sexual content on reality shows (Cohen & Weimann, 2008). As a result of these reported concerns, viewers were willing to limit the number of produced reality shows, as well as creating regulatory restrictions for reality shows.

With the introduction of reality tv shows over the years, society is being flooded with representations of romantic relationships. Society has always utilized multimedia platforms represent elements of romantic relationships through movies and books. Given the presumed impact that these multimedia platforms have on one's working models or schema of romantic relationships, it is important to consider its influence on society's romantic relationship development, maintenance, and dissolution. Movies and books sometimes provide an idealized and perhaps inaccurate view of romantic relationships. Although they exist to a lesser degree, there are movies and books that reflect the grief and loss experienced by breakups or the normal ups and downs of romantic relationships. However, society often refers to romantic relationships depicted in movies and books as models of types of relationships to be obtained. Due to the lack of accurate representations, one is left with a disillusioned view of relationships. In addition, couples to a lesser degree acknowledge conflict in their romantic relationships and how they resolve them. The lack of honest communication of romantic relationships adds to one's disillusionment of romantic relationships. Most of reality television shows display acceptance of behaviors involving infidelity, distrust, dishonesty, and emotional abuse. Although these behaviors occur at times within relationships, some reality shows only display these behaviors. For individuals developing their working models and schemas of romantic relationships, these representations provide a model of relationships that might promote acceptance of behaviors that negatively impact one's emotional experience and add to the conflict experienced in a relationship, which has an effect on the stability of the relationship.

Conclusion

The intent of this text was to provide evidence for the proposal that romantic relationship dissolution has a process that resembles grief. Multiple theories of love and romantic attachment were provided to serve as a foundation for the discussion of romantic relationship development. Each of the various types of theories offered a representation of love experiences but also reflected the complexity in discussing love. What does appear to be true is that brain chemistry has a significant influence in the process of love and involves particular regions of the brain which result in relevant emotional outcomes. Oxytocin also serves a major role in its importance in both maternal and romantic relationships. Animal and human studies were explored to solidify the argument that the root of relationships is connection. Connection seems to be the unifying theme of most, if not all, studies and theories of love.

Attachment theory was defined as the framework to further explain and serve as the foundation for the experience of the bonds that are created in loving relationships. The importance of early childhood relationships and relationship models was explored in creating the prototype for future relationships. Romantic partners as attachment figures were explored and the powerful impact that these relationships have was illustrated. Attachment styles were described as they provide insight into how attachment related behaviors are enacted within close romantic bonds. It is the strength and complexity of these bonds that are offered as the reason for the experience of grief in situations when attachments are lost or broken, as in the case of romantic relationship breakups and divorce. Attachment styles were described and were illustrated in how they have different trajectories relevant to each particular attachment style within romantic relationships.

Individuals often come to understand the origin of their patterns and have the desire to change their patterns but are unable to because of fear and anxiety. Despite the knowledge that a change in their behavior would most likely result in enhanced relationships (moving from an insecure orientation to a secure one), these individuals feel more comfortable choosing *familiar* partners (i.e., partners that reflect some childhood attachment issue). Individuals have spent quite some time perfecting behaviors interacting with a particular type of parental figure and can consciously or unconsciously lead one to seek out a particular romantic partner. This experience creates a familiarity that individuals are often resistant to let go. Until the resistance regarding fear and anxiety is addressed it is very difficult for change to occur and new relationship patterns to form. On the other hand, reparative relationships can alter this trajectory and result in one obtaining more secure relationships. Connection is important and essential to the health of all relationships but also to one's own physical and mental health. It is imperative for the nurturance of connective relationships that society redefines connection and acknowledges and promotes its benefits. It needs to be acknowledged not as weakness but as strength. When relationship building, nurturance, and reparation can be prioritized, not only will the quality of relationships improve but also the quality of mental and physical health. Eventually, this shift would prove to have evolutionary benefits in cultivating a healthier and more connected human population.

A special section related to digital relationships was offered in this text to reflect the strong influence that technology and social media have on today's society. A review of the various methods of technology and social media in forming and creating romantic relationships provide insight into how romantic relationship development is changing. Mainstream culture argues that technology and social media allow for greater connection; however, it appears that these mechanisms allow opportunities for more contact. The question continues to be whether the increased contact leads to greater connection. It is assumed that for some relationships these mechanisms potentially offer avenues for deeper connection, but it appears that for the majority of users this might not be the case and only adds a decrease in, or a lack of, a true deep connection. It is clear that more study in this field needs to be undertaken to fully understand its ramifications. However, research was provided that greater connection was obtained for long-distance romantic couples who utilized video chat platforms. Perhaps due to the absence of proximity this option allows couples to interact in ways that would not be possible without it.

Consequences of romantic relationship dissolution were discussed with special attention on grief reactions, physically, physiologically, and emotionally. Conceptualizations of grief related to romantic relationship breakups and divorce were provided with an introduction of what is already understood about the experience of loss related to death. Studies involving the brain chemistry of loss were explored, as well as resulting physical and emotional consequences of loss. Types of loss were identified and several of the major theories of grief were provided in explaining the process of loss. Strengths and weaknesses of the various models were discussed in an attempt to highlight the difficulty in accurately explaining the experience of individual loss within universal concepts. A more in-depth analysis of grief experienced in romantic relationship dissolution was provided and categorized into intrapersonal, interpersonal, religious, community, and societal factors to illustrate the multiple consequences associated with loss. Special attention was placed on the role that culture (i.e., race, sexual orientation) has on the experience of grief following breakups and divorce.

Technology was observed and explored as it relates to the influence on dating and maintenance as well as dissolution of romantic relationships. The existence of online dating on romantic relationships as well as the role of social media networking sites on romantic relationships was also provided. Parasocial relationships were presented in order to reflect the impact of media influences on one's attachment experience. There is limited research in the area of grief as a result of romantic relationship dissolution as it relates to online dating and the influence of social media. However, speculations were made as to the existence of grief related reactions within the realm of online dating and social media platforms. The grief experienced in parasocial relationships was identified and explored to further the argument of the complexity within relationship development, and also the identification of grief when relationships end.

The complexity in diagnosing loss was reviewed, which revealed the absence of diagnostic criteria specifically relating to grief that is experienced as a result of the ending of romantic relationships. Although the psychiatric field is moving toward that direction with new diagnostic language and methods to assess for bereavement and also for the influence of divorce, it is also important to find similar methods to diagnose grief related to unmarried romantic relationships as well. Regarding treatment, value lies in utilizing interventions from attachment theory, grief treatment, and marital and couples psychotherapy. Using attachment principles in psychotherapy illustrates the associations between childhood and adult attachment related behaviors. In addition, attachment based concepts can provide insight into attachment figures that might serve as better romantic partners in meeting one's needs. Right now, there is not a model that addresses grief experienced as loss within romantic relationship breakups. In time, it is hoped that grief treatment will focus on loss within romantic relationships and offer guidelines that would inform treatment. Related to couples and marital therapy, Emotionally Focused Couples Therapy, was reviewed as an appropriate psychotherapy theoretical model relevant to treating the attachment and relationship needs of romantic partners. Other clinical themes were provided to consider its use within psychotherapy to address the many components of loss related to romantic relationship endings.

Clinical vignettes were provided to further illustrate how loss and attachment styles can be addressed in psychotherapy. Using Kubler-Ross's stage model and attachment theory, individual vignettes were explored related to each stage of the model. In addition, an entire case was highlighted to reveal an example of the experience of the grief and loss experienced in romantic relationship dissolution, along with an exploration of the influence of attachment styles on the experience of loss. Finally, evidence was provided that showed the power of parasocial relationships in one's overall relationship behavior. *Sex and the City: The Movie* was provided as an example to explain the experience of loss reflected in a movie based on a popular television episode. In addition, hypotheses of the potential affective results of the ending of the episode and movies were offered for further thought. A brief note on reality tv shows was provided to reflect the recent influence of media behavior and its influence on viewers.

It is hoped that an enlightened understanding of loss that involves the experience of romantic relationship breakups has been obtained. In addition, it was a goal of this text to provide a better understanding and respect for the impact of romantic relationship dissolution on individual emotional experiences in the process of grief. Truly understanding the impact of attachment as is inherent in romantic relationships and activated during times of loss will allow for more healing in times of grief and better understanding and expression of societal responses.

FUTURE IMPLICATIONS

Especially related to the formation and maintenance of relationships as well as the dissolution of those relationships, there needs to be continued study into same sex romantic relationships, as well as the romantic relationships of trans individuals. As K. R. Allen (2007) argued, there needs to be a priority to institute legalized divorce for same sex marriages. With the 2015 ruling for legalized marriage for all citizens, this would now allow the same process of formalized endings of unions traditionally held by heterosexual couples. It would allow for opportunities of custody agreements and arrangements that did not exist in the past or at least on a consistent basis. In some ways, legalized divorce will remove some of the uncertainty that K. R. Allen (2007) described and will mark a definitive ending to the romantic relationship process. Finally, it will be important to implement increased support for same sex couples and trans couples, when it comes to grief experienced following the dissolution of romantic relationships. One significant aspect of this support would include an awareness and acknowldgement of the various social and sexual prejudices that these populations experience. In addition to sexuality, there needs to be additional investigation into the role that ethnicity plays in grief reactions post dissolution. Variables related to the intersection of racism, prejudice, and bias result in a historical trend of stress experienced by different ethnicities. These issues influence the romantic relationship formation and subsequent dissolution of these ethnic groups and therefore deserve attention and study.

A more informed outlook would allow for better creation of support programs based on individual needs. Understanding how religion plays a major role for particular ethnicities, it would be beneficial for religious institutions to consider offering divorce support programs to better meet the needs of its religious community. Given what could be experienced as a trauma to some regarding breakups and divorce, it seems imperative that additional support interventions are provided. Considering that individuals will potentially remarry and to help promote healthier parenting practices, it is important to provide services that acknowledge and normalize the grief reaction related to divorce and breakups to help ensure healthier future romantic relationships. Grief practices that are easily provided for situations of grief related to death and divorce, including funerals, ceremonies, and support groups, should also be extended to grief experiences, including romantic relationship breakups. Recognizing these resources as needed interventions for the purpose of healing will provide support to individuals who have experienced romantic relationship dissolution as well as signal to others the significance of loss following breakups.

It is clear that there needs to be additional study in the experience of grief, especially in the case of romantic relationship dissolution. As part of that study, it is also important to consider the diagnosis and treatment of these particular types of loss experiences. Grief as it is related to romantic relationships should be better identified as traumatic attachment experiences in the literature, as well as in diagnostic and treatment settings. Divorce has been incorporated into the diagnostic coding for emotional disorders and it is hoped that unmarried romantic relationship breakups will also be recognized. In addition, related to the divorce and relationship breakup process, the experience of grief should be a part of any psychotherapeutic treatment. Finally, mental health professionals should obtain education and training in how to address the grief needs of those who require treatment in the area of romantic relationship dissolution. Grief and loss should be explored in any psychotherapy model utilized to treat the grief and loss experienced in situations of breakup and divorce. Related to this idea, grief as a result of romantic relationship dissolution should be incorporated into the curriculum of psychology graduate and psychiatry medical school programs.

Increasing advancement in technology and continued use of social media and enjoyment of multimedia demands a better understanding of the consequences of its use. In a desire to better understand the depth of connection, it is imperative to consider the influence that technology and social media have on both romantic relationship building and breakups. It would be important to recognize which factors improve the opportunities for connection using these mechanisms of contact and communication. However, it will be equally as important to understand the factors that lead to decreased connection as well. Related to grief, it would be interesting to understand how grief is impacted in the use of these platforms. In addition, it would be advantageous to create interventions that can be tailored to improve the grief experience of those individuals who use these digital platforms. Finally, multimedia outlets have a valuable opportunity to reflect media that portray accurate representations of relationships, breakups, and the experience of grief.

As we continue the study of the experience of grief in all romantic relationships, observations need to also be made in the area of the community experience of grief following breakups. Following the lead of investigation into the influence of divorce on the community, similar conclusions need to be made as it relates to breakups. Romantic relationship breakups also have an effect on family members, friends, coworkers, religious communities, and the culture as a whole, and so having a better understanding of the impact would be valuable. It will be important for society to obtain education and training regarding understanding and supporting others who experience divorce and romantic relationship breakups. Part of this education will include better insight into how grief affects not only the individuals but the community as a whole. In addition, it will be important to gain a better understanding of the ramifications of relationship dissolution in order to have more empathic interactions with others. Training can involve healthy ways of supporting others when experiencing grief reactions from breakups and divorce (i.e., such as what to say or what not to say, how to reinforce the normalization of the grief process, etc.). Finally, training can also remind individuals, whose loved ones experience dissolution, of their own grief processes and how to obtain their own support.

One last but very important point involves the role of culture. It is important in the study of relationship formation, maintenance, and dissolution, as well as with grief, to observe the role of culture when discussing any of these experiences. Rosenblatt (2011) hypothesizes that the expression of grief may not fit into any universal theory of grief that explains the grief experience for all individuals. Therefore, it is always important to remember the individual experience of all of these concepts and be aware of the limitations of attempts at universal models. Future study needs to continue to incorporate culture within any discussion of grief.

Bonnano (2004) acknowledged the pathological stigmatization of grief. He described how individuals who experience limited posttraumatic stress disorder reactions are viewed as resilient and those individuals that experience more symptomatology tend to be stigmatized. More work needs to be accomplished in normalizing and appreciating grief that is experienced not only with the death of loved ones but also with the endings of marriages and romantic relationships. By decreasing the stigma of grief, one is allowed the freedom to experience the natural emotional and behavioral process of loss and will create a society that better supports the experience of grief.

References

Adelmann, P. K., Chadwick, C., & Baerger, D. R. (1996). Marital quality of Black and White adults over the life course. *Journal of Social and Personal Relationships, 13*, 361–384. doi: 10.1177/0265407596133004

Adkins, V. K. (1999). Grandparents as a national asset: A brief note. *Activities, Adaptation and Aging, 24*, 13–18. doi: 10.1300/J016v24n01_02

Agnew, C. R. (2000). Cognitive interdependence and the experience of relationship loss. In J. Harvey & E. Miller (Eds.), *Loss and trauma: General and close relationship perspectives* (pp. 385–398). Philadelphia: Brunner-Routledge.

Agnew, C. R., Van Lange, P. A., Rusbult, C. E., & Langston, C. A. (1998). Cognitive interdependence: Commitment and the mental representation of close relationships. *Journal of Personality and Social Psychology, 74*, 939–954. doi: 10.1037//0022-3514.74.4.939

Ainsworth, M. D. (1979). Infant-mother attachment. *American Psychologist, 34*(10), 932–937.

Ainsworth, M. D. (1985). Attachments across the lifespan. *Bulletin of the New York Academy of Medicine, 61*, 792–812.

Akhtar, S. (1996). Love and its discontents: A concluding overview. In S. Akhtar & S. Kramer (Eds.), *Intimacy and Infidelity: Separation-Individuation Perspectives* (pp.145–178). Northvale, NJ: Jason Aronson.

Akhtar, S., & Blue, S. (2017). The emotional impact of divorce: An overview. In S. Akhtar (Ed.), *Divorce: Emotional impact and therapeutic interventions* (pp. 1–30). Lanham, MD: Rowman & Littlefield.

Albert, A., & Bulcroft, K. (1987). Pets and urban life. Anthrozoos, *1*(1), 9–25. doi: 10.2752/089279388787058740

Albert, A., & Bulcroft, K. (1988). Pets, families and the life course. *Journal of Marriage and the Family, 50*(2), 543–552. doi: 10.2307/352019

Allen, K. (2003). Are pets a healthy pleasure? The influence of pets on blood pressure. *Current Directions in Psychological Science, 12*(6), 236–239. doi: 10.1046/j.0963-7214.2003.01269.x

Allen, K. R. (2007). Ambiguous loss after lesbian couples with children break up: A case for same-gender divorce. *Family Relations: Interdisciplinary Journal of Applied Family Studies, 56*(2), 175–183. doi: 10.1111/j.1741-3729.2007.00450.x

American Psychiatric Association. (2000). *Diagnostic and statistical manual of mental disorders,* 4th ed. text (rev.) Washington, DC. Author

American Psychiatric Association. (2013). *Diagnostic and statistical manual of mental disorders,* 5th ed. Washington, DC. Author.

Ano, G. G., & Vasconcelles, E. B. (2005). Religious coping and psychological adjustment to stress: A meta-analysis. *Journal of Clinical Psychology, 61*(4), 461–480. doi: 10.1002/jclp.20049

Archer, J. (1997). Why do people love their pets? *Evolution and Human Behavior, 18*(4), 237–259. doi: 10.1016/S0162-3095(99)80001-4

Archer, J., & Winchester, J. (1994). Bereavement following death of a pet. *British Journal of Psychology, 85*(2), 259–271. doi: 10.1111/j.2044-8295.1994.tb02522.x

Aron, A., & Aron, E. (1986). *Love and the expansion of self.* New York: Hemisphere.

Aron, A., Aron, E., Tudor, M., & Nelson, G. (1991). Close relationship as including other in the self. *Journal of Personality and Social Psychology, 60*, 241–253. doi: 10.1037/0022-3514.60.2.241

Aron, A., Paris, M., & Aron, E. (1995). Falling in love: Prospective studies of self-concept change. *Journal of Personality and Social Psychology, 69*, 1102–1112. doi: 10.1037/0022-3514.69.6.1102

Aseltine, R. H., & Kessler, R. C. (1993). Marital disruption and depression in a community sample. *Journal of Health and Social Behavior, 34*(3), 237–251. doi: 10.2307/2137205

Ayduk, O., Downey, G., & Kim, M. (2001). Rejection sensitivity and depressive symptoms in women. *Personality and Social Psychology Bulletin, 27*, 868–877. doi: 10.1177/0146167201277009

Bach, G., & Bernard, Y. (1971). *Aggression Lab.* Dubuque, IA: Kendall-Hunt Publishing Company.

Balsam, K. F., & Szymanski, D. M. (2005). Relationship quality and domestic violence in women's same-sex relationships: The role of minority stress. *Psychology of Women Quarterly, 29*, 258–269. doi: 10.1111/j.1471-6402.2005.00220

Balsters, M. J., Krahmer, E. J., Swerts, M. G., & Vingerhoets, A. J. (2013). Emotional tears facilitate the recognition of sadness and the perceived need for social support. *Evolutionary Psychology, 11*(1), 148–158. doi: 10.1177/147470491301100114

Barranti, C. C. (1985). The grandparent–grandchild relationship: Family resource in an era of voluntary bond. *Family Relations, 34*, 343–352.

Bartels, A., & Zeki, S. (2000). The neural basis of romantic love. *NeuroReport, 2*(17), 12–15. doi: 10.1097/0001756-200011270-00046

Bartholomew, K., & Horowitz, L. (1991). Attachment styles among young adults: A test of a four category model. *Journal of Personality and Social Psychology, 61*(2), 226–244. doi: 10.1037/0022-3514.61.2.226

Barutcu, K. F., & Aydin, Y. C. (2013). The scale for emotional reactions following the breakup. *Social and Behavioral Sciences, 84*, 786–790. doi: 10.1016/j.sbspro.2013.06.647

Baumeister, R. F., & Leary, M. R. (1995). The need to belong: Desire for interpersonal attachments as a fundamental human motivation. *Psychological Bulletin, 117*(3), 497–529. doi: 10.1037/0033-2909.117.3.497

Baxter, L. A. (1984). Trajectories of relationship disengagement. *Journal of Social and Personal Relationships, 2*, 253–269. doi: 10.1177/0265407584011003

Beck, A. T. (1976). *Cognitive therapy and the emotional disorders*. New York: International University Press.

Beck, L., & Madresh, E. A. (2008). Romantic partners and four-legged friends: An extension of attachment theory to relationships with pets. *Anthozoos, 21*(1), 43–56. doi: 10.2752/089279308X274056

Billingsley, A. (1988). *Black families in White America*. New York: Simon & Schuster.

Billingsley, A. (1992). *Climbing Jacob's ladder: The enduring legacy of African American families*. New York: Simon & Schuster.

Birnbaum, G. E., Orr, I., Mikulincer, M., & Florian, V. (1997). When marriage breaks up: Does attachment contribute to coping and mental health? *Journal of Social Personal Relationships, 14*, 643–654. doi: 10.1177/0265407597145004

Blue, S. L. (2006). *Childhood attachment and adult romantic attachment in African Americans* (Unpublished doctoral dissertation). The Georgia School of Professional Psychology at Argosy University, Georgia.

Bockting, W., Benner, A., & Coleman, E. (2009). Gay and bisexual identity development among female-to-male transsexuals in North America: Emergence of a transgender sexuality. *Archives of Sexual Behavior, 38*(5), 688–701. doi: 10.1007/s10508-009-9489-3

Boelen, P. A., de Keijser, J., van den Hout, M. A., & van den Bout, J. (2007). Treatment of complicated grief: A comparison between cognitive-behavioral therapy and supportive counseling. *Journal of Consulting and Clinical Psychology, 75*(2), 277–284. doi: 10.1037/0022-006X.75.2.277

Bogart, L. (1980). Television news as entertainment. In P. Tannenbaum (Ed.), *The entertainment functions of television* (pp. 209–249). Hillsdale, NJ: Lawrence Erlbaum.

Bohannan, P. (1968). The six stations of divorce. In P. Bohannan (Ed.), *Divorce and after: An analysis of the emotional and social problems of divorce* (pp. 33–62). Garden City, NY: Doubleday.

Bonanno, G. A. (2004). Loss, trauma and human resilience: Have we underestimated the human capacity to thrive after extremely aversive events? *American Psychologist*, 59, 20–28. doi: 10.1037/0003-066X.59.1.20

Bonanno, G. A., Wortman, C. B., Lehman, D. R., Tweed, R. G., Haring, M., Sonnega, J., Carr, D., et al. (2002). Resilience to loss and chronic grief: A prospective study from preloss to 18 months postloss. *Journal of Personality and Social Psychology, 83*, 1150–1164. doi: 10.1037//0022-3514.83.5.1150

Bonanno, G. A., Wortman, C. B., & Nesse, R. M. (2004). Prospective patterns of resilience and maladjustment during widowhood. *Psychology and Aging, 19*, 260–271. doi: 10.1037/0882-7974.19.2.260

Boon, S. D., & Lomore, C. D. (2001). Admirer-celebrity relationships among young adults: Explaining perceptions of celebrity influence on identity. *Human Communication Research, 27*(3), 432–465. doi: 10.1111/j.1468-2958.2001.tb00788.x

Booth, A., & Amato, P. (1991). Divorce and psychological stress. *Journal of Health and Social Behavior, 32*, 396–407. doi: 10.2307/2137106

Bowlby, J. (1973). *Attachment and loss: Vol. 2: Separation: Anxiety and anger*. New York: Basic Books.

Bowlby, J. (1979). *The making and breaking of affectional bonds*. London, England: Tavistock.

Bowlby, J. (1980). *Attachment and loss: Vol. 3: Loss*. New York: Basic Books.

Bowlby, J. (1982). *Attachment and loss. Vol.1: Attachment* (2nd ed.). New York: Basic Books. (original work published 1969).

Bowlby, J. (1988). *A secure base: Parent-child attachment and healthy human development*. New York: Basic Books.

Bratter, J. L., & King, R. B. (2008). "But will it last?": Marital instability among interracial and same-race couples. *Family Relations, 57*, 160–171. doi: 10.1111/j.1741-3729.2008.00491.x

Broman, C. L. (1993). Race differences in marital well-being. *Journal of Marriage and Family, 55*, 724–732. doi: 10.2307/353352

Brown, L. S. (1995). Therapy with same-sex couples: An introduction. In N. S. Jacobson & A. S. Gurman (Eds.), *Clinical handbook of couple therapy* (pp. 274–294). New York: Guilford Press.

Brown, N. (2010). The sexual relationships of sexual minority women partnered with trans men: A qualitative study. *Archives of Sexual Behavior, 39*(2), 561–572. doi: 10.1007/s10508-009-9511-9

Brown, E. J., & Goodman, R. F. (2005). Childhood traumatic grief: An exploration of the construct in children bereaved on September 11th. *Journal of Child Clinical and Adolescent Psychology, 34*, 248–259. doi: 10.1207/s15374424jccp3402_4

Brown, P., Felton, B. J., Whiteman, V., & Manela, R. (1980). Attachment and distress following marital separation. *Journal of Divorce, 3*, 303–317. doi: 10.1300/J279v03n04_01

Burnette, J. L., Davis, D. E., Green, J. D., Worthington, E. L., & Bradfield, E. (2009). Insecure attachment and depressive symptoms: The mediating role of rumination, empathy, and forgiveness. *Personal Individual Differences, 46*, 276–280. doi: 10.1016/j.paid.2008.10.016

Buxton, A. P. (2007). Counseling heterosexual spouses of bisexual or transgender partners. In B. A. Firestein (Ed.), *Becoming visible: Counseling bisexuals across the lifespan* (pp. 395–416). New York: Columbia University Press.

Bylsma, L. M., Croon, M. A., Vingerhoets, A. J., & Rottenberg, J. (2011). When and for whom does crying improve mood? A daily diary study of 1004 crying episodes. *Journal of Research in Personality, 45*(4), 385–392. doi: 10.1016/j.jrp.2011.04.007

Bylsma, L. M., Vingerhoets, A. J., & Rottenberg, J. (2008). When is crying cathartic? An international study. *Journal of Social and Clinical Psychology, 27*(10), 1165–1187. doi: 10.1521/jscp.2008.27.10.1165

Cain, A. O. (1985). Pets as family members. In M. B. Sussman (Ed.), *Pets and the family* (pp.5–10). New York: Haworth Press.

Calhoun, L. G., & Tedeschi, R. G. (1990). Positive aspects of critical life problems: Recollections of grief. *Omega: Journal of Death and Dying, 20*(4), 265–272. doi: 10.2190/QDY6-6PQC-KQWV-SU7K

Calhoun, L. G., Tedeschi, R. G., Cann, A., & Hanks, E. A. (2010). Positive outcomes following bereavement: Paths to posttraumatic growth. *Psychologica Belgica, 50*(1–2), 125–143. doi: 10.5334/pb-50-1-2-125

Cardinal, R. N., & Howes, N. J. (2005). Effects of lesions of the nucleus accumbens core on choice between small certain rewards and large uncertain rewards in rats. *BMC Neuroscience, 6*, 37. doi: 10.1186/1471-2202-6-37

Carmack, J. (1985). The effects on family members and functioning after death of a pet. *Marriage and Family Reviews, 8*, 149–161. doi: 10.1300/J002v08n03_11

Cassidy, J. (2008). The nature of the child's ties. In J. Cassidy & P. Shaver (Eds.), *Handbook of attachment: Theory, Research and Clinical Applications, Second Edition*, (pp.3–22). New York: The Guilford Press.

Cassidy, J. (2016). The nature of the child's ties. In J. Cassidy & P. Shaver (Eds.), *Handbook of attachment: Theory, Research and Clinical Applications*, 3rd ed. (pp.3–24). New York: The Guilford Press.

Cassidy, J., & Shaver, P. R. (2008). *Handbook of attachment: Theory, research, and clinical Applications*, 2nd ed. New York: Guilford Press.

Cassidy, J., & Shaver, P. R. eds. (2016). *Handbook of attachment: Theory, research, and clinical Applications*, 3rd ed. New York: Guilford Press.

Caughey, J. L. (1978). Artificial social relations in modern America. *American Quarterly, 30*(1), 70–89. doi: 10.2307/2712280

Caughey, J. L. (1984). *Imaginary social worlds: A cultural approach*. Lincoln: University of Nebraska Press.

Caughey, J. L. (1988). Masking the self: Fictional identities and the construction of self in adolescence. *Adolescent Psychiatry, 14*, 319–322.

Chafetz, J. S. (1975). *Masculine/feminine or human?* Itasca, IL: Peacock.

Chen, J. H., Bierhals, A. J., Prigerson, H. G., Kasl, S. V., Mazure, C. M., & Jacobs, S. (1999). Gender differences in the effects of bereavement-related psychological distress in health outcomes. *Psychological Medicine, 29*, 367–380. doi: 10.1017/S0033291798008137

Chivers, M. L., & Bailey, M. J. (2000). Sexual orientation of female-to-male transsexuals: A comparison of homosexual and nonhomosexual types. *Archives of Sexual Behavior, 29*(7), 259–278. doi: 10.1080/09540121.2013.855701

Chodorow, N. (1978). *The reproduction of mothering*. Berkeley, CA: University of California Press.

Clayton, R. B., Nagurney, A., & Smith, J. R. (2013). Cheating, breakup, and divorce: Is facebook use to blame? *Cyberpsychology, Behavior and Social Networking, 16*(10), 717–720. doi: 10.1089/cyber.2012.0424

Cohen, J. (1997). Parasocial relations and romantic attraction: Gender and dating status differences. *Journal of Broadcasting and Electronic Media, 41*(4), 516–529. doi: 10.1080/08838159709364424

Cohen, J. (2003). Parasocial breakups: Measuring individual differences in response to the dissolution of parasocial relationships. *Mass Communication and Society, 6*, 191–202. doi: 10.1207/S15327825MCS0602_5

Cohen, J. (2004). Parasocial break-up from favorite television characters: The role of attachment styles and relationship intensity. *Journal of Social and Personal Relationships, 21*, 187–202. doi: 10.1177/0265407504041374

Cohen, J., & Weimann, G. (2008). Who's afraid of reality shows? Exploring the effects of perceived influence of reality shows and the concern over their social effects on willingness to censor. *Communication Research, 35*(3), 382–397. doi: 10.1177/0093650208315964

Cohen, J. A., Mannarino, A., Greenberg, T., Padlo, S., & Shipley, C. (2002). Childhood grief—Concepts and controversies. *Trauma, Violence, and Abuse, 3*(4), 307–327. doi: 10.1177/1524838002237332

Cole, T., & Leets, L. (1999). Attachment styles and intimate television viewing: Insecurely forming relationships in a parasocial way. *Journal of Social and Personal Relationships, 16*, 495–511. doi: 10.1177/0265407599164005

Collier, L. (2014). Why we cry: New research is opening eyes to the psychology of tears. *Monitor on Psychology, 45*(2), 47.

Collins, N., & Read, S. J. (1990). Adult attachment, working models and relationship quality in dating couples. *Journal of Personality and Social Psychology, 58*, 644–663. doi: 10.1037/0022-3514.58.4.644

Corr, C. A. (2011a). Anticipatory grief and mourning. In K. Doka & A. Tucci (Eds.), *Beyond Kubler-Ross: New perspectives in death, dying and grief* (pp. 17–30). Washington, DC: Hospice Foundation of America.

Corr, C. A. (2011b). Strengths and limitations of the stage theory proposed by Elisabeth Kubler-Ross. In K. J. Doka & A. S. Tucci (Eds.), *Beyond Kubler-Ross: New perspectives in death, dying and grief* (pp. 3–16). Washington, DC: Hospice Foundation of America.

Cotton, S. R. (1999). Marital status and mental health revisited: Examining the importance of risk factors and resources. *Family Relations, 48*, 225–233. doi: 10.2307/585631

Cowles, K. U. (1985). The death of a pet: Human responses to the breaking of the bond. In M. B. Sussman (Ed.), *Pets and the family* (pp.135–148). New York: Haworth Press.

Cromwell, J. (1999). *Transmen and FTMs: Identities, bodies, genders and sexualities*. Urbana: University of Illinois Press.

Crosby, J. F., Gage, B. A., & Raymond, M. C. (1983). The grief resolution process in divorce. *Journal of Divorce, 7*(1), 3–18. doi:10.1300/J279v07n01_02

Crosby, J. F., Lybarger, S. K., & Mason, R. L. (1987). The grief resolution process in divorce: Phase II. *Journal of Divorce, 10*(1–2), 17–40. doi: 10.1300/J279v10n01_02

Currier, J. M., Neimeyer, R. A., & Berman, J. S. (2008). The effectiveness of psychotherapeutic interventions for bereaved persons: A comprehensive quantitative review. *Psychological Bulletin, 134*, 648–661.

Cusak, O. (1988). *Pets and mental health.* New York: Haworth Press.

Darvell, M. J., Walsh, S. P., & White, K. M. (2011). Facebook tells me so: Applying the theory of planned behavior to understand partner-monitoring behavior on Facebook. *Cyberpsychology, Behavior, and Social Networking, 14*(12), 717–722. doi: 10.1089/cyber.2011.0035

Davila, J., & Bradbury, T. N. (2001). Attachment insecurity and the distinction between unhappy spouses who do and do not divorce. *Journal of Family Psychology, 15*, 371–393. doi: 10.1037//0893–3200.15.3.371

Davis, D., Shaver, P. R., & Vernon, M. L. (2003). Physical, emotional, and behavioral reactions to breaking up: The roles of gender, age, emotional involvement, and attachment style. *Personality and Social Psychology Bulletin, 29*, 871–884. doi: 10.1177/0146167203029007006

Davis, S. (1990). Men as success objects and women as sex objects: A study of personal advertisements. *Sex Roles, 23*, 43–50. doi: 10.1007/BF00289878

De Groot, M., de Keijser, J., Neeleman, J., Kerkhor, A., Nolen, W., & Burger, H. (2007). Cognitive behaviour therapy to prevent complicated grief among relatives and spouses bereaved by suicide: Cluster randomized controlled trial. *British Medical Journal, 334*, 1–6. doi: 10.1136/bmj.39161.457431.55

Denham, T., E., & Smith, C. W. (1989). The influence of grandparents on grandchildren: A review of the literature and resources. *Family Relations, 38*(3), 345–350. doi: 10.2307/585064

Devor, H. (1997). *FTM: Female-to-male transsexuals in society*. Bloomington: Indiana University Press.

Diener, E., Gohm, C. L., Suh, E., & Oishi, S. (2000). Similarity of the relations between marital status and subjective well-being across cultures. *Journal of Cross Cultural Psychology, 31*(4), 419–436. doi:10.1177/0022022100031004001

Dixon, P. (2009). Marriage among African Americans: What does the research reveal? *Journal of African American Studies, 13*(1), 29–46. doi:10.1007/s12111-008-9062-5

Doka, K. J. (2011). Task models and the dying process. In K. J. Doka & A. S. Tucci (Eds.), *Beyond Kubler-Ross: New perspectives in death, dying and grief* (pp. 31–42). Washington, DC: Hospice Foundation of America.

Dozier, R. (2005). Beards, breasts, and bodies: Doing sex in a gendered world. *Gender and Society, 19*, 297–316. doi: 10.1177/0891243204272153

Duck, S. W. (1982). A topography of relationship disengagement and dissolution. In S. W. Duck (Ed). *Personal relationships: Vol. 4, Dissolving personal relationships* (pp.1–30). London: Academic Press.

Duggan, L. (2003). *The twilight of equality? Neoliberalism, cultural politics and the attack on democracy*. Boston: Beacon Press.

Duggan, M., Ellison, N., Lampe, C., Lenhart, A., & Madden, M. (2015). *Social media update 2014*. Washington, DC: Pew Research Center's Internet and American Life Project. Retrieved from Pew Research Center, http://pewinternet.org/2015/01/09/social-media-update-2014/.

Dunbar, R. (2012). *The science of love*. Hoboken, New Jersey: John Wiley & Sons, Inc.

Duran-Aydintug, C. (1998). Emotional support during separation: Its sources and determinants. *Journal of Divorce and Remarriage, 29*,121–141

Efran, J., & Greene, M. (2012). Why we cry: A clinician's guide. *Psychotherapy Networker*, accessed online at http://www.psychotherapynetworker.org/magazine/currentissue

Ehrlich, J. (2014). *Divorce and loss: Helping adults and children mourn when a marriage comes apart*. Lanham, MD: Rowman & Littlefield.

Eisenberger, N. I., & Lieberman, M. D. (2003). Why rejection hurts: A common neural alarm system for physical and social pain. *Science, 302*, 290–292. doi: 10.1016/j.tics.2004.05.010

Elizur, Y., & Mintzer, A. (2003). Gay males' intimate relationship quality: The roles of attachment security, gay identity, social support and income. *Personal Relationships, 10*(3), 411–435. doi: 10.1111/1475-6811.00057

Ellis, K. M., & Erikson, K. (2002). Transsexual and transgenderist experiences and treatment options. *Family Journal—Counseling and Therapy for Couples and Families, 10*(3), 289–299. doi: 10.1177/10680702010003005

Ellison, C. G., Wolfinger, N. H., & Ramos-Wada, A. I. (2012). Attitudes toward marriage, divorce, cohabitation, and casual sex among working-age Latinos: Does religion matter? *Journal of Family Issues, 34*(3), 295–322. doi: 10.1177/0192513X12445458

Elphinston, R. A., & Noller, P. (2011). Time to face it! Facebook intrusion and the implications for romantic jealousy and relationship satisfaction. *Cyberpsychology, Behavior, and Social Networking, 14*(11), 631–635. doi: 10.1089/cyber.2010.0318

Eyal, K., & Cohen, J. (2006). When good friends say goodbye: A parasocial breakup study. *Journal of Broadcasting and Electronic Media, 50*(3), 502–523. doi: 10.1207/s15506878jobem5003_9

Fagundes, C. P. (2012). Getting over you: Contributions of attachment theory for postbreakup emotional adjustment. *Personal Relationships, 19*, 37–50. doi: 10.1111/j.1475-6811.2010.01336.x

Fassinger, R. E., & Arseneau, J. R. (2007). "I'd rather get wet than be under that umbrella": Differentiating the experiences and identities of lesbian, gay, bisexual, and transgender people. In K. Bieschke, R. Perez, & K. DeBord (Eds.), *Handbook of counseling and psychotherapy with lesbian, gay, bisexual, and transgender clients* (2nd ed.) (pp. 19–49). Washington, DC: American Psychological Association.

Feeney, B. C., & Monin, J. K. (2008). An attachment-theoretical perspective on divorce. In J. Cassidy & P. Shaver (Eds.), *Handbook of attachment: Theory, Research and Clinical Applications*, 2nd ed. (pp.934–957). New York: The Guilford Press.

Feeney, B. C., & Monin, J. K. (2016). Divorce through the lens of attachment theory. In J. Cassidy & P. Shaver (Eds.), *Handbook of attachment: Theory, Research and Clinical Applications*, 3rd ed. (pp.941–965). New York: The Guilford Press.

Feeney, J. A., & Noller, P. (1990). Attachment style as a predictor of adult romantic relationships. *Journal of Personality and Social Psychology*, *58*, 281–291.

Field, T. (2011). Romantic breakups, heartbreak and bereavement. *Psychology, 2*(4), 382–387. doi: 10.4236/psych.2011.24060

Fisher, H. (2004). *Why we love? The nature and chemistry of romantic love*. New York: St. Martin's Press.

Fisher, H. E., Aron, A., & Brown, L. L. (2006). Romantic love: a mammalian brain system for mate choice. *Philosophical Transactions of the Royal Society B: Biological Sciences, 361*(1476), 2173–2186. doi: 10.1098/rstb.2006.1938

Fleming, M., Bradford, R., MacGowan, B. R., & Salt, P. (1984). Female to-male transsexualism and sex roles: Self and spouse ratings on the PAQ. *Archives of Sexual Behavior, 13*(1), 51–57. doi: 10.1007/BF01542977

Folkman, S., Chesney, M., Collette, L., Boccellari, A., & Cooke, M. (1996). Postbereavement depressive mood and its prebereavement predictors in HIV+ and HIV- gay men. *Journal of Personality and Social Psychology, 70*(2), 336–348.

Forgatch, M. S., & DeGarmo, D. S. (1999). Parenting through change: An effective prevention program for single mothers. *Journal of Consulting and Clinical Psychology, 67*(5), 711–724.

Fox, J., & Warber, K. M. (2013). Romantic relationship development in the age of Facebook: An exploratory study of emerging adults' perceptions, motives, and behaviors. *Cyberpsychology, Behavior, and Social Networking, 16*(1), 3–7. doi: 10.1089/cyber.2012.0288

Fox, J., & Warber, K. M. (2014). Social networking sites in romantic relationships: Attachment, uncertainty, and partner surveillance on Facebook. *Cyberpsychology, Behavior, and Social Networking, 17*(1), 3–7. doi: 10.1089/cyber.2012.0667.

Fox, J., Warber, K. M., & Makstaller, D. C. (2013). The role of Facebook in romantic relationship development: An exploration of Knapp's relational stage model. *Journal of Social and Personal Relationships, 30*(6), 771–794. doi: 10.1177 /0265407512468370

Fredrickson, B. L. (2013). *Love 2.0: Creating happiness and health in moments of connection*. New York: Plume.

Freud, S. (1912). On the universal tendency to debasement in the sphere of love. *Standard Edition, 7*, 135–243.

Freud, S. (1914). On narcissism. *Standard Edition, 14*, 69–102.

Freud, S. (1915). Observations on transference love. *Standard Edition, 12*, 158–171.

Freud, S. (1917). Mourning and Melancholia. In J. Strachey, (Ed.), *The Standard Edition of the Complete Psychological Works of Sigmund Freud. Vol. 14*, Reprint, London: Hogarth Press.

Freud, S. (1920). Beyond the pleasure principle. *Standard Edition*, Vol. 20 (pp.3–64). London: Hogarth Press.

Freud, S. (1930). Civilization and its discontents. *Standard Edition, 21*, 59–145.

Freud S. (1963). *Sexuality and the psychology of love*. New York: Simon & Schuster Inc.

Fromm, E. (1956). *The art of loving*. New York: Harper & Row.

Gaines, S. O., & Henderson, M. C. (2002). Impact of attachment style on responses to accommodative dilemmas among same-sex couples. *Personal Relationships, 9*, 89–93. doi: 10.1111/1475-6811.00006

Gamino, L. A. (2011). Putting to rest the debate over grief counseling. In K. Doka & A. Tucci (Eds.), *Beyond Kubler-Ross: New perspectives in death, dying and grief* (pp. 113–130). Washington, DC: Hospice Foundation of America.

Garimella, V. R., Weber, I., & Cin, S. D. (2014). From "i love you babe" to "leave me alone"—Romantic relationship breakups on Twitter. *Social Informatics, 8851*, 199–215. doi: 10.1007/978-3-319-13734-6_14

Garvin, V., Kalter, N., & Hansell, J. (1993). Divorced women: Individual differences in stressors, mediating factors, and adjustment outcomes. *American Journal of Orthopsychiatry, 63*, 232–240.

Gerwolls, M. K., & Labott, S. M. (1994). Adjustment to the death of a companion animal. *Anthrozoos, 7*(3), 172–187. doi: 10.2752/089279394787001826

Glahn, J. V. (2012). Therapeutic crying: In praise of therapy's best kept secret. *Psychotherapy Networker*, accessed online at http://www.psychotherapynetworker.org/magazine/currentissue

Goldberg, W. A., Greenberger, E., Hamill, S., & O'Neil, R. (1992). Role demands in the lives of employed single mothers with preschoolers. *Journal of Family Issues, 13*, 312–333.

Goode, W. J. (1956). *Women in divorce*. New York: Free Press.

Gottman, J. (1994). *What predicts divorce? The relationship between marital process and marital outcomes*. Hillsdale,New Jersey: Lawrence Erlbaum.

Gottman, J. M., Levenson, R.W., Gross, J., Fredrickson, B., McCoy, K., Rosenthal, L., Yoshimoto, D. (2003). Correlates of gay and lesbian couples' relationship satisfaction and relationship dissolution, *Journal of Homosexuality, 45*(1), 23–43. doi: 10.1300/Jo82v45n01_02

Gray, J. D., & Silver, R. C. (1990). Opposite sides of the same coin: Former spouses' divergent perspectives in coping with their divorce. *Journal of Personality and Social Psychology, 59*, 1180–1191.

Greenwood, D. N., & Long, C. R. (2011). Attachment, belongingness, needs and relationship status predict imagined intimacy with media figures. *Communication Research, 38*(2), 278–297. doi: 10.1177/0093650210362687

Greenwood, D. N., Pietromonaco, P. R., & Long, C. R. (2008). Young women's attachment style and interpersonal engagement with female TV stars. *Journal of Social and Personal Relationships, 25*(3), 387–407. doi: 10.1177/0265407507087964

Greenwood, S., Perrin, A., & Duggan, M. (2016). *Social media update 2016*. Washington, DC: Pew Research Center's Internet and American Life Project. Retrieved from Pew Research Center, http://www.pewinternet.org/2016/11/11/social-media-update-2016/.

Hall, J. A. (2014). First comes social networking, then comes marriage? Characteristics of Americans married 2005–2012 who met through social networking sites. *Cyberpsychology, Behavior, and Social Networking, 17*(5), 322–326. doi: 10.1089/cyber.2013.0408

Harvey, J. H., & Miller, E. D. (1998). Toward a psychology of loss. *Psychological Science, 9*(6), 429–434. doi: 10.1111/1467-9280.00081

Hay, L. L., & Kessler, D. (2014). *You can heal your heart: Finding peace after a break-up, divorce or death*. California: Hay House, Inc.

Hazan, C., & Shaver, P. R. (1987). Romantic love conceptualized as an attachment process. *Journal of Personality and Social Psychology, 52*, 511–524. doi: 10.1037/0022-3514.52.3.511

Hazan, C., & Shaver, P. R. (1994). Author's response: Deeper into attachment theory. *Psychological Inquiry*, *5*(1), 68–79. doi: 10.1207/S15327965pli0501_15

Hendrix, H. (1988). *Getting the love you want: A guide for couples*. New York: Henry Holt and Company.

Herek, G. M. (2006). Legal recognition of same-sex relationships in the United States: A social science perspective. *American Psychologist, 61*(6), 607–621. doi: 10.1037/0003-066X.61.6.607

Hershberger, S. L., & D'Augelli, A. R. (1995). The impact of victimization on the mental health and suicidality of lesbian, gay and bisexual youths. *Developmental Psychology, 31*(1) 65–74. doi: 10.1037/0012-1649.31.1.65

Hetherington, E. M., Cox, M., & Cox, R. (1982). The effects of divorce on parents and children. In M. Lamb (Ed.), *Nontraditional families* (pp. 233–288). Hillsdale, NJ: Erlbaum.

Hight, E. S. (1977). A contractual, working separation: A step between resumption and/or divorce. *Journal of Divorce, 1*(1), 21–30.

Hill, A. (2005). *Reality tv—Audiences and popular factual television*. New York: Routledge.

Hines, S. (2006). Intimate transitions: Transgender practices of partnering and parenting. *Sociology, 40*(2), 353–371. doi: 10.1177/0038038506062037

Hirsh-Pasek, K., & Treiman, R. (1982). Doggerel: Motherese in a new context. *Journal of Child Language, 9*(1), 229–237. doi: 10.1017/S0305000900003731

Horton, D., & Wohl, R. R. (1956). Mass communication and para-social interaction: Observations on intimacy at a distance. *Psychiatry, 19*, 215–229.

Houston, B. (1984). Viewing television: The metapsychology of endless consumption. *Quarterly Review of Film Studies*, *9*(3) 183–195. doi: 10.1080/10509208409361211

Huxley, P. J., Kenna, J. C., & Brandon, S. (1981a). Partnership in transsexualism. Part I. The nature of the partnership. *Archives of Sexual Behavior, 10*, 133–142.

Huxley, P. J., Kenna, J. C., & Brandon, S. (1981b). Partnership in transsexualism. Part II. The nature of the partnership. *Archives of Sexual Behavior, 10*(2), 143–160. doi: 10.1007/BF01542175

Ickees, W. (1993). Traditional gender roles: Do they make, and then break, our relationships? *Journal of Social Issues, 49*, 71–86. doi: 10.1111/j.1540-4560.1993.tb01169.x

Jacobs S. C., Nelson J. C., & Zisook S. (1987). Treating depressions of bereavement with antidepressants. A pilot study. *The Psychiatric Clinics of North America, 10*(3), 501–510.

Janoff-Bulman, R. (2006). Schema-change perspectives on posttraumatic growth. In L. Calhoun & R. Tedeschi (Eds.), *Handbook of posttraumatic growth: Research and practice* (pp.81–99). Mahweh, NJ: Lawrence Erlbaum Associates.

Jellison, W. A., & McConnell, A. R. (2003). The mediating effects of attitudes toward homosexuality between secure attachment and disclosure outcomes among gay men. *Journal of Homosexuality, 46*, 159–177. doi: 10.1300/J082v46n01_05

Jin, B., & Park, N. (2010). In-person contact begets calling and texting: Interpersonal motives for cell phone use, face-to-face interaction, and loneliness. *Cy-*

berpsychology, Behavior and Social Networking, 13(6), 611–618. doi: 10.1089/cyber.2009.0314

Johnson, S. (2004). *The Practice of Emotionally Focused Couple Therapy: Creating Connection, 2nd Edition.* New York: Routledge.

Johnson, S. (2013). *Love sense: The revolutionary new science of romantic relationships*. New York: Little, Brown and Company.

Johnson C. L., & Barer, B. M. (1987). Marital stability and the changing kinship networks of grandparents. *Gerontologist, 27*, 330–335.

Joslin-Roher, E., & Wheeler, D. P. (2009). Partners in transition: The transition experience of lesbian, bisexual, and queer identified partners of transgender men. *Journal of Gay and Lesbian Social Services, 21*(1), 30–48. doi: 10.1080/10538720802494743

Joung, I. M. A., Stronks, K., van de Mheen, H., van Poppel, F. W. A., van der Meer, J. B. W., & Mackenbach, J. P. (1997). The contribution of intermediary factors to marital status differences in self-reported health. *Journal of Marriage and the Family, 8*, 39–66.

Julien, D. Chartrand, E., & Begin, J. (1999). Social networks, structural interdependence, and conjugal adjustment in heterosexual, gay and lesbian couples. *Journal of Marriage and the Family, 61*(2), 516–530.

Kanazawa, S. (2002). Bowling with our imaginary friends. *Evolution and Human Behavior, 23*, 167–171. doi: 10.1016/S1090-5138(01)00098-8

Kaslow, F. (1991). The sociocultural context of divorce. *Contemporary Family Therapy, 13*(6), 583–607.

Katz J., Beach S. R., Joiner T. E. (1998). When does partner devaluation predict emotional distress? Prospective moderating effects of reassurance-seeking and self-esteem. *Personal Relationships, 5*, 409–421.

Keddie, K. M. G. (1977). Pathological mourning after the death of a domestic pet. *British Journal of Psychiatry, 131*, 21–25. doi: 10.1192/bjp.131.1.21

Keicolt-Glaser, J. K., & Newton, T. L. (2001). Marriage and health: His and hers. *Psychological Bulletin, 127*, 475–503.

Keith, V. M. (1997). Life stress and psychological well-being among married and unmarried blacks. In R. J. Taylor, J. S. Jackson, & L. M. Chatters (Eds.), *Family life in Black America* (pp.94–116). Thousand Oaks, CA: Sage.

Kessler, D., & Hay, L. (2014). *You can heal your heart: Finding peace after a breakup, divorce or death*. California: Hay House.

Kessler, S. (1975). *The American way of divorce: Prescriptions for change*. Chicago: Nelson-Hall.

King, M. P., Melfi, J. P., Parker, S. J., & Star, D. (Producers), & King, M. P. (Director). (2008). *Sex and the City: The movie* [Motion Picture]. United States: New Line.

Kins, E., Hoebeke, P., Heylens, G., Rubens, R., & De Cuypere, G. (2008). The female-to-male transsexual and his female partner versus the traditional couple: A comparison. *Journal of Sex and Marital Therapy, 34*, 429–438. doi: 10.1080/00926230802156236

Kirkpatrick, L. A., & Davis, K. E. (1994). Attachment style, gender and relationship stability: A longitudinal analysis. *Journal of Personality and Social Psychology, 66*, 502–512. doi: 10.1037/10022-3514.66.3.502

Kitson, G. C. (1982). Attachment to the spouse in divorce: A scale and its application. *Journal of Marriage and the Family, 44*, 379–393.

Kitson, G. C., & Morgan, L. A. (1990). The multiple consequences of divorce: A decade review. *Journal of Marriage and the Family, 52*, 913–924.

Koenig, F., & Lessan, G. (1985). Viewers' relationship to television personalities. *Psychological Reports, 57*, 263–266. doi: 10.2466/pr0.1985.57.1.263

Krumrei, E. J., Mahoney, A., & Pargament, K. I. (2009). Divorce and the divine: The role of spirituality in adjustment to divorce. *Journal of Marriage and Family, 71*(2), 373–383. doi: 10.1111/j.1741-3737.2009.00605.x

Krumrei, E. J., Mahoney, A., & Pargament, K. I. (2011). Spiritual stress and coping model of divorce: A longitudinal study. *Journal of Family Psychology, 25*(6), 973–985. doi: 10.1037/a0025879

Kubler-Ross, E. (2014). *On death and dying: What the dying have to teach doctors, nurses, clergy and their own families*. New York: Scribner.

Kubler-Ross, E. (2014). *On grief and grieving: Finding the meaning of grief through the five stages of loss*. New York: Scribner.

Kubler-Ross, E., & Kessler, D. (2005). *On grief and grieving. Finding the meaning of grief through the five stages of loss*. New York: Scribner.

Kubler-Ross, E. (1969). *On death and dying: What the dying have to teach doctors, nurses, clergy and their own families*. New York: Scribner.

Kurdek, L. A. (1997). Adjustment to relationship dissolution in gay, lesbian and heterosexual partners. *Personal Relationships, 4*(2), 145–161. doi: 10.1111/j.1475-6811.1997.tb00136.x

Kurdek, L. A. (1998). Relationship outcomes and their predictors: Longitudinal evidence from heterosexual married, gay cohabitating, and lesbian cohabitating couples. *Journal of Marriage and the Family, 60*, 553–568. doi: 10.2307/353528

Kurdek, L. A. (2002). On being insecure about the assessment of attachment styles. *Journal of Social and Personal Relationships, 19*, 803–826. doi: 10.1177/0265407502196005

Kurdek, L. A. (2005). What do we know about gay and lesbian couples? *Current Directions in Psychological Science, 14*, 251–254. doi: 10.1111/j.0963-7214.2005.00375.x

Laan A. J., van Assen, M. A., & Vingerhoets, A. J. (2012). Individual differences in adult crying: The role of attachment styles. *Social Behavior and Personality: An International Journal, 40*(3), 453–471. doi: 10.2224/sbp.2012.40.3.453

Lago, D., Kafer, R., Delaney, M., & Conell, C. (1988). Assessment of favorable attitudes toward pets: Development and preliminary validation of self-report pet relationship scales. *Anthrozoos, 1*(4), 240–254. doi: 10.2752/089279388787058308

Landale, N. S., & Fennelly, K. (1992). Informal unions among mainland Puerto Ricans: Cohabitation or an alternative to legal marriage? *Journal of Marriage and the Family, 54*, 269–280.

Lawson, E. J., & Thompson, A. (1996). Black men's perceptions of divorce-related stressors and strategies for coping with divorce. *Journal of Family Issues, 17*, 249–273.

Lawton, L. E., & Bures, R. (2001). Parental divorce and the "switching" of religious identity. *Journal for the Scientific Study of Religion, 40*, 99–111. doi: 10.1111/0021-8294.00041

Lee, J. A. (1988). Love Styles. In R. Sternber & M. Barnes (Eds.), *The Psychology of Love* (pp.38–67). New Haven, CT: Yale University Press.

Lee, S. M., & Edmonston, B. (2005). New marriages, new families: U.S. racial and Hispanic intermarriage. *Population Bulletin, 60*, 1–40.

LeFebvre, L., Blackburn, K., & Brody, N. (2015). Navigating romantic relationships on Facebook: Extending the relationship dissolution model to social networking environments. *Journal of Social and Personal Relationships, 32*(1), 78–98. doi: 10.1177/0265407514524848

Lehman, D. R., Davis, C. G., DeLongis, A., Wortman, C. B., Bluck, S., Mandel, D., & Ellard, J. H. (1993). Positive and negative life changes following bereavement and their relations to adjustment. *Journal of Personality and Social Psychology, 12*, 90–112. doi: 10.1521/jscp.1993.12.1.90

Lenhart, A., & Duggan, M. (2014). Couples, the internet and social media: Main report. Washington, DC: Pew Research Center's Internet and American Life Project. Retrieved from Pew Research Center, http://pewinternet.org/2014/02/11/main-report-30/.

Leonoff, A. (2015). *The good divorce: A psychoanalyst's exploration of separation, divorce, and children*. London: Karnac.

Lepore, S. J., & Greenberg, M. A. (2002). Mending broken hearts: Effects of expressive writing on mood, cognitive processing, social adjustment, and health following a relationship breakup. *Psychology and Health, 17*(5), 547–560. doi: 10.1080/08870440290025768

Lev, A. (2004). *Transgender emergence: Therapeutic guidelines for working with gender-variant people and their families*. New York: Hawthorn Clinical Practice Press.

Levenson, R. W., & Gottman, J. M. (1983). Marital interaction: Physiological linkage and affective exchange. *Journal of Personality and Social Psychology, 45*, 587–597.doi: 10.1037//0022-3514.45.3.587

Levenson, R.W., & Gottman, J. M. (1985). Physiological and affective predictors of change in relationship satisfaction. *Journal of Personality and Social Psychology, 49*(1), 85–94. doi: 10.1037/0022-3514.49.1.85

Levine, A., & Heller, R. (2010). *Attached: The new science of adult attachment and how it can help you find-and keep-love*. New York: Penguin Group.

Levinger, G. (1979). A social exchange view of the dissolution of pair relationships. In R. L. Burgess & T. L. Huston (Eds.), *Social exchange in developing relationships* (pp. 169–193). New York: Academic Press.

Levy, M. R. (1979). Watching tv news as para-social interaction. *Journal of Broadcasting, 23*, 69–80. doi: 10.1080/08838157909363919

Lewandowski, G. W. (2009). Promoting positive emotions following relationship dissolution through writing. *The Journal of Positive Psychology, 4*(1), 21–31. doi: 10.1080/17439760802068480

Lewis, P. H. (1983). Innovative divorce rituals: Their psycho-social functions. *Journal of Divorce, 6*(3), 71–81.

Lobb, E. A., Kristjanson, L. J., Aoun, S. M., Monterosso, L., Halkett, G. K., & Davies, A. (2010). Predictors of complicated grief: A systematic review of empirical studies, *Death Studies, 34(*8), 673–698. doi: 10.1080/07481187.2010.496686

Lyndon, A., Bonds-Raacke, J., & Cratty, A. D. (2011). College students' Facebook stalking of ex-partners. *Cyberpsychology, Behavior, and Social Networking 14(*12), 711–716. doi: 10.1089/cyber.2010.0588

MacDonald, G., Kingsbury, R., & Shaw, S. (2005). Adding insult to injury: Social pain theory and response to social exclusion. In K. Williams, J. Forgas & W. Von Hippel (Eds.), *The Social Outcast: Ostracism, Social Exclusion, Rejection and Bullying*, (pp.77–90). New York: Psychology Press.

Madey, S. F., & Jilek, L. (2012). Attachment style and dissolution of romantic relationships: Breakup is hard to do, or is it? *Individual Differences Research, 10*, 202–210. doi: 10.1371/journal.pone.0075161

Mahler, M. (1974). Symbiosis and Individuation: The psychological birth of the human infant. *The Psychological Study of the Child, 29*, 98–106.

Mahoney, A., Krumrei, E. J., & Pargament, K. I. (2008). Broken vows: Divorce as a spiritual trauma and its implications for growth and decline. In S. Joseph & P. Alex Linley (Eds.), *Trauma, Recovery, and Growth: Positive Psychological Perspectives on Posttraumatic Stress* (pp. 105–124). Hoboken, NJ: Wiley.

Mahoney, A., Pargament, K. I., Jewell, T., Swank, A. B., Scott, E., Emery, E., & Rye, M. (1999). Marriage and the spiritual realm: The role of proximal and distal religious constructs in marital functioning. *Journal of Family Psychology, 13*, 321–338. doi: 10.1037/0893-3200.13.3.321

Mahoney, A., Pargament, K. I., Murray-Swank, A., & Murray-Swank, N. (2003). Religion and the sanctification of family relationships. *Review of Religious Research, 44*, 220–236. doi: 10.2307/3512384

Main, M., Kaplan, N., & Cassidy, J. (1985). Security in infancy, childhood and adulthood: A move to the level of representations. In I. Bretherton & E. Waters (Eds.), *Growing points of attachment theory and research. Monographs of the Society for Research in Child Development, 50* (1–2, Serial No. 209), 66–104.

Marks, N. F. (1996). Flying solo at midlife: Gender, marital status and psychological well being. *Journal of Marriage and Family, 58*, 917–932. doi: 10.2307/353980

Marshall, T. C. (2012). Facebook surveillance of former romantic partners: Associations with postbreakup recovery and personal growth. *Cyberpsychology, Behavior, and Social Networking, 15*(10), 521–526. doi: 10.1089/cyber.2012.0125

Marshall, T. C., Bejanyan, K., & Ferenczi, N. (2013). Attachment styles and personal growth following romantic breakups: The mediating roles of distress, rumination, and tendency to rebound. *PLoS ONE 8*(9), 1–11. doi: 10.1371/journal.pone.0075161

Mastekaasa, A. (1997). Marital dissolution as a stressor: Some evidence on psychological, physical, and behavioral changes during the preseparation period. *Journal of Divorce and Remarriage, 26*, 155–183.

Mathews, L. T., & Marwit, S. J. (2004). Complicated grief and the trend toward cognitive-behavioral therapy. *Death Studies, 28*, 849–863. doi: 10.1080/07481180490490924

Matusow, B. (1983). *The evening stars: The making of the network news anchor*. Boston: Houghton Mifflin.

McCulloch, M. (1981). The pet as prosthesis: Defining criteria for the adjunctive use of companion animals in the treatment of medically ill, depressed outpatients. In

B. Fogle (Ed.), *Interrelations between people and pets* (pp.101–123). Springfield, IL: Charles C. Thomas.

McKiernan, A., Ryan, P., McMahon, E., & Butler, E. (2017). Qualitative analysis of interactions on an online discussion forum for young people with experience of romantic relationship breakup. *Cyberpsychology, Behavior, and Social Networking, 20*(2), 78–82. doi: 10.1089/cyber.2016.0450

Meier, S. C., Pardo, S., Labuski, C., & Babcock, J. (2013). Measures of clinical health among female-to-male transgender persons as a function of sexual orientation. *Archives of Sexual Behavior, 42*(3), 463–474. doi: 10.1007/s10508-012-0052-2

Meier, S. C., Sharp, C., Michonski, J., Babcock, J. C., & Fitzgerald, K. (2013). Romantic relationships of female-to-male trans men: A descriptive study. *International Journal of Transgenderism, 14*(2), 75–85. doi: 10.1080/15532739.2013.791651

Melhem, N. M., Day, N., Shear, M. K., Day, R., Reynolds, C. F., & Brent, D. (2004). Traumatic grief among adolescents exposed to a peer's suicide. *American Journal of Psychiatry, 161*(8), 1411–1416. doi: 10.1176/appi.ajp.161.8.1411

Melson, G. F. (1989). Studying children's attachment to their pets: A Conceptual and methodological review. *Anthrozoos, 4*(2), 91–99. doi: 10.2752/089279391787057297

Mesman, J., van IJzendoorn, M. H., & Sagi-Schwartz (2016). Cross-cultural patterns of attachment: Universal and contextual dimensions. In J. Cassidy & P. Shaver (Eds.), *Handbook of attachment: Theory, Research and Clinical Applications* (3rd ed.) (pp.852–877). New York: The Guilford Press.

Meyrowitz, J. (1994). The life and death of media friends: New genres of intimacy and mourning. In R. Cathcart & S. Drucker (Eds.), *American heroes in a media age* (pp. 52–81). Cresskill, NJ: Hampton.

Mikulincer, M., & Florian, V. (1996). Emotional reactions to interpersonal losses over the life span: An attachment theoretical perspective. In C. Magai & S. McFadden (Eds.), *Handbook of emotions, adult development, and aging* (pp. 269–285). San Diego: Academic Press.

Mikulincer, M., & Shaver, P. R. (2007). *Attachment in adulthood: Structure, dynamics and change*. New York: The Guilford Press.

Mikulincer, M., & Shaver, P. R. (2016). *Attachment in adulthood: Structure, dynamics and Change* (2nd ed.). New York: The Guilford Press.

Miller, A. (2014). Digital heartbreak: Psychologists are finding that how romance blooms—and withers—is different in the digital age. *gradPSYCH Magazine*, 22.

Miller, J. G., & Bersoff, D. M. (1994). Cultural influences on the moral status of reciprocity and the discounting of endogenous motivation. *Personality and Social Psychology Bulletin, 20*(5), 592–602.

Miller, J. G., Bersoff, D. M., & Harwood, R. L. (1990). Perceptions of social responsibilities in India and in the United States: Moral imperatives or personal decisions? *Journal of Personality and Social Psychology, 58*, 33–47. doi:10.1037/0022-3514.58.1.33

Moen, P., Kim, J. E., & Hofmeister, H. (2001). Couples' work/retirement transitions, gender, and marital quality. *Social Psychology Quarterly, 64*(1), 55–71. doi: 10.2307/3090150

Mohr, J. (2008). Same-sex romantic attachment. In J. Cassidy & P. Shaver (Eds.). *Handbook of attachment: Theory, Research and Clinical Applications* (2nd ed.) (pp. 482–502). New York: The Guilford Press.

Mohr, J., & Fassinger, R. E. (2003). Self-acceptance and self-disclosure of sexual orientation in lesbian, gay, and bisexual adults: An attachment perspective. *Journal of Counseling Psychology, 50*(4), 482–495. doi: 10.1037/0022-0167.50.4.482.

Mohr, J. J., & Fassinger, R. E. (2006). Sexual orientation identity and romantic relationship quality in same-sex couples. *Personality and Social Psychology Bulletin, 32*, 1085–1099. doi: 10.1177/0146167206288281

Mohr, J. J., & Jackson, S. D. (2016). Same-sex attachment. In J. Cassidy & P. Shaver (Eds.). *Handbook of attachment: Theory, Research and Clinical Applications* (3rd ed.) (pp. 484–506). New York: The Guilford Press.

Morgan, D. L., Carder, P., & Neal, M. B. (1997). Are some relationships more useful than others? The value of similar others in the networks of recent widows. *Journal of Social and Personal Relationships, 14*(6):745–759. doi: 10.1177/0265407597146002

Murphy, B. C. (1989). Lesbian couples and their parents: The effects of perceived parental attitudes on the couple. *Journal of Counseling and Development, 68*, 46–51. doi: 10.1002/j.1556–6676.1989.tb02492.x

Murray, S. L., Holmes, J. G., MacDonald, G., & Ellsworth, P. (1998). Through the looking glass darkly? When self-doubts turn into relationship insecurities. *Journal of Personality and Social Psychology, 75*, 1459–1480.

Murstein, B. I. (1976). *Who will marry whom?* New York: Springer.

Muscanell, N. L., Guadagno, R. E., Rice, L., & Murphy, S. (2013) Don't it make my brown eyes green? An analysis of Facebook use and romantic jealousy. *Cyberpsychology, Behaviour and Social Networking, 16*(4), 237–242.

Muschel, I. (1984). Pet therapy with terminal cancer patients. *Social Casework, 65*(8), 451–458.

Myers, J. E., & Perrin, N. (1993). Grandparents affected by parental divorce: A population at risk? *Journal of Counseling and Development, 72*: 62–66. doi:10.1002/j.1556–6676.1993.tb02278.x

Najib, A., Lorberbaum, J. P., Kose, S., Bohning, D. E., & George, M.S. (2004). Regional brain activity in women grieving a romantic relationship breakup. *American Journal of Psychiatry 161*(12): 2245–2256. doi: 10.1176/appi.ajp.161.12.2245

Nathanson, I. G. (1995). Divorce and women's spirituality. *Journal of Divorce and Remarriage, 22*, 179–188. doi: 10.1300/J087v22n03_11

Nelson, J. K. (2005). *Seeing through tears: Crying and attachment*. New York: Routledge.

Neustaedter, C., & Greenberg, S. (2011). Intimacy in long-distance relationships over video chat. *Research Report 2011–1014–26*, Department of Computer Science, University of Calgary, Calgary, AB, Canada T2N IN4, August. doi: 10.1145/2207676.2207785

Newton, B. J., & Buck, E. B. (1985). Television as significant other: Its relationship to self-descriptors in five countries. *Journal of Cross Cultural Psychology, 16*, 289–312. doi: 10.1177/0022002185016003003

Nitzburg, G. C., & Farber, B. A. (2013). Putting up emotional (Facebook) walls? Attachment status and emerging adults' experiences of social networking sites. *Journal of Clinical Psychology, 69*(11), 1183–1190. doi: 10.1002/jclp.22045

O'Connor, T. G., Hawkins, N., Dunn, J., Thorpe, K., & Golding, J. (1998). Family type and depression in pregnancy: Factors mediating risk in a community sample. *Journal of Marriage and the Family, 60*, 757–770.

Olmert, M. D. (2009). *Made for each other: The biology of the human-animal bond.* Cambridge: Da Capo Press.

Orbuch, T. L., & Brown, E. (2006). Divorce in the context of being African American. In M. A. Fine & J. H. Harvey (Eds.), *Handbook of divorce and relationship dissolution* (pp.481–498). Mahwah, NJ: Lawrence Erlbaum Associates.

Oswald, R.F., & Clausell, E. (2006). Same-sex relationships and their dissolution. In M. A. Fine & J. H. Harvey (Eds.), *Handbook of divorce and relationship dissolution* (pp. 499–514). Mahwah, NJ: Lawrence Erlbaum Associates.

Otis, M. D., Riggle, E. D., & Rotosky, S. S. (2006). Dyadic effects of mental health on lesbian couple relationships. *Journal of Lesbian Studies, 10*, 267–283.

Palmgreen, P. Wenner, L. A., & Rayburn, J. D. (1980). Relations between gratifications sought and obtained: A Study of television news. *Communication Research, 7*, 161–192. doi: 10.1177/009365028000700202

Papp, L. M., Danielewicz, J., & Cayemberg, C. (2012). "Are we facebook official?" Implications, of dating partners' Facebook use and profiles for intimate relationship satisfaction. *Cyberpsychology, Behavior, and Social Networking, 15*(2), 85–90. doi:10.1089/cyber.2011.0291

Pargament, K. I. (1997). *The psychology of religion and coping: Theory, research, practice*. New York: Guilford Press.

Pargament, K. I. (2011). Religion and coping: The current state of knowledge. In S. Folkman (Ed.), *Oxford handbook of stress, health, and coping* (pp. 269–288). New York: Oxford University Press.

Park, L. E., Sanchez, D. T., & Brynildsen, K. (2011). Maladaptive responses to relationship dissolution: The role of relationship contingent self-worth. *Journal of Applied Social Psychology, 41*(7), 1749–1773. doi: 10.1111/j.1559-1816.2011.00769.x

Parkes, C. M., Laugani, P., & Young, B. (2015). Culture and Religion. In C. Parkes, P. Laugani, & B. Young (Eds.). *Death and Bereavement across Cultures* (2nd ed.) (pp. 9–20). London: Routledge.

Parkes, C. M., Reif, M., & Couldrick, A. (1996). *Counseling in terminal care and childhood bereavement*. Baltimore, MD: BPS Books.

Pasternak, R. E., Reynolds, C. F., Schlernitzauer, M. A., Hoch, C. C., Buysse, D. J., Houck, P. R., & Perel, J. M. (1991). Acute open-trial nortriptyline therapy of bereavement-related depression in late life. *Journal of Clinical Psychiatry, 52*, 307–310.

Patterson, D. G., Ciabattari, T., & Schwartz, P. (1999). The constraints of innovation: Commitment and stability among same-sex couples. In J. M. Adams & W. H. Jones (Eds.), *Handbook of interpersonal commitment and relationship stability: Perspectives on individual differences* (pp. 339–359). Dordrecht, Netherlands: Kluwer Academic Publishers.

Pauly, I. (1974). Female transsexualism, Part I. *Archives of Sexual Behavior, 3*(6), 487–508. doi: 10.1007/BF01541134

Perse, E. M., & Rubin, R. B. (1989). Attribution in social and parasocial relationships. *Communication Research, 16*(59), 59–77. doi: 10.1177/009365089016001003

Perse, E. M., & Rubin, A. M. (1990). Chronic loneliness and television use. *Journal of Broadcasting and Electronic Media, 34,* 37–53. doi: 10.1080/08838159009386724

Peters, A., & Liefbroer, A. C. (1997). Beyond marital status: Partner history and well-being in old age. *Journal of Marriage and the Family, 59*, 687–699.

Pfeffer, C. (2008). Bodies in relation—Bodies in transition: Lesbian partners of trans men and body image. *Journal of Lesbian Studies, 12*(4), 325–345. doi: 10.1080/10894160802278184

Pines, A. M. (2005). *Falling in love: Why we choose the lovers we choose* (2nd ed.). New York: Routledge.

Pistole, M. C. (1996). After love: Attachment styles and grief themes. *The Family Journal, 4*(3), 199–207. doi: 10.1177/1066480796043003

Powers, R. (1978). *The newscasters: The news business as show business*. New York: St. Martin's Press.

Prigerson, H. G., Bierhals, A. J., Kasl, S. V., Reynolds, C. F., Shear, M. K., Day, N., & Jacobs, S. (1997). Traumatic grief as a risk factor for mental and physical morbidity. *American Journal of Psychiatry, 154*, 616–623. doi: 10.1176/ajp.154.5.616

Prigerson, H. G., Bierhals, A. J., Kasl, S. V., Reynolds, C. F., Shear, M. K., Newsom, J. T., & Jacobs, S. (1996). Complicated grief as a disorder distinct from bereavement-related depression and anxiety: a replication study. *American Journal of Psychiatry. 153*, 1484–1486. doi: 10.1176/ajp.153.11.1484

Prigerson, H. G., Frank, E., Kasl, S. V., Reynolds, C. F., Anderson, B., Zubenko, G. S., & Kupfer, D. J. (1995). Complicated grief and bereavement related depression as distinct disorders: preliminary empirical validation in elderly bereaved spouses. *American Journal of Psychiatry, 152*, 22–30. doi: 10.1176/ajp.152.1.22

Prigerson, H., & Jacobs, S. (2001). Traumatic grief as a distinct disorder: A rationale, consensus criteria, and a preliminary empirical test. In M. Stroebe, R. Hansson, W. Stroebe & H. Schut, (Eds.), *Handbook of bereavement research: consequences, coping, and care.* (pp. 613–645). Washington, DC: American Psychological Association. doi:10.1037/10436-026

Prigerson, H. G., Maciejewski, P. K., Reynolds, C. F., Bierhals, A. J., Newsom, J. T., Fasiczka, A., & Miller, M. (1995). Inventory of complicated grief: A scale to measure maladaptive symptoms of loss. *Psychiatry Research, 59*, 65–79. doi: 10.1016/0165-1781(95)02757-2

Prigerson, H. G., Shear, M. K., Frank, E., Beery, L. C., Silberman, R., Prigerson, J., & Reynolds, C. F. (1997). Traumatic grief: A case of loss-induced trauma. *American Journal of Psychiatry, 154*, 1003–1009. doi: 10.1176/ajp.154.7.1003

Prigerson, H. G., Shear, M. K., Newsom, J. T., Frank, E., Reynolds, C. F., Maciejewski, P. K., & Kupfer, D. J. (1995). Anxiety among widowed elders: Is it distinct from depression and grief? *Anxiety, 2*(1), 1–12. doi: 10.1002/(SICI)1522-7154.

Quackenbush, J. E. (1984) Pet bereavement in older owners. In B. K. Anderson, B. L. Hart, & L. A. Hart (Eds.), *The Pet Connection: Its Influence on Our Health and Quality of Life* (pp. 292–299). Minneapolis, MN: University of Minnesota Press.

Reczek, C., Elliott, S., & Umberson, D. (2009). Commitment without marriage: Union formation among long-term same-sex couples. *Journal of Family Issues, 30*(6), 738–756.

Reeves, B., & Nass, C. (1996). *The media equation: How people treat computers, television, and new media like real people and places*. Cambridge, MA: Cambridge University Press.

Reibstein, J. (1998). Attachment, pain and detachment for the adults in divorce. *Sexual and Marital Therapy, 13*, 351–360. doi: 10.1080/02674659808404253

Ridge, S. R., & Feeney, J. A. (1998). Relationship history and relationship attitudes in gay males and lesbians: Attachment style and gender differences. *Austrialian New Zealand Journal of Psychiatry, 32*(6), 848–859. doi: 10.3109/00048679809073875

Riggle, E. D., Rostosky, S. S., & Horne, S. G. (2010). Psychological distress, well-being, and legal recognition in same-sex couple relationships. *Journal of Family Psychology, 24*(1), 82–86. doi: 10/1037/a0017942

Roisman, G. I., Clausell, E., Holland, A., Fortuna, K., & Elieff, C. (2008). Adult romantic relationships as contexts of human development: A multimethod comparison of same-sex couples with opposite-sex dating, engaged and married dyads. *Developmental Psychology, 44*(1), 91–101. doi: 1.1037/0012-1649.44.1.91

Rollie, S. S., & Duck, S. W. (2006). Divorce and dissolution of romantic relationships: Stage models and their limitations. In M. A. Fine & J. H. Harvey (Eds.), *Handbook of divorce and relationship dissolution* (pp. 223–240). Mahweh, NJ: Lawrence Erlbaum Associates, Inc.

Rosenblatt, P. C. (1983). *Bitter, bitter tears: Nineteenth-century diarists and twentieth century grief theories*. Minneapolis: University of Minnesota Press.

Rosenblatt, P. C. (2011). Beyond Kubler-Ross: What we have learned about grief from cross-cultural research. In K. Doka & A. Tucci (Eds.), *Beyond Kubler-Ross: New perspectives in death, dying and grief* (pp. 77–90). Washington, DC: Hospice Foundation of America.

Rosenblatt, P. C. (2015). Grief in small societies. In C. Parkes, P. Laugani, & B. Young (Eds.). *Death and Bereavement Across Cultures* (2nd ed.) (pp. 23–41). London: Routledge.

Rosenblatt, P. C., Walsh, R. P., & Jackson, D. A. (1976). *Grief and mourning in cross-cultural perspective*. Michigan: HRAF Press.

Rosenfeld, M. J., & Thomas, R. J. (2012). Searching for a mate: The rise of the internet as a social intermediary. *American Sociological Review, 77*(4), 523–547. doi: 10:1177/0003122412448050

Ross, C. E. (1995). Reconceptualizing marital status as a continuum of social attachment. *Journal of Marriage and the Family, 57*, 129–140.

Rothbaum, F., Weisz, J., Pott, M., Miyake, K., & Morelli, G. (2000). Attachment and culture: Security in the United States and Japan. *American Psychologist, 55*(10), 1093–1104. doi: 10.1037//0003-066X.55.10.1093

Rubin, A., & Perse, E. (1987). Audience activity and soap opera involvement: A uses and effects approach. *Human Communication Research, 14*, 246–268. doi: 10.1111/j.1468-2958.1987.tb00129.x

Rubin, A., Perse, E., & Powell, R. (1985). Loneliness, parasocial interaction, and local television viewing. *Human Communication Research, 12*, 155–180. doi: 10.1111/j.1468-2958.1985.tb00071.x

Rubin, H. (2003). *Self-made men: Identity and embodiment among transsexual men*. Nashville, TN: Vanderbilt University Press.

Rubin, L. B. (1983). *Intimate strangers: Men and women together*. New York: Harper & Row.

Rubin, R., & McHugh, M. (1987). Development of parasocial interaction relationships. *Journal of Broadcasting and Electronic Media, 31*, 279–292. doi: 10.1080/08838158709386664

Rynearson, E. K. (1978). Humans and pets and attachment. *British Journal of Psychiatry, 133*, 550–555.

Sable, P. (1989). Attachment, anxiety, and loss of a husband. American Journal of *Orthopsychiatry, 59*(4), 550–556. doi: 10.1111/j.1939–0025.1989.tb02745.x

Sable, P. (1991). Attachment, loss of spouse, and grief in elderly adults. *Omega, 23*(2), 129–142. doi: 10.2190/PU6V-H0NW61NY-1W5G.

Sable, P. (1995). Pets, attachment, and well-being across the life cycle. *Social Work, 40*(3), 334–341. doi: 10.1093/sw/40.3.334

Sable, P. (2000). *Attachment and adult psychotherapy*. Northvale, NJ: Jason Aronson.

Sable, P. (2013). The pet connection: An attachment perspective. *Clinical Social Work Journal, 41*, 93–99. doi: 10.1007/s10615-012-0405-2

Saffrey, C., & Ehrenberg, M. (2007). When thinking hurts: Attachment, rumination, and postrelationship adjustment. *Personal Relationships, 14*(3), 351–368. doi: 10.1111/j.1475–6811.2007.00160.x

Sanchez, D. T., Good, J. J., Kwang, T., & Saltzman, E. (2008). When finding a mate feels urgent: Why relationship contingency predicts men's and women's body shame. *Social Psychology, 39*(2), 90–102. doi: 10.1027/1864-9335.39.2.90

Sanchez, D. T., & Kwang, T. (2007). When the relationship becomes her: Revisiting women's body concerns from a relationship contingency perspective. *Psychology of Women Quarterly, 31*, 401–414.

Sanders, C. M., Mauger, P. A., & Strong, P. N. (1985). *A Manual for the Grief Experience Inventory*. Palo Alto, CA: Consulting Psychologist Press.

Sanders, C. F., & Trygstad, D. W. (1989). Stepgrandparents and grandparents: The view from young adults. *Family Relations, 38*, 71–75.

Sbarra, D. A. (2006). Predicting the onset of emotional recovery following nonmarital relationship dissolution: Survival analysis of sadness and anger. *Personality and Social Psychological Bulletin, 32*, 298–312. doi: 10.1177/0146167205280913

Sbarra, D. A., & Emery, R. E. (2005). The emotional sequelae of nonmarital relationship dissolution: Analysis of change and intraindividual variability over time. *Personal Relationships, 12*, 213–232.

Schachner, D. A., Shaver, P. R., & Gillath, O. (2008). Attachment style and long-term singlehood. *Personal Relationships, 15*, 479–491. doi: 10.1111/j.1475-6811.2008.00211.x

Schiappa, E., Allen, M., & Gregg, P. (2007). *Mass media effects research: Advances through meta-analysis*. New Jersey: Lawrence Erlbaum Associates.

Schneller, D. P., & Arditti, J. A. (2004). After the breakup: Interpreting divorce and rethinking intimacy. *Journal of Divorce and Remarriage, 42*, 1–37. doi: 10.1300/J087v42n01_01

Schrock, D. P., & Reid, L. L. (2006). Transsexuals' sexual stories. *Archives of Sexual Behavior, 35*(1), 75–86. doi: 10.1007/s10508-006-8996-8

Schut, H., Stroebe, M. S., van den Bout, J., & Terheggen, M. (2001). The efficacy of bereavement interventions: Determining who benefits. In M. Stroebe, R. Hansson, W. Stroebe, & H. Schut (Eds.), *Handbook of bereavement research: Consequences, coping and care* (pp. 705–737). Washington, DC: American Psychological Association.

Serpell, J. A. (1996). Evidence for an association between pet behaviour and owner attachment levels. *Applied Animal Behavior Science, 47*, 49–60. doi: 10.1016/0168-1591(95)01010-6

Sharpsteen, D. J., & Kirkpatrick, L. A. (1997). Romantic jealousy and adult romantic attachment. *Journal of Personality and Social Psychology, 72*, 627–640. doi: 10.1037//0022-3514.72.3.627

Shear, K. (2010). Complicated grief treatment: The theory, practice and outcomes. *Bereavement Care, 29*(3), 10–14. doi: 10.1080/02682621.2010.522373

Shear, K., Frank, E., Houck, P., & Reynolds, C. (2005). Treatment of complicated grief. A randomized controlled trial. *Journal of the American Medical Association, 293*(21), 2601–2608. doi: 10.1001/jama.293.21.2601

Shear, K., Simon, N., Wall, M., Zisook, S., Neimeyer, R., Duan, N., Keshaviah, A. (2011). Complicated grief and related bereavement issues for DSM–5. *Depression and Anxiety, 28*, 103–117. doi: 10.1002/da.20780

Silverman, G. K., Johnson, J. G., & Prigerson, H. G. (2001). Preliminary explorations of the effects of prior trauma and loss on risk for psychiatric disorders in recently widowed people. *The Israel Journal of Psychiatry and Related Sciences, 38*, 202–215.

Simpson, J. A. (1990). Influence of attachment styles on romantic relationships. *Journal of Personality and Social Psychology, 59*, 971–980. doi: 10.1037/0022-3514.59.5.971

Slotter, E. B., Gardner, W. L., & Finkel, E. J. (2010). Who am I without you? The influence of romantic breakup on the self-concept. *Personality and Social Psychology Bulletin, 36*(2), 147–160. doi: 10.1177/0146167209352250

Slotter, E. B., & Ward, D. E. (2014). Finding the silver lining: The relative roles of redemptive narratives and cognitive reappraisal in individuals' emotional distress after the end of a romantic relationship, *Journal of Social and Personal Relationships, 32*(6), 737–756. doi: 10.1177/0265407514546978

Smith, A., & Duggan, M. (2013). *Online dating and relationships*. Washington, DC: Pew Research Center's Internet and American Life Project. Retrieved from Pew Research Center, http://pewinternet.org/Reports/2013/Online-Dating.aspx

Smith, R. B., & Brown, R. A. (1997). The impact of social support on gay male couples. *Journal of Homosexuality, 33*, 39–61. doi: 10.1300/J082v33n02_03

Smith, S. L. (1983). Interactions between pet dog and family members: An ethological study. In A.H. Katcher & A. M. Beck (Eds.), *New Perspectives on Our Lives with Companion Animals* (pp.29–36). Philadelphia: University of Pennsylvania Press.

Spielmann, S. S., MacDonald, G., & Wilson, A. E. (2009). On the rebound: Focusing on someone new helps anxiously attached individuals let go of ex-partners. *Personality and Social Psychological Bulletin, 35*, 1382–1394. doi: 10.1177/0146167209341580

Sprecher, S., Felmlee, D., Metts, S., Fehr, B., & Vanni, D. (1998). Factors associated with distress following the breakup of a close relationship. *Journal of Social and Personal Relationships, 15*(6), 791–809. doi: 10.1177/0265407598156005

Starka, L. (2007). Endocrine factors of pair bonding. *Prague Medical Report, 108*(4), 297–305.

Steele, H., & Steele, M. (2008). Ten clinical uses of the adult attachment interview. In H. Steele & M. Steele (Eds.), *Clinical applications of the adult attachment interview*. New York: The Guilford Press.

Steiner, B., & Bernstein, S. M. (1981). Female-to-male transsexuals and their partners. *Canadian Journal of Psychiatry, 26*(3), 178–182. doi: 10.1177/070674378102600308

Sternberg, R. J. (1986). A triangular theory of love. *Psychological Review, 93*(2), 119–135.

Stever, G. S. (2009). Parasocial and social interaction with celebrities: Classification of media fans. *Journal of Media Psychology, 14*(3), 1–39.

Stewart, M. (1983). Loss of a pet—loss of a person: A comparative study of bereavement. In A.H. Katcher & A. M. Beck (Eds.), *New Perspectives on Our Lives with Companion Animals* (pp.390–404). Philadelphia: University of Pennsylvania Press.

Stiers, G. A. (1999). *From this day forward: Commitment, marriage, and family in lesbian and gay relationships*. New York: St. Martin's Press.

Stoessel, C., Stiller, J., Bleich, S., Boensch, D., Doerfler, A., Garcia, M., Richter-Schmidinger, T., Kornhuber, J., & Forster, C. (2011). Differences and similarities on neuronal activities of people being happily and unhappily in love: a functional magnetic resonance imaging study. *Neuropsychobiology 64*(1): 52–60. doi: 10.1159/000325076

Stoller, K. P. (2012). *Oxytocin: The hormone of healing and hope*. Santa Fe, NM: Dream Treader Press.

Stroebe, M., & Schut, H. (1999). The dual process model of coping with bereavement: Rationale and description. *Death Studies*, 23, 197–224. doi: 10.1080/074811899201046

Stroebe, M., & Schut, H. (2010). The dual process model of coping with bereavement: A decade on. *Omega, 61*(4), 273–289. doi: 10.2190/OM.61.4.b

Stroud, L. R., Tanofsky-Kraff, M., Wilfley, D. E., & Salovey, P. (2000). The Yale Interpersonal Stressor (YIPS): affective, physiological, and behavioral responses to a novel interpersonal rejection paradigm. *Annals of Behavioral Medicine: A publication of the Society of Behavioral Medicine, 22*, 204–213.

Talbot, K. (1998). Mothers now childless: Personal transformation after the death of an only child. *Omega: Journal of Death and Dying*, 38, 167–186. doi: 10.2190/LT9P-9PJ7-ORXH-ED2C

Tashiro, T., & Frazier, P. (2003). "I'll never be in a relationship like that again": Personal growth following romantic relationship breakups. *Personal Relationships*, 10: 113–128. doi: 10.1111/1475-6811/00039

Taylor, R. J., Chatters, L. M., & Levin, J. (2004). *Religion in the loves of African Americans: Social, psychological, and health perspectives*. Thousand Oaks, CA: Sage.

Taylor, R. J., Chatters, L. M., Tucker, B. J., & Lewis, E. (1990). Developments in research on Black families: A decade review. *Journal of Marriage and Family, 52*(4), 993–1014. doi: 10.2307/353315

Taylor, R. J., Keith, V. M., & Tucker, M. B. (1993). Gender, marital, familial, and friendship roles. In J. S. Jackson, L. M. Chatters, & R. J. Taylor (Eds.), *Aging in Black America* (pp. 49–68). Newbury Park, CA: Sage.

Taylor, R. J., Tucker, L. M., Chatters, L. M., & Jayakody, R. (1997). Recent demographic trends in African American family structure. In R. J. Taylor, J. S. Jackson, & L. M. Chatters (Eds.), *Family life in Black America* (pp.94–116). Thousand Oaks, CA: Sage.

Taylor S.E. (2002). *The tending instinct: How nurturing is essential to who we are and how we live*. New York: Holt.

Tedeschi, R. G., & Calhoun, L. G. (1996). The posttraumatic growth inventory: Measuring the positive legacy of trauma. *Journal of Traumatic Stress*, 9, 455–471. doi: 10.1007/BF02103658

Tedeschi, R. G., & Calhoun, L. G. (2004). *Helping bereaved parents: A clinician's guide*. New York: Brunner-Routledge.

Terhell, E. L., Broese van Groenou, M. I., & van Tilburg, T. (2004). Network dynamics in the long-term period after divorce. *Journal of Social and Personal Relationships, 21*(6), 719–738.

Thabes, V. (1997). A survey analysis of women's long-term postdivorce adjustment. *Journal of Divorce and Remarriage, 27*, 163–175.

Tong, S. T. (2013). Facebook use during relationship termination: uncertainty reduction and surveillance. *Cyberpsychology, Behavior, and Social Networking, 16*(11), 788–793. doi: 10.1089/cyber.2012.0549

Triandis, H. C., Bontempo, R., Villareal, M. J., Asai, M., & Lucca, N. (1988). Individualism and collectivism: Cross-cultural perspectives on self-ingroup relationships. *Journal of Personality and Social Psychology, 54*, 323–338.

Tsao, J. (1996). Compensatory media use: An exploration of two paradigms. *Communication Studies, 47*, 89–109. doi: 10.1080/10510979609368466

Umana-Taylor, A. J., & Alfaro, E. C. (2006). Divorce and relationship dissolution among Latino populations in the United States. In M. A. Fine & J.H. Harvey (Eds.), *Handbook of divorce and relationship dissolution* (pp. 515–530). Mahwah, NJ: Lawrence Erlbaum Associates.

Umberson, D., Chen, M. D., House, J. S., Hopkins, K., & Slaten, E. (1996). The effect of social relationships on psychological well-being: Are men and women really so different? *American Sociological Review*, *61*(5), 837–857.

Valentine, D. (2003). "I went to bed with my own kind once": The erasure of desire in the name of identity. *Language and Communication, 23*(2), 123–138. doi: 10.1016/S0271–5309(02)00045–9

Vanderwerker, L. C., Jacobs, S. C., Murray-Parkes, C., & Prigerson, H. G. (2006). An exploration of associations between separation anxiety in childhood and complicated grief in later-life. *Journal of Nervous and Mental Disease, 194*, 121–123. doi: 10.1097/01.nmd.0000198146.28182.d5 van Hemert, D. A., van de Vijver, F. J., & Vingerhoets, A. J. (2011). Culture and crying: Prevalences and gender differences. *Cross-Cultural Research, 45*(4), 399–431. doi: 10.1177/1069397111404519

van IJzendoorn, M. H., & Sagi-Schwartz, A. (2008). Cross-cultural patterns of attachment: Universal and contextual dimensions. In J. Cassidy & P. Shaver (Eds.), *Handbook of attachment: Theory, Research and Clinical Applications* (2nd ed.) (pp. 880–905). New York: The Guilford Press.

Wachtel, P. L. (1993). *Therapeutic communication: Knowing what to say when*. New York: The Guilford Press.

Wallerstein, J. S., & Blakeslee, S. (2004). *Second chances: Men, women, and children a decade after divorce*. New York: Houghton Mifflin Company.

Webb, A. P., Ellison, C. G., McFarland, M. J., Lee, J. W., Morton, K., & Walters, J. (2010). Divorce, religious coping, and depressive symptoms in a conservative protestant religious group. *Family Relations: An Interdisciplinary Journal of Applied Family Studies, 59*, 544–557. doi:10.1111/j.1741-3729.2010.00622.x

Weisskirch, R. S., & Delevi, R. (2012). Its ovr b/n u n me: Technology use, attachment styles, and gender roles in relationship dissolution, *Cyberpsychology, Behavior, and Social Networking, 15*(9), 486–490. doi: 10.1089/cyber.2012.0169

Weiss, R. S. (1975). *Marital separation*. New York: Basic Books.

Weiss, R. S. (1976). The emotional impact of marital separation. *Journal of Social Issues, 32*, 135–145. doi: 10.1111/j.1540-4560.1976.tb02484.x

Wells, G. B., & Hansen, N. D. (2003). Lesbian shame: Its relationship to identity integration and attachment. *Journal of Homosexuality, 45*, 93–110.

Westman, J. C., & Cline, D. W. (1973). Divorce is a family affair. In Lasswell & Lasswell (Eds.), *Love, Marriage and the Family, A Developmental Approach*. Glenview, IL: Scott, Foresman & Company.

White, L. K. (1990). Determinants in divorce: A review of research in the eighties. *Journal of Marriage and the Family, 53*, 904–912.

Winnicott, D. W. (1960). Ego distortion in terms of true and false self. In *Maturational processes and the facilitating environment* (pp. 140–152). New York: International Universities Press.

Wiseman, R. S. (1975). Crisis theory and the process of divorce. *Social Casework, 56*, 205–212.

Worden, J. W. (1982). *Grief counseling and grief therapy: A handbook for the mental health practitioner*. New York: Springer.

Worden, J. W. (2009). *Grief counseling and grief therapy: A handbook for the mental health practitioner* (4th Ed.). New York: Springer.

Yancey, G. (2003). *Who is White: Latinos, Asians, and the New Black/non-Black divide*. Boulder, CO: Lynne Rienner.

Yang, B., & Lester, D. (1991). Correlates of statewide divorce rates. *Journal of Divorce and Remarriage, 15*, 219–223.

Young, L., & Alexander, B. (2012). *The chemistry between us: Love, sex and the science of attraction*. New York: The Penguin Group.

Index

AAI. *See* Adult Attachment Interview
absent grief, 178
Adult Attachment Interview, 178
Ainsworth, 178
anticipatory grief, 178
attachment: adulthood, 178; affect regulation, 178; childhood, 178; interpersonal dynamics, 178; same sex romantic relationships, 178; singlehood, 178; transgender romantic relationships, 178
attachment styles, 178
attachment theory, 178
attraction, 2, 3, 4, 9, 12, 14, 15, 31, 32, 110

befriending, 178
belongingness hypothesis, 178
bereavement, 178
Bowlby, John, 178
broken heart syndrome, 178

complicated grief, 178
complicated grief and attachment theory, 178
crying, 178
cyber obsessional pursuit, 178
cyclical psychodynamics, 178

Darwin, Charles, 178
Davis, Deborah, 178
deactivation, 178
differentiation, 178
disenfranchised grief, 178
dopamine, 2
dual process model, 178
Dunbar, 178

Emotionally Focused Couples Therapy, 178
evolutionary theory, 2

Fisher, 178
Fredrickson, Barbara, 178
Freud, Sigmund, 178
Fromm, Erich, 178

Greenberg, Les, 178
grief: divorce, 178; romantic relationship breakups, 178; romantic relationships with transgender individuals, 178; same sex romantic relationship breakups, 178

Hendrix, Harville, 178
hyperactivation, 178

Johnson, Sue, 178

Kubler-Ross, Elizabeth, 178

Lee, John Alan, 178
loss in limbo, 178

Mahler, Margaret, 178
Main, Mary, 178
mate selection, 178
mourning, 178

norephinephrine, 2

object relations theory, 2
obsessive relational intrusion, 178
oxytocin, 2

parental investment, 178
Pines, Ayala Malach, 178
psychoanalytic theory, 2
psychobiological attunement, 178
psychological birth, 178

reactance theory, 178
repetition compulsion, 178
resiliency, 178

separation distress, 178
serotonin, 178
social regulation model, 178
social theory, 2
Sternberg, Robert, 178

Taylor, Shelley, 178
tears, 178
tending, 178

Wachtel, 178
Worden, William, 178
working models, 178

About the Author

Shawn Blue, PsyD, is a clinical psychologist, and currently works as an assistant professor at Thomas Jefferson University in the Sidney Kimmel Medical College and staff psychologist in the Student Personal Counseling Center and Emotional Health & Wellness Program for House Staff. Dr. Blue conducts individual, couples, and group therapy and has specializations in grief, trauma, energy psychology, and eating disorders. She has particular interests in interpersonal relationships, diversity, energy work, and wellness programming. Her professional website is www.drshawnblue.com.

CPSIA information can be obtained
at www.ICGtesting.com
Printed in the USA
BVOW03*0059101017
496769BV00008B/4/P

9 781498 568555